Essential PySpark for Scalable Data Analytics

A beginner's guide to harnessing the power and ease of PySpark 3

Sreeram Nudurupati

BIRMINGHAM—MUMBAI

Essential PySpark for Scalable Data Analytics

Publishing Product Manager: Aditi Gour

Senior Editor: Mohammed Yusuf Imaratwale

Content Development Editor: Sean Lobo

Technical Editor: Manikandan Kurup

Copy Editor: Safis Editing

Project Coordinator: Aparna Ravikumar Nair

Proofreader: Safis Editing

Indexer: Sejal Dsilva

Production Designer: Joshua Misquitta

First published: October 2021

Production reference: 1230921

Published by Packt Publishing Ltd.

Livery Place

35 Livery Street

Birmingham

B3 2PB, UK.

ISBN 978-1-80056-887-7

www.packt.com

Contributors

About the author

Sreeram Nudurupati is a data analytics professional with years of experience in designing and optimizing data analytics pipelines at scale. He has a history of helping enterprises, as well as digital natives, build optimized analytics pipelines by using the knowledge of the organization, infrastructure environment, and current technologies.

About the reviewers

Karen J. Yang is a software engineer with computer science training in programming, data engineering, data science, and cloud computing. Her technical skills include Python, Java, Spark, Kafka, Hive, Docker, Kubernetes, CI/CD, Spring Boot, machine learning, data visualization, and cloud computing with AWS, GCP, and Databricks. As an author for Packt Publishing LLC, she has created three online instructional video courses, namely *Apache Spark in 7 Days*, *Time Series Analysis with Python 3.x*, and *Fundamentals of Statistics and Visualization in Python*. In her technical reviewer role, she has reviewed *Mastering Big Data Analytics with PySpark*, *The Applied Data Science Workshop*, and, most recently, *Essential PySpark for Scalable Data Analytics*.

Ayan Putatunda has 11 years of experience working with data-related technologies. He is currently working as an engineering manager of data engineering at Noodle.ai, based in San Francisco, California. He has held multiple positions, such as tech lead, principal data engineer, and senior data engineer, at Noodle.ai. He specializes in utilizing SQL and Python for large-scale distributed data processing. Before joining Noodle.ai he worked at Cognizant for 9 years in countries such as India, Argentina, and the US. At Cognizant, he worked with a wide range of data-related tools and technologies. Ayan holds a bachelor's degree in computer science from India and a master's degree in data science from the University of Illinois at Urbana-Champaign, USA.

Table of Contents

Preface

Section 1: Data Engineering

1

Distributed Computing Primer

Technical requirements	4	Higher-order functions	10
Distributed Computing	4	Apache Spark cluster architecture	11
Introduction to Distributed Computing	5	Getting started with Spark	12
Data Parallel Processing	5	**Big data processing with Spark SQL and DataFrames**	**15**
Data Parallel Processing using the MapReduce paradigm	6	Transforming data with Spark DataFrames	15
Distributed Computing with Apache Spark	**8**	Using SQL on Spark	18
Introduction to Apache Spark	8	What's new in Apache Spark 3.0?	20
Data Parallel Processing with RDDs	9	**Summary**	**20**

2

Data Ingestion

Technical requirements	24	Ingesting from relational data sources	26
Introduction to Enterprise Decision Support Systems	24	Ingesting from file-based data sources	27
Ingesting data from data sources	25	Ingesting from message queues	28

Ingesting data into data
sinks   30
Ingesting into data warehouses   30
Ingesting into data lakes   31
Ingesting into NoSQL and
in-memory data stores   32

Using file formats for data
storage in data lakes   33
Unstructured data storage
formats   34
Semi-structured data storage
formats   36
Structured data storage
formats   37

Building data ingestion
pipelines in batch and
real time   39
Data ingestion using batch
processing   39
Data ingestion in real time
using structured streaming   43

Unifying batch and real
time using Lambda
Architecture   48
Lambda Architecture   48
The Batch layer   49
The Speed layer   49
The Serving layer   50

Summary   51

3

Data Cleansing and Integration

Technical requirements   54
Transforming raw data
into enriched meaningful
data   54
Extracting, transforming, and
loading data   55
Extracting, loading, and
transforming data   57
Advantages of choosing ELT
over ETL   58

Building analytical data
stores using cloud
data lakes   58
Challenges with cloud data lakes   58
Overcoming data lake challenges
with Delta Lake   62

Consolidating data using
data integration   74
Data consolidation via ETL and
data warehousing   74
Integrating data using data
virtualization techniques   79
Data integration through
data federation   79

Making raw data analytics-
ready using data cleansing   81
Data selection to eliminate
redundancies   82
De-duplicating data   82
Standardizing data   84
Optimizing ELT processing
performance with
data partitioning   86

Summary   88

4
Real-Time Data Analytics

Technical requirements	90	Financial fraud detection	97
Real-time analytics systems architecture	90	IT security threat detection	98
Streaming data sources	91	**Simplifying the Lambda Architecture using Delta Lake**	**98**
Streaming data sinks	93		
Stream processing engines	95	**Change Data Capture**	**102**
Real-time data consumers	96	**Handling late-arriving data**	**106**
Real-time analytics industry use cases	96	Stateful stream processing using windowing and watermarking	106
Real-time predictive analytics in manufacturing	97	**Multi-hop pipelines**	**110**
Connected vehicles in the automotive sector	97	**Summary**	**113**

Section 2: Data Science

5
Scalable Machine Learning with PySpark

Technical requirements	118	Introduction to Apache Spark's ML library	124
ML overview	118		
Types of ML algorithms	119	**Data wrangling with Apache Spark and MLlib**	**127**
Business use cases of ML	121	Data preprocessing	127
Scaling out machine learning	123	Data cleansing	128
		Data manipulation	129
Techniques for scaling ML	123	**Summary**	**130**

6

Feature Engineering – Extraction, Transformation, and Selection

Technical requirements	132	Batch inferencing using the offline feature store	144
The machine learning process	132	**Delta Lake as an offline feature store**	**145**
Feature extraction	133		
Feature transformation	136	Structure and metadata with Delta tables	145
Transforming categorical variables	136	Schema enforcement and evolution with Delta Lake	145
Transforming continuous variables	139	Support for simultaneous batch and streaming workloads	146
Transforming the date and time variables	140	Delta Lake time travel	146
Assembling individual features into a feature vector	140	Integration with machine learning operations tools	146
Feature scaling	141	Online feature store for real-time inferencing	147
Feature selection	142	**Summary**	**149**
Feature store as a central feature repository	143		

7

Supervised Machine Learning

Technical requirements	152	Classification using decision trees	161
Introduction to supervised machine learning	152	Naïve Bayes	162
Parametric machine learning	153	Support vector machines	163
Non-parametric machine learning	153	**Tree ensembles**	**164**
Regression	154	Regression using random forests	165
Linear regression	155	Classification using random forests	166
Regression using decision trees	156	Regression using gradient boosted trees	167
Classification	158	Classification using GBTs	168
Logistic regression	158		

**Real-world supervised
learning applications**   **169**

Regression applications   169

Classification applications   171

Summary   **172**

8
Unsupervised Machine Learning

Technical requirements   **174**

**Introduction to unsupervised
machine learning**   **174**

**Clustering using machine
learning**   **175**

K-means clustering   175

Hierarchical clustering using
bisecting K-means   177

Topic modeling using latent
Dirichlet allocation   178

Gaussian mixture model   179

**Building association rules
using machine learning**   **180**

Collaborative filtering using
alternating least squares   181

**Real-world applications
of unsupervised learning**   **183**

Clustering applications   183

Association rules and collaborative
filtering applications   185

Summary   **186**

9
Machine Learning Life Cycle Management

Technical requirements   **188**

**Introduction to the ML
life cycle**   **188**

Introduction to MLflow   190

**Tracking experiments
with MLflow**   **191**

ML model tuning   198

**Tracking model versions
using MLflow
Model Registry**   **199**

**Model serving and
inferencing**   **201**

Offline model inferencing   201

Online model inferencing   202

Continuous delivery for ML   **203**

Summary   **205**

10
Scaling Out Single-Node Machine Learning Using PySpark

Technical requirements   **208**

Scaling out EDA   **208**

EDA using pandas   209

EDA using PySpark   210

Scaling out model
inferencing   211
Model training using
embarrassingly
parallel computing   213

Distributed hyperparameter
tuning   214
Scaling out arbitrary Python
code using pandas UDF   216
Upgrading pandas to
PySpark using Koalas   217
Summary   218

Section 3: Data Analysis

11
Data Visualization with PySpark

Technical requirements   222
Importance of data
visualization   222
Types of data visualization tools   223
Techniques for visualizing
data using PySpark   224
PySpark native data visualizations 225

Using Python data visualizations
with PySpark   231
Considerations for PySpark
to pandas conversion   236
Introduction to pandas   236
Converting from PySpark
into pandas   238
Summary   239

12
Spark SQL Primer

Technical requirements   242
Introduction to SQL   242
DDL   243
DML   243
Joins and sub-queries   244
Row-based versus columnar
storage   244
Introduction to Spark
SQL   245

Catalyst optimizer   246
Spark SQL data sources   247
Spark SQL language
reference   249
Spark SQL DDL   250
Spark DML   251
Optimizing Spark SQL
performance   252
Summary   254

13
Integrating External Tools with Spark SQL

Technical requirements   256
Apache Spark as a
distributed SQL engine   257
Introduction to Hive Thrift
JDBC/ODBC Server   257

Spark connectivity to SQL
analysis tools   259

Spark connectivity to
BI tools   263
Connecting Python
applications to Spark
SQL using Pyodbc   268
Summary   270

14
The Data Lakehouse

Moving from BI to AI   272
Challenges with data
warehouses   272
Challenges with data lakes   274

The data lakehouse
paradigm   276
Key requirements of a
data lakehouse   276

Data lakehouse architecture   277
Examples of existing
lakehouse architectures   278
Apache Spark-based data
lakehouse architecture   279

Advantages of data
lakehouses   282
Summary   283

Other Books You May Enjoy

Index

Preface

Apache Spark is a unified data analytics engine designed to process huge volumes of data in a fast and efficient way. PySpark is the Python language API of Apache Spark that provides Python developers an easy-to-use scalable data analytics framework.

Essential PySpark for Scalable Data Analytics starts by exploring the distributed computing paradigm and provides a high-level overview of Apache Spark. You'll then begin your data analytics journey with the data engineering process, learning to perform data ingestion, data cleansing, and integration at scale.

This book will also help you build real-time analytics pipelines that enable you to gain insights much faster. Techniques for building cloud-based data lakes are presented along with Delta Lake, which brings reliability and performance to data lakes.

A newly emerging paradigm called the Data Lakehouse is presented, which combines the structure and performance of a data warehouse with the scalability of cloud-based data lakes. You'll learn how to perform scalable data science and machine learning using PySpark, including data preparation, feature engineering, model training, and model productionization techniques. Techniques to scale out standard Python machine learning libraries are also presented, along with a new pandas-like API on top of PySpark called Koalas.

Who this book is for

This book is intended for practicing data engineers, data scientists, data analysts, citizen data analysts, and data enthusiasts who are already using data analytics to delve into the world of distributed and scalable data analytics. It's recommended that you have knowledge of the field of data analytics and data manipulation to gain actionable insights.

What this book covers

Chapter 1, *Distributed Computing Primer*, introduces the distributed computing paradigm. It also talks about how distributed computing became a necessity with the ever-increasing data sizes over the last decade and ends with the in-memory data-parallel processing concept with the Map Reduce paradigm, and finally, contains introduction to the latest features in Apache Spark 3.0 engine.

Chapter 2, *Data Ingestion*, covers various data sources, such as databases, data lakes, message queues, and how to ingest data from these data sources. You will also learn about the uses, differences, and efficiency of various data storage formats at storing and processing data.

Chapter 3, *Data Cleansing and Integration*, discusses various data cleansing techniques, how to handle bad incoming data, data reliability challenges and how to cope with them, and data integration techniques to build a single integrated view of the data.

Chapter 4, *Real-time Data Analytics*, explains how to perform real-time data ingestion and processing, discusses the unique challenges that real-time data integration presents and how to overcome, and also the benefits it provides.

Chapter 5, *Scalable Machine Learning with PySpark*, briefly talks about the need to scale out machine learning and discusses various techniques available to achieve this from using natively distributed machine learning algorithms to embarrassingly parallel processing to distributed hyperparameter search. It also provides an introduction to PySpark MLlib library and an overview of its various distributed machine learning algorithms.

Chapter 6, *Feature Engineering – Extraction, Transformation, and Selection*, explores various techniques for converting raw data into features that are suitable to be consumed by machine learning models, including techniques for scaling, transforming features.

Chapter 7, *Supervised Machine Learning*, explores supervised learning techniques for machine learning classification and regression problems including linear regression, logistic regression, and gradient boosted trees.

Chapter 8, *Unsupervised Machine Learning*, covers unsupervised learning techniques such as clustering, collaborative filtering, and dimensionality reduction to reduce the number of features prior to applying supervised learning.

Chapter 9, Machine Learning Life Cycle Management, explains that it is not just sufficient to just build and train models, but in the real world, multiple versions of the same model are built and different versions are suitable for different applications. Thus, it is necessary to track various experiments, their hyperparameters, metrics, and also the version of the data they were trained on. It is also necessary to track and store the various models in a centrally accessible repository so models can be easily productionized and shared; and finally, mechanisms are needed to automate this repeatedly occurring process. This chapter introduces these techniques using an end-to-end open source machine learning life cycle management library called MLflow.

Chapter 10, Scaling Out Single-Node Machine Learning Using PySpark, explains that in *Chapter 5, Scalable Machine Learning with PySpark*, you learned how to use the power of Apache Spark's distributed computing framework to train and score machine learning models at scale. Spark's native machine learning library provides good coverage of standard tasks that data scientists typically perform; however, there is a wide variety of functionality provided by standard single-node Python libraries that were not designed to work in a distributed manner. This chapter deals with techniques for horizontally scaling out standard Python data processing and machine learning libraries such as pandas, scikit-learn, and XGBoost. This chapter covers scaling out typical data science tasks such as exploratory data analysis, model training, model inference, and finally also covers a scalable Python library named Koalas that lets you effortlessly write PySpark code using very familiar and easy-to-use pandas-like syntax.

Chapter 11, Data Visualization with PySpark, covers data visualizations, which are an important aspect of conveying meaning from data and gleaning insights into it. This chapter covers how the most popular Python visualization libraries can be used along with PySpark.

Chapter 12, Spark SQL Primer, covers SQL, which is an expressive language for ad hoc querying and data analysis. This chapter will introduce Spark SQL for data analysis and also show how to interchangeably use PySpark with data analysis.

Chapter 13, Integrating External Tools with Spark SQL, explains that once we have clean, curated, and reliable data in our performant data lake, it would be a missed opportunity to not democratize this data across the organization to citizen analysts. The most popular way of doing this is via various existing **Business Intelligence (BI)** tools. This chapter deals with requirements for BI tool integration.

Chapter 14, The Data Lakehouse, explains that traditional descriptive analytics tools such as BI tools are designed around data warehouses and expect data to be presented in a certain way and modern advanced analytics and data science tools are geared toward working with large amounts of data that's easily accessible in data lakes. It is also not practical or cost-effective to store redundant data in separate storage locations to be able to cater to these individual use cases. This chapter will present a new paradigm called Data Lakehouse that tries to overcome the limitations of data warehouses and data lakes and bridge the gap by combining the best elements of both.

To get the most out of this book

Basic to intermediate knowledge of the disciplines of data engineering, data science, and SQL analytics is expected. A general level of proficiency using any programming language, especially Python, and a working knowledge of performing data analytics using frameworks such as pandas and SQL will help you to get the most out of this book.

Software/hardware covered in the book	Operating system requirements
Apache Spark 3	Windows, macOS, or Linux or the cloud
Python 2, 3	

The book makes use of Databricks Community Edition to run all code: `https://community.cloud.databricks.com`. Sign-up instructions can be found at `https://databricks.com/try-databricks`.

The entire code base used in this book can be downloaded from `https://github.com/PacktPublishing/Essential-PySpark-for-Scalable-Data-Analytics/blob/main/all_chapters/ess_pyspark.dbc`.

The datasets used for this chapter can be found at `https://github.com/PacktPublishing/Essential-PySpark-for-Data-Analytics/tree/main/data`.

If you are using the digital version of this book, we advise you to type the code yourself or access the code from the book's GitHub repository (a link is available in the next section). Doing so will help you avoid any potential errors related to the copying and pasting of code.

Download the example code files

You can download the example code files for this book from GitHub at `https://github.com/PacktPublishing/Essential-PySpark-for-Scalable-Data-Analytics`. If there's an update to the code, it will be updated in the GitHub repository.

We also have other code bundles from our rich catalog of books and videos available at `https://github.com/PacktPublishing/`. Check them out!

Download the color images

We also provide a PDF file that has color images of the screenshots and diagrams used in this book. You can download it here: `https://static.packt-cdn.com/downloads/9781800568877_ColorImages.pdf`

Conventions used

There are a number of text conventions used throughout this book.

`Code in text`: Indicates code words in text, database table names, folder names, filenames, file extensions, pathnames, dummy URLs, user input, and Twitter handles. Here is an example: "The `readStream()` method of the DataStreamReader object is used to create the streaming DataFrame."

A block of code is set as follows:

```
lines = sc.textFile("/databricks-datasets/README.md")
words = lines.flatMap(lambda s: s.split(" "))
word_tuples = words.map(lambda s: (s, 1))
word_count = word_tuples.reduceByKey(lambda x, y: x + y)
word_count.take(10)
word_count.saveAsTextFile("/tmp/wordcount.txt")
```

Any command-line input or output is written as follows:

```
%fs ls /FileStore/shared_uploads/delta/online_retail
```

Bold: Indicates a new term, an important word, or words that you see onscreen. For instance, words in menus or dialog boxes appear in **bold**. Here is an example: "There can be multiple **Map** stages followed by multiple **Reduce** stages."

> **Tips or important notes**
> Appear like this.

Get in touch

Feedback from our readers is always welcome.

General feedback: If you have questions about any aspect of this book, email us at customercare@packtpub.com and mention the book title in the subject of your message.

Errata: Although we have taken every care to ensure the accuracy of our content, mistakes do happen. If you have found a mistake in this book, we would be grateful if you would report this to us. Please visit www.packtpub.com/support/errata and fill in the form.

Piracy: If you come across any illegal copies of our works in any form on the internet, we would be grateful if you would provide us with the location address or website name. Please contact us at copyright@packt.com with a link to the material.

If you are interested in becoming an author: If there is a topic that you have expertise in and you are interested in either writing or contributing to a book, please visit authors.packtpub.com.

Share your thoughts

Once you've read *Essential PySpark for Scalable Data Analytics*, we'd love to hear your thoughts! Scan the QR code below to go straight to the Amazon review page for this book and share your feedback.

https://packt.link/r/1-800-56887-8

Your review is important to us and the tech community and will help us make sure we're delivering excellent quality content.

Section 1: Data Engineering

This section introduces the uninitiated to the Distributed Computing paradigm and shows how Spark became the de facto standard for big data processing.

Upon completion of this section, you will be able to ingest data from various data sources, cleanse it, integrate it, and write it out to persistent storage such as a data lake in a scalable and distributed manner. You will also be able to build real-time analytics pipelines and perform change data capture in a data lake. You will understand the key differences between the ETL and ELT ways of data processing, and how ELT evolved for the cloud-based data lake world. This section also introduces you to Delta Lake to make cloud-based data lakes more reliable and performant. You will understand the nuances of Lambda architecture as a means to perform simultaneous batch and real-time analytics and how Apache Spark combined with Delta Lake greatly simplifies Lambda architecture.

This section includes the following chapters:

- *Chapter 1, Distributed Computing Primer*
- *Chapter 2, Data Ingestion*
- *Chapter 3, Data Cleansing and Integration*
- *Chapter 4, Real-Time Data Analytics*

1
Distributed Computing Primer

This chapter introduces you to the **Distributed Computing** paradigm and shows you how Distributed Computing can help you to easily process very large amounts of data. You will learn about the concept of **Data Parallel Processing** using the **MapReduce** paradigm and, finally, learn how Data Parallel Processing can be made more efficient by using an in-memory, unified data processing engine such as Apache Spark.

Then, you will dive deeper into the architecture and components of Apache Spark along with code examples. Finally, you will get an overview of what's new with the latest 3.0 release of Apache Spark.

In this chapter, the key skills that you will acquire include an understanding of the basics of the Distributed Computing paradigm and a few different implementations of the Distributed Computing paradigm such as MapReduce and Apache Spark. You will learn about the fundamentals of Apache Spark along with its architecture and core components, such as the Driver, Executor, and Cluster Manager, and how they come together as a single unit to perform a Distributed Computing task. You will learn about Spark's **Resilient Distributed Dataset (RDD)** API along with higher-order functions and lambdas. You will also gain an understanding of the Spark SQL Engine and its DataFrame and SQL APIs. Additionally, you will implement working code examples. You will also learn about the various components of an Apache Spark data processing program, including transformations and actions, and you will learn about the concept of **Lazy Evaluation**.

In this chapter, we're going to cover the following main topics:

- Introduction Distributed Computing
- Distributed Computing with Apache Spark
- Big data processing with Spark SQL and DataFrames

Technical requirements

In this chapter, we will be using the Databricks Community Edition to run our code. This can be found at `https://community.cloud.databricks.com`.

Sign-up instructions can be found at `https://databricks.com/try-databricks`.

The code used in this chapter can be downloaded from `https://github.com/PacktPublishing/Essential-PySpark-for-Data-Analytics/tree/main/Chapter01`.

The datasets used in this chapter can be found at `https://github.com/PacktPublishing/Essential-PySpark-for-Data-Analytics/tree/main/data`.

The original datasets can be taken from their sources, as follows:

- Online Retail: `https://archive.ics.uci.edu/ml/datasets/Online+Retail+II`
- Image Data: `https://archive.ics.uci.edu/ml/datasets/Rice+Leaf+Diseases`
- Census Data: `https://archive.ics.uci.edu/ml/datasets/Census+Income`
- Country Data: `https://public.opendatasoft.com/explore/dataset/countries-codes/information/`

Distributed Computing

In this section, you will learn about Distributed Computing, the need for it, and how you can use it to process very large amounts of data in a quick and efficient manner.

Introduction to Distributed Computing

Distributed Computing is a class of computing techniques where we use a group of computers as a single unit to solve a computational problem instead of just using a single machine.

In data analytics, when the amount of data becomes too large to fit in a single machine, we can either split the data into smaller chunks and process it on a single machine iteratively, or we can process the chunks of data on several machines in parallel. While the former gets the job done, it might take longer to process the entire dataset iteratively; the latter technique gets the job completed in a shorter period of time by using multiple machines at once.

There are different kinds of Distributed Computing techniques; however, for data analytics, one popular technique is **Data Parallel Processing**.

Data Parallel Processing

Data Parallel Processing involves two main parts:

- The actual data that needs to be processed
- The piece of code or business logic that needs to be applied to the data in order to process it

We can process large amounts of data by splitting it into smaller chunks and processing them in parallel on several machines. This can be done in two ways:

- First, bring the data to the machine where our code is running.
- Second, take our code to where our data is actually stored.

One drawback of the first technique is that as our data sizes become larger, the amount of time it takes to move data also increases proportionally. Therefore, we end up spending more time moving data from one system to another and, in turn, negating any efficiency gained by our parallel processing system. We also find ourselves creating multiple copies of data during data replication.

The second technique is far more efficient because instead of moving large amounts of data, we can easily move a few lines of code to where our data actually resides. This technique of moving code to where the data resides is referred to as Data Parallel Processing. This Data Parallel Processing technique is very fast and efficient, as we save the amount of time that was needed earlier to move and copy data across different systems. One such Data Parallel Processing technique is called the **MapReduce paradigm**.

Data Parallel Processing using the MapReduce paradigm

The MapReduce paradigm breaks down a Data Parallel Processing problem into three main stages:

- The Map stage
- The Shuffle stage
- The Reduce stage

The **Map** stage takes the input dataset, splits it into (key, value) pairs, applies some processing on the pairs, and transforms them into another set of (key, value) pairs.

The **Shuffle** stage takes the (key, value) pairs from the Map stage and shuffles/sorts them so that pairs with the same *key* end up together.

The **Reduce** stage takes the resultant (key, value) pairs from the Shuffle stage and reduces or aggregates the pairs to produce the final result.

There can be multiple **Map** stages followed by multiple **Reduce** stages. However, a **Reduce** stage only starts after all of the **Map** stages have been completed.

Let's take a look at an example where we want to calculate the counts of all the different words in a text document and apply the **MapReduce** paradigm to it.

The following diagram shows how the MapReduce paradigm works in general:

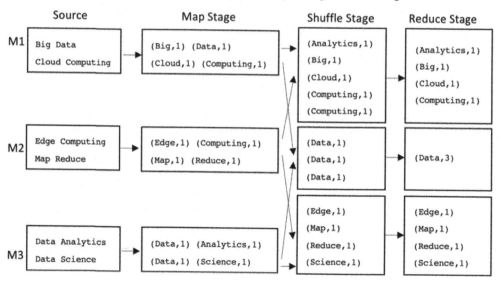

Figure 1.1 – Calculating the word count using MapReduce

The previous example works in the following manner:

1. In *Figure 1.1*, we have a cluster of three nodes, labeled **M1**, **M2**, and **M3**. Each machine includes a few text files containing several sentences in plain text. Here, our goal is to use MapReduce to count all of the words in the text files.

2. We load all the text documents onto the cluster; each machine loads the documents that are local to it.

3. The **Map Stage** splits the text files into individual lines and further splits each line into individual words. Then, it assigns each word a count of **1** to create a (word, count) pair.

4. The **Shuffle Stage** takes the (word, count) pairs from the **Map stage** and shuffles/sorts them so that word pairs with the same keyword end up together.

5. The **Reduce Stage** groups all keywords together and sums their counts to produce the final count of each individual word.

The MapReduce paradigm was popularized by the **Hadoop** framework and was pretty popular for processing big data workloads. However, the MapReduce paradigm offers a very low-level API for transforming data and requires users to have proficient knowledge of programming languages such as Java. Expressing a data analytics problem using Map and Reduce is not very intuitive or flexible.

MapReduce was designed to run on commodity hardware, and since commodity hardware was prone to failures, resiliency to hardware failures was a necessity. MapReduce achieves resiliency to hardware failures by saving the results of every stage to disk. This round-trip to disk after every stage makes MapReduce relatively slow at processing data because of the slow I/O performance of physical disks in general. To overcome this limitation, the next generation of the MapReduce paradigm was created, which made use of much faster system memory, as opposed to disks, to process data and offered much more flexible APIs to express data transformations. This new framework is called Apache Spark, and you will learn about it in the next section and throughout the remainder of this book.

Important note

In Distributed Computing, you will often encounter the term **cluster**. A cluster is a group of computers all working together as a single unit to solve a computing problem. The primary machine of a cluster is, typically, termed the **Master Node**, which takes care of the orchestration and management of the cluster, and secondary machines that actually carry out task execution are called **Worker Nodes**. A cluster is a key component of any Distributed Computing system, and you will encounter these terms throughout this book.

Distributed Computing with Apache Spark

Over the last decade, Apache Spark has grown to be the de facto standard for big data processing. Indeed, it is an indispensable tool in the hands of anyone involved with data analytics.

Here, we will begin with the basics of Apache Spark, including its architecture and components. Then, we will get started with the PySpark programming API to actually implement the previously illustrated word count problem. Finally, we will take a look at what's new with the latest 3.0 release of Apache Spark.

Introduction to Apache Spark

Apache Spark is an in-memory, unified data analytics engine that is relatively fast compared to other distributed data processing frameworks.

It is a unified data analytics framework because it can process different types of big data workloads with a single engine. The different workloads include the following

- Batch data processing
- Real-time data processing
- Machine learning and data science

Typically, data analytics involves all or a combination of the previously mentioned workloads to solve a single business problem. Before Apache Spark, there was no single framework that could accommodate all three workloads simultaneously. With Apache Spark, various teams involved in data analytics can all use a single framework to solve a single business problem, thus improving communication and collaboration among teams and drastically reducing their learning curve.

We will explore each of the preceding workloads, in depth, in *Chapter 2, Data Ingestion* through to *Chapter 8, Unsupervised Machine Learning,* of this book.

Further, Apache Spark is fast in two aspects:

- It is fast in terms of data processing speed.
- It is fast in terms of development speed.

Apache Spark has fast job/query execution speeds because it does all of its data processing in memory, and it has other optimizations techniques built-in such as **Lazy Evaluation**, **Predicate Pushdown**, and Partition Pruning to name a few. We will go over Spark's optimization techniques in the coming chapters.

Secondly, Apache Spark provides developers with very high-level APIs to perform basic data processing operations such as *filtering, grouping, sorting, joining*, and *aggregating*. By using these high-level programming constructs, developers can very easily express their data processing logic, making their development many times faster.

The core abstraction of Apache Spark, which makes it fast and very expressive for data analytics, is called an RDD. We will cover this in the next section.

Data Parallel Processing with RDDs

An RDD is the core abstraction of the Apache Spark framework. Think of an RDD as any kind of immutable data structure that is typically found in a programming language but one that resides in the memory of several machines instead of just one. An RDD consists of partitions, which are logical divisions of an RDD, with a few of them residing on each machine.

The following diagram helps explain the concepts of an RDD and its partitions:

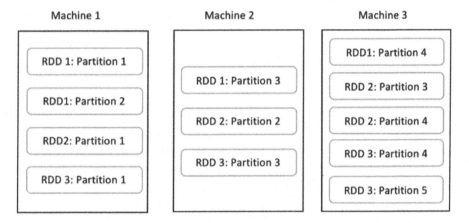

Figure 1.2 – An RDD

In the previous diagram, we have a cluster of three machines or nodes. There are three RDDs on the cluster, and each RDD is divided into partitions. Each node of the cluster contains a few partitions of an individual RDD, and each RDD is distributed among several nodes of the cluster by means of partitions.

The RDD abstractions are accompanied by a set of high-level functions that can operate on the RRDs in order to manipulate the data stored within the partitions. These functions are called **higher-order functions**, and you will learn about them in the following section.

Higher-order functions

Higher-order functions manipulate RDDs and help us write business logic to transform data stored within the partitions. Higher-order functions accept other functions as parameters, and these inner functions help us define the actual business logic that transforms data and is applied to each partition of the RDD in parallel. These inner functions passed as parameters to the higher-order functions are called **lambda functions** or **lambdas**.

Apache Spark comes with several higher-order functions such as map, flatMap, reduce, fold, filter, reduceByKey, join, and union to name a few. These functions are high-level functions and help us express our data manipulation logic very easily.

For example, consider our previously illustrated word count example. Let's say you wanted to read a text file as an RDD and split each word based on a delimiter such as a whitespace. This is what code expressed in terms of an RDD and higher-order function would look like:

```
lines = sc.textFile("/databricks-datasets/README.md")
words = lines.flatMap(lambda s: s.split(" "))
word_tuples = words.map(lambda s: (s, 1))
```

In the previous code snippet, the following occurs:

1. We are loading a text file using the built-in sc.textFile() method, which loads all text files at the specified location into the cluster memory, splits them into individual lines, and returns an RDD of lines or strings.

2. We then apply the flatMap() higher-order function to the new RDD of lines and supply it with a function that instructs it to take each line and split it based on a white space. The lambda function that we pass to flatMap() is simply an anonymous function that takes one parameter, an individual line of StringType, and returns a list of words. Through the flatMap() and lambda() functions, we are able to transform an RDD of lines into an RDD of words.

3. Finally, we use the map() function to assign a count of 1 to every individual word. This is pretty easy and definitely more intuitive compared to developing a MapReduce application using the Java programming language.

To summarize what you have learned, the primary construct of the Apache Spark framework is an RDD. An RDD consists of *partitions* distributed across individual nodes of a cluster. We use special functions called higher-order functions to operate on the RDDs and transform the RDDs according to our business logic. This business logic is passed along to the Worker Nodes via higher-order functions in the form of lambdas or anonymous functions.

Before we dig deeper into the inner workings of higher-order functions and lambda functions, we need to understand the architecture of the Apache Spark framework and the components of a typical Spark Cluster. We will do this in the following section.

> **Note**
>
> The *Resilient* part of an RDD comes from the fact that every RDD knows its lineage. At any given point in time, an RDD has information of all the individual operations performed on it, going back all the way to the data source itself. Thus, if any Executors are lost due to any failures and one or more of its partitions are lost, it can easily recreate those partitions from the source data making use of the lineage information, thus making it *Resilient* to failures.

Apache Spark cluster architecture

A typical Apache Spark cluster consists of three major components, namely, the Driver, a few Executors, and the Cluster Manager:

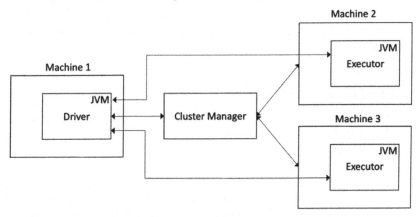

Figure 1.3 – Apache Spark Cluster components

Let's examine each of these components a little closer.

Driver – the heart of a Spark application

The Spark Driver is a Java Virtual Machine process and is the core part of a Spark application. It is responsible for user application code declarations, along with the creation of RDDs, DataFrames, and datasets. It is also responsible for coordinating with and running code on the Executors and creating and scheduling tasks on the Executors. It is even responsible for relaunching Executors after a failure and finally returning any data requested back to the client or the user. Think of a Spark Driver as the `main()` program of any Spark application.

> **Important note**
> The Driver is the single point of failure for a Spark cluster, and the entire
> Spark application fails if the driver fails; therefore, different Cluster Managers
> implement different strategies to make the Driver highly available.

Executors – the actual workers

Spark Executors are also Java Virtual Machine processes, and they are responsible for
running operations on RDDs that actually transform data. They can cache data partitions
locally and return the processed data back to the Driver or write to persistent storage.
Each Executor runs operations on a set of partitions of an RDD in parallel.

Cluster Manager – coordinates and manages cluster resources

The **Cluster Manager** is a process that runs centrally on the cluster and is responsible for
providing resources requested by the Driver. It also monitors the Executors regarding task
progress and their status. Apache Spark comes with its own Cluster Manager, which is
referred to as the Standalone Cluster Manager, but it also supports other popular Cluster
Managers such as YARN or Mesos. Throughout this book, we will be using Spark's built-in
Standalone Cluster Manager.

Getting started with Spark

So far, we have learnt about Apache Spark's core data structure, called RDD, the functions
used to manipulate RDDs, called higher-order functions, and the components of an
Apache Spark cluster. You have also seen a few code snippets on how to use higher-order
functions.

In this section, you will put your knowledge to practical use and write your very first
Apache Spark program, where you will use Spark's Python API called **PySpark** to create
a word count application. However, first, we need a few things to get started:

- An Apache Spark cluster
- Datasets
- Actual code for the word count application

We will use the free **Community Edition of Databricks** to create our Spark cluster. The
code used can be found via the GitHub link that was mentioned at the beginning of this
chapter. The links for the required resources can be found in the *Technical requirements*
section toward the beginning of the chapter.

> **Note**
>
> Although we are using Databricks Spark Clusters in this book, the provided code can be executed on any Spark cluster running Spark 3.0, or higher, as long as data is provided at a location accessible by your Spark cluster.

Now that you have gained an understanding of Spark's core concepts such as RDDs, higher-order functions, lambdas, and Spark's architecture, let's implement your very first Spark application using the following code:

```
lines = sc.textFile("/databricks-datasets/README.md")
words = lines.flatMap(lambda s: s.split(" "))
word_tuples = words.map(lambda s: (s, 1))
word_count = word_tuples.reduceByKey(lambda x, y:  x + y)
word_count.take(10)
word_count.saveAsTextFile("/tmp/wordcount.txt")
```

In the previous code snippet, the following takes place:

1. We load a text file using the built-in `sc.textFile()` method, which reads all of the text files at the specified location, splits them into individual lines, and returns an RDD of lines or strings.

2. Then, we apply the `flatMap()` higher-order function to the RDD of lines and supply it with a function that instructs it to take each line and split it based on a white space. The lambda function that we pass to `flatMap()` is simply an anonymous function that takes one parameter, a line, and returns individual words as a list. By means of the `flatMap()` and `lambda()` functions, we are able to transform an RDD of lines into an RDD of words.

3. Then, we use the `map()` function to assign a count of 1 to every individual word.

4. Finally, we use the `reduceByKey()` higher-order function to sum up the count of similar words occurring multiple times.

5. Once the counts have been calculated, we make use of the `take()` function to display a sample of the final word counts.

6. Although displaying a sample result set is usually helpful in determining the correctness of our code, in a big data setting, it is not practical to display all the results on to the console. So, we make use of the `saveAsTextFile()` function to persist our finals results in persistent storage.

> **Important note**
>
> It is not recommended that you display the entire result set onto the console using commands such as `take()` or `collect()`. It could even be outright dangerous to try and display all the data in a big data setting, as it could try to bring way too much data back to the driver and cause the driver to fail with an `OutOfMemoryError`, which, in turn, causes the entire application to fail.
>
> Therefore, it is recommended that you use `take()` with a very small result set, and use `collect()` only when you are confident that the amount of data returned is, indeed, very small.

Let's dive deeper into the following line of code in order to understand the inner workings of lambdas and how they implement Data Parallel Processing along with higher-order functions:

```
words = lines.flatMap(lambda s: s.split(" "))
```

In the previous code snippet, the `flatMmap()` higher-order function bundles the code present in the lambda and sends it over a network to the Worker Nodes, using a process called *serialization*. This *serialized lambda* is then sent out to every executor, and each executor, in turn, applies this lambda to individual RDD partitions in parallel.

> **Important note**
>
> Since higher-order functions need to be able to serialize the lambdas in order to send your code to the Executors. The lambda functions need to be `serializable`, and failing this, you might encounter a *Task not serializable* error.

In summary, higher-order functions are, essentially, transferring your data transformation code in the form of serialized lambdas to your data in RDD partitions. Therefore, instead of moving data to where the code is, we are actually moving our code to where data is situated, which is the exact definition of Data Parallel Processing, as we learned earlier in this chapter.

Thus, Apache Spark along with its RDDs and higher-order functions implements an in-memory version of the Data Parallel Processing paradigm. This makes Apache Spark fast and efficient at big data processing in a Distributed Computing setting.

The RDD abstraction of Apache Spark definitely offers a higher level of programming API compared to MapReduce, but it still requires some level of comprehension of the functional programming style to be able to express even the most common types of data transformations. To overcome this challenge, Spark's already existing SQL engine was expanded, and another abstraction, called the DataFrame, was added on top of RDDs. This makes data processing much easier and more familiar for data scientists and data analysts. The following section will explore the DataFrame and SQL API of the Spark SQL engine.

Big data processing with Spark SQL and DataFrames

The Spark SQL engine supports two types of APIs, namely, DataFrame and Spark SQL. Being higher-level abstractions than RDDs, these are far more intuitive and even more expressive. They come with many more data transformation functions and utilities that you might already be familiar with as a data engineer, data analyst, or a data scientist.

Spark SQL and DataFrame APIs offer a low barrier to entry into big data processing. They allow you to use your existing knowledge and skills of data analytics and allow you to easily get started with Distributed Computing. They help you get started with processing data at scale, without having to deal with any of the complexities that typically come along with Distributed Computing frameworks.

In this section, you will learn how to use both DataFrame and Spark SQL APIs to get started with your scalable data processing journey. Notably, the concepts learned here will be useful and are required throughout this book.

Transforming data with Spark DataFrames

Starting with Apache Spark 1.3, the Spark SQL engine was added as a layer on top of the RDD API and expanded to every component of Spark, to offer an even easier to use and familiar API for developers. Over the years, the Spark SQL engine and its DataFrame and SQL APIs have grown to be even more robust and have become the de facto and recommended standard for using Spark in general. Throughout this book, you will be exclusively using either DataFrame operations or Spark SQL statements for all your data processing needs, and you will rarely ever use the RDD API.

Think of a Spark DataFrame as a Pandas DataFrame or a relational database table with rows and named columns. The only difference is that a Spark DataFrame resides in the memory of several machines instead of a single machine. The following diagram shows a Spark DataFrame with three columns distributed across three worker machines:

Machine 1

uid	last_name	first_name	birth_year
1	Asimov	Isaac	January
2	Brown	Dan	June
3	Burroughs	Edgar Rice	September

Machine 2

uid	last_name	first_name	birth_year
1	Asimov	Isaac	January
2	Brown	Dan	June
3	Burroughs	Edgar Rice	September

Machine 3

uid	last_name	first_name	birth_year
1	Asimov	Isaac	January
2	Brown	Dan	June
3	Burroughs	Edgar Rice	September

Figure 1.4 – A distributed DataFrame

A Spark DataFrame is also an immutable data structure such as an RDD, consisting of rows and named columns, where each individual column can be of any type. Additionally, DataFrames come with operations that allow you to manipulate data, and we generally refer to these set of operations as **Domain Specific Language (DSL)**. Spark DataFrame operations can be grouped into two main categories, namely, transformations and actions, which we will explore in the following sections.

One advantage of using DataFrames or Spark SQL over the RDD API is that the Spark SQL engine comes with a built-in query optimizer called **Catalyst**. This Catalyst optimizer analyzes user code, along with any available statistics on the data, to generate the best possible execution plan for the query. This query plan is further converted into Java bytecode, which runs natively inside the Executor's Java JVM. This happens irrespective of the programming language used, thus making any code processed via the Spark SQL engine equally performant in most cases, whether it be written using Scala, Java, Python, R, or SQL.

Transformations

Transformations are operations performed on DataFrames that manipulate the data in the DataFrame and result in another DataFrame. Some examples of transformations are `read`, `select`, `where`, `filter`, `join`, and `groupBy`.

Actions

Actions are operations that actually cause a result to be calculated and either printed onto the console or, more practically, written back to a storage location. Some examples of actions include `write`, `count`, and `show`.

Lazy evaluation

Spark transformations are lazily evaluated, which means that transformations are not evaluated immediately as they are declared, and data is not manifested in memory until an action is called. This has a few advantages, as it gives the Spark optimizer an opportunity to evaluate all of your transformations until an action is called and generate the most optimal plan of execution to get the best performance and efficiency out of your code.

The advantage of Lazy Evaluation coupled with Spark's Catalyst optimizer is that you can solely focus on expressing your data transformation logic and not worry too much about arranging your transformations in a specific order to get the best performance and efficiency out of your code. This helps you be more productive at your tasks and not become perplexed by the complexities of a new framework.

> **Important note**
> Compared to Pandas DataFrames, Spark DataFrames are not manifested in memory as soon as they are declared. They are only manifested in memory when an action is called. Similarly, DataFrame operations don't necessarily run in the order you specified them to, as Spark's Catalyst optimizer generates the best possible execution plan for you, sometimes even combining a few operations into a single unit.

Let's take the word count example that we previously implemented using the RDD API and try to implement it using the DataFrame DSL:

```
from pyspark.sql.functions import split, explode
linesDf = spark.read.text("/databricks-datasets/README.md")
wordListDf = linesDf.select(split("value", " ").alias("words"))
wordsDf = wordListDf.select(explode("words").alias("word"))
wordCountDf = wordsDf.groupBy("word").count()
wordCountDf.show()
wordCountDf.write.csv("/tmp/wordcounts.csv")
```

In the previous code snippet, the following occurs:

1. First, we import a few functions from the PySpark SQL function library, namely, split and explode.

2. Then, we read text using the `SparkSession read.text()` method, which creates a DataFrame of lines of `StringType`.

3. We then use the `split()` function to separate out every line into its individual words; the result is a DataFrame with a single column, named `value`, which is actually a list of words.

4. Then, we use the `explode()` function to separate the list of words in each row out to every word on a separate row; the result is a DataFrame with a column labeled `word`.

5. Now we are finally ready to count our words, so we group our words by the `word` column and count individual occurrences of each word. The final result is a DataFrame of two columns, that is, the actual `word` and its `count`.

6. We can view a sample of the result using the `show()` function, and, finally, save our results in persistent storage using the `write()` function.

Can you guess which operations are actions? If you guessed `show()` or `write()`, then you are correct. Every other function, including `select()` and `groupBy()`, are transformations and will not induce the Spark job into action.

> **Note**
>
> Although the `read()` function is a transformation, sometimes, you will notice that it will actually execute a Spark job. The reason for this is that with certain structured and semi-structured data formats, Spark will try and infer the schema information from the underlying files and will process a small subset of the actual files to do this.

Using SQL on Spark

SQL is an expressive language for ad hoc data exploration and business intelligence types of queries. Because it is a very high-level declarative programming language, the user can simply focus on the input and output and what needs to be done to the data and not worry too much about the programming complexities of how to actually implement the logic. Apache Spark's SQL engine also has a SQL language API along with the DataFrame and Dataset APIs.

With Spark 3.0, Spark SQL is now compliant with ANSI standards, so if you are a data analyst who is familiar with another SQL-based platform, you should be able to get started with Spark SQL with minimal effort.

Since DataFrames and Spark SQL utilize the same underlying Spark SQL engine, they are completely interchangeable, and it is often the case that users intermix DataFrame DSL with Spark SQL statements for parts of the code that are expressed easily with SQL.

Now, let's rewrite our word count program using Spark SQL. First, we create a table specifying our text file to be a CSV file with a white space as the delimiter, a neat trick to read each line of the text file, and also split each file into individual words all at once:

```
CREATE TABLE word_counts (word STRING)
USING csv
OPTIONS ("delimiter"=" ")
LOCATION "/databricks-datasets/README.md"
```

Now that we have a table of a single column of words, we just need to GROUP BY the word column and do a COUNT() operation to get our word counts:

```
SELECT word, COUNT(word) AS count
FROM word_counts
GROUP BY word
```

Here, you can observe that solving the same business problem became progressively easier from using MapReduce to RRDs, to DataFrames and Spark SQL. With each new release, Apache Spark has been adding many higher-level programming abstractions, data transformation and utility functions, and other optimizations. The goal has been to enable data engineers, data scientists, and data analysts to focus their time and energy on solving the actual business problem at hand and not worry about complex programming abstractions or system architectures.

Apache Spark's latest major release of version 3 has many such enhancements that make the life of a data analytics professional much easier. We will discuss the most prominent of these enhancements in the following section.

What's new in Apache Spark 3.0?

There are many new and notable features in Apache Spark 3.0; however, only a few are mentioned here, which you will find very useful during the beginning phases of your data analytics journey:

- **Speed**: Apache Spark 3.0 is orders of magnitude faster than its predecessors. Third-party benchmarks have put Spark 3.0 to be anywhere from 2 to 17 times faster for certain types of workloads.

- **Adaptive Query Execution**: The Spark SQL engine generates a few logical and physical query execution plans based on user code and any previously collected statistics on the source data. Then, it tries to choose the most optimal execution plan. However, sometimes, Spark is not able to generate the best possible execution plan either because the statistics are either stale or non-existent, leading to suboptimal performance. With adaptive query execution, Spark is able to dynamically adjust the execution plan during runtime and give the best possible query performance.

- **Dynamic Partition Pruning**: Business intelligence systems and data warehouses follow a data modeling technique called **Dimensional Modeling**, where data is stored in a central fact table surrounded by a few dimensional tables. Business intelligence types of queries utilizing these dimensional models involve queries with multiple joins between the dimension and fact tables, along with various filter conditions on the dimension tables. With dynamic partition pruning, Spark is able to filter out any fact table partitions based on the filters applied on these dimensions, resulting in less data being read into the memory, which, in turn, results in better query performance.

- **Kubernetes Support**: Earlier, we learned that Spark comes with its own Standalone Cluster Manager and can also work with other popular resource managers such as YARN and Mesos. Now Spark 3.0 natively supports **Kubernetes**, which is a popular open source framework for running and managing parallel container services.

Summary

In this chapter, you learned the concept of Distributed Computing. We discovered why Distributed Computing has become very important, as the amount of data being generated is growing rapidly, and it is not practical or feasible to process all your data using a single specialist system.

You then learned about the concept of Data Parallel Processing and reviewed a practical example of its implementation by means of the MapReduce paradigm.

Then, you were introduced to an in-memory, unified analytics engine called Apache Spark, and learned how fast and efficient it is for data processing. Additionally, you learned it is very intuitive and easy to get started for developing data processing applications. You also got to understand the architecture and components of Apache Spark and how they come together as a framework.

Next, you came to understand RDDs, which are the core abstraction of Apache Spark, how they store data on a cluster of machines in a distributed manner, and how you can leverage higher-order functions along with lambda functions to implement Data Parallel Processing via RDDs.

You also learned about the Spark SQL engine component of Apache Spark, how it provides a higher level of abstraction than RRDs, and that it has several built-in functions that you might already be familiar with. You learned to leverage the DataFrame DSL to implement your data processing business logic in an easier and more familiar way. You also learned about Spark's SQL API, how it is ANSI SQL standards-compliant, and how it allows you to seamlessly perform SQL analytics on large amounts of data efficiently.

You also came to know some of the prominent improvements in Apache Spark 3.0, such as adaptive query execution and dynamic partition pruning, which help make Spark 3.0 much faster in performance than its predecessors.

Now that you have learned the basics of big data processing with Apache Spark, you are ready to embark on a data analytics journey using Spark. A typical data analytics journey starts with acquiring raw data from various source systems, ingesting it into a historical storage component such as a data warehouse or a data lake, then transforming the raw data by cleansing, integrating, and transforming it to get a single source of truth. Finally, you can gain actionable business insights through clean and integrated data, leveraging descriptive and predictive analytics. We will cover each of these aspects in the subsequent chapters of this book, starting with the process of data cleansing and ingestion in the following chapter.

2
Data Ingestion

Data ingestion is the process of moving data from disparate operational systems to a central location such as a data warehouse or a data lake to be processed and made conducive for data analytics. It is the first step of the data analytics process and is necessary for creating centrally accessible, persistent storage, where data engineers, data scientists, and data analysts can access, process, and analyze data to generate business analytics.

You will be introduced to the capabilities of Apache Spark as a data ingestion engine for both batch and real-time processing. Various data sources supported by Apache Spark and how to access them using Spark's DataFrame interface will be presented.

Additionally, you will learn how to use Apache Spark's built-in functions to access data from external data sources, such as a **Relational Database Management System (RDBMS)**, and message queues such as Apache Kafka, and ingest them into data lakes. The different data storage formats, such as structured, unstructured, and semi-structured file formats, along with the key differences between them, will also be explored. Spark's real-time streams processing engine called **Structured Streaming** will also be introduced. You will learn to create end-to-end data ingestion pipelines using batch processing as well as real-time stream processing. Finally, will explore a technique to unify batch and streams processing, called **Lambda Architecture**, and its implementation using Apache Spark.

In this chapter, you will learn about the essential skills that are required to perform both batch and real-time ingestion using Apache Spark. Additionally, you will acquire the knowledge and tools required for building end-to-end scalable and performant big data ingestion pipelines.

In this chapter, we will cover the following main topics:

- Introduction to Enterprise Decision Support Systems
- Ingesting data from data sources
- Ingesting data into data sinks
- Using file formats for data storage in data lakes
- Building data ingestion pipelines in batches and real time
- Unifying batch and real-time data ingestion using Lambda architecture

Technical requirements

In this chapter, we will be using the Databricks Community Edition to run our code. This can be found at `https://community.cloud.databricks.com`.

Sign-up instructions can be found at `https://databricks.com/try-databricks`.

The code used in this chapter can be downloaded from `https://github.com/PacktPublishing/Essential-PySpark-for-Data-Analytics/tree/main/Chapter02`.

The datasets used for this chapter can be found at `https://github.com/PacktPublishing/Essential-PySpark-for-Data-Analytics/tree/main/data`.

Introduction to Enterprise Decision Support Systems

An **Enterprise Decision Support System (Enterprise DSS)** is an end-to-end data processing system that takes operational and transactional data generated by a business organization and converts them into actionable insights. Every Enterprise DSS has a few standard components, such as data sources, data sinks, and data processing frameworks. An Enterprise DSS takes raw transactional data as its input and converts this into actionable insights such as operational reports, enterprise performance dashboards, and predictive analytics.

The following diagram illustrates the components of a typical Enterprise DSS in a big data context:

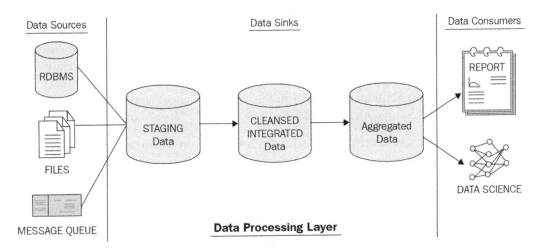

Figure 2.1 – The Enterprise DSS architecture

A big data analytics system is also an Enterprise DSS operating at much larger *Volumes*, with more *Variety* of data, and arriving at much faster *Velocity*. Being a type of Enterprise DSS, a big data analytics system has components that are similar to that of a traditional Enterprise DSS. The first step of building an Enterprise DSS is data ingestion from data sources into data sinks. You will learn about this process throughout this chapter. Let's elaborate on the different components of a big data analytics system, starting with data sources.

Ingesting data from data sources

In this section, we will learn about various data sources that a big data analytics system uses as a source of data. Typical data sources include transactional systems such as RDBMSes, file-based data sources such as **data lakes**, and **message queues** such as **Apache Kafka**. Additionally, you will learn about Apache Spark's built-in connectors to ingest data from these data sources and also write code so that you can view these connectors in action.

Ingesting from relational data sources

A **Transactional System**, or an **Operational System**, is a data processing system that helps an organization carry out its day-to-day business functions. These transactional systems deal with individual business transactions, such as a point-of-service transaction at a retail kiosk, an order placed on an online retail portal, an airline ticket booked, or a banking transaction. A historical aggregate of these transactions forms the basis of data analytics, and analytics systems ingest, store, and process these transactions over long periods. Therefore, such Transactional Systems form the source of data of analytics systems and a starting point for data analytics.

Transactional systems come in many forms; however, the most common ones are RDBMSes. In the following section, we will learn how to ingest data from an RDBMS.

Relational data sources are a collection of relational databases and relational tables that consist of rows and named columns. The primary programming abstraction used to communicate with and query an RDBMS is called **Structured Query Language** (**SQL**). External systems can communicate with an RDBMS via communication protocols such as JDBC and ODBC. Apache Spark comes with a built-in JDBC data source that can be used to communicate with and query data stored in RDBMS tables.

Let's take a look at the code required to ingest data from an RDBMS table using PySpark, as shown in the following code snippet:

```
dataframe_mysql = spark.read.format("jdbc").options(
    url="jdbc:mysql://localhost:3306/pysparkdb",
    driver = "org.mariadb.jdbc.Driver",
    dbtable = "authors",
    user="#####",
    password="@@@@@").load()
dataframe_mysql.show()
```

In the previous code snippet, we use the `spark.read()` method to load data from a JDBC data source by specifying the format to be `jdbc`. Here, we connect to a popular open source RDBMS called **MySQL**. We pass a few options such as a `url` that specifies the `jdbc url` for the MySQL server along with its `hostname`, `port number`, and `database name`. The `driver` option specifies the JDBC driver to be used by Spark to connect and communicate with the RDBMS. The `dtable`, `user`, and `password` options specify the table name to be queried and the credentials that are needed to authenticate with the RDBMS. Finally, the `show()` function reads sample data from the RDBMS table and displays it onto the console.

> **Important note**
>
> The previous code snippet, which uses dummy database credentials, shows them in plain text. This poses a huge data security risk and is not a recommended practice. The appropriate best practices to handle sensitive information such as using config files or other mechanisms provided by big data software vendors such as obscuring or hiding sensitive information should be followed.

To run this code, you can either use your own MySQL server and configure it with your Spark cluster, or you can use the sample code provided with this chapter to set up a simple MySQL server. The required code can be found at `https://github.com/PacktPublishing/Essential-PySpark-for-Data-Analytics/blob/main/Chapter02/utils/mysql-setup.ipynb`.

> **Note**
>
> Apache Spark provides a JDBC data source and is capable of connecting to virtually any RDBMS that supports JDBC connections and has a JDBC driver available. However, it doesn't come bundled with any drivers; they need to be procured from the respective RDBMS provider, and the driver needs to be configured to your Spark cluster to be available to your Spark application.

Ingesting from file-based data sources

File-based data sources are very common when data is exchanged between different data processing systems. Let's consider an example of a retailer who wants to enrich their internal data sources with external data such as Zip Code data, as provided by a postal service provider. This data between the two organizations is usually exchanged via file-based data formats such as XML or JSON or more commonly using a delimited plain-text or CSV formats.

Apache Spark supports various file formats, such as plain-text, CSV, JSON as well as binary file formats such as Apache Parquet and ORC. These files need to be located on a distributed filesystem such as **Hadoop Distributed File System** (**HDFS**), or a cloud-based data lake such as **AWS S3**, **Azure Blob**, or **ADLS** storage.

Let's take a look at how to ingest data from CSV files using PySpark, as shown in the following block of code:

```
retail_df = (spark
        .read
        .format("csv")
```

```
        .option("inferSchema", "true")
        .option("header","true")
        .load("dbfs:/FileStore/shared_uploads/snudurupati@
outlook.com/")
     )
retail_df.show()
```

In the previous code snippet, we use the `spark.read()` function to read a CSV file. We specify the `inferSchema` and `header` options to be `true`. This helps Spark infer the column names and data type information by reading a sample set of data.

> **Important note**
>
> The file-based data source needs to be on a distributed filesystem. The Spark Framework leverages data parallel processing, and each Spark Executor tries to read a subset of the data into its own local memory. Therefore, it is essential that the file be located on a distributed filesystem and accessible by all the Executors and the Driver. HDFS and cloud-based data lakes, such as AWS S3, Azure Blob, and ADLS storage, are all distributed data storage layers that are good candidates to be used as file-based data sources with Apache Spark.

Here, we read the CSV files from a `dbfs/` location, which is Databricks' proprietary filesystem called **Databricks Filesystem (DBFS)**. DBFS is an abstraction layer that actually utilizes either AWS S3 or Azure Blob or ADLS storage underneath.

> **Tip**
>
> Given that each Executor tries to read only a subset of data, it is important that the file type being used is splittable. If the file cannot be split, an Executor might try to read a file larger than its available memory, run out of memory, and throw an "Out of Memory" error. One example of such an unsplittable file is a `gzipped` CSV or a text file.

Ingesting from message queues

Another type of data source commonly used in real-time streaming analytics is a **message queue**. A message queue offers a publish-subscribe pattern of data consumption, where a publisher publishes data to a queue while multiple subscribers could consume the data asynchronously. In a **Distributed Computing** context, a message queue needs to be distributed, fault-tolerant, and scalable, in order to serve as a data source for a distributed data processing system.

One such message queue is Apache Kafka, which is quite prominent in real-time streaming workloads with Apache Spark. Apache Kafka is more than just a message queue; it is an end-to-end distributed streams processing platform in itself. However, for our discussion, we will consider Kafka to be just a distributed, scalable, and fault-tolerant message queue.

Let's take a look at what the code to ingest from Kafka using PySpark looks like, as shown in the following block of code:

```
kafka_df = (spark.read
        .format("kafka")
        .option("kafka.bootstrap.servers", "localhost:9092")
        .option("subscribe", "wordcount")
        .option("startingOffsets", "earliest")
        .load()
        )
kafka_df.show()
```

In the previous code example, we use `spark.read()` to load data from a Kafka server by providing its *hostname* and *port number*, a *topic* named `wordcount`. We also specify that Spark should start reading *events* from the very beginning of the queue, using the `StartingOffsets` option. Even though Kafka is more commonly used for streaming use cases with Apache Spark, this preceding code example makes use of Kafka as a data source for batch processing of data. You will learn to use Kafka with Apache Spark for processing streams in the *Data ingestion in real time using Structured Streaming* section.

> **Tip**
> In Kafka terminology, an individual queue is called a *topic*, and each event is called an *offset*. Kafka is a queue, so it serves events in the same order in which they were published onto a topic, and individual consumers can choose their own starting and ending offsets.

Now that you are familiar with ingesting data from a few different types of **data sources** using Apache Spark, in the following section, let's learn how to ingest data into **data sinks**.

Ingesting data into data sinks

A data sink, as its name suggests, is a storage layer for storing raw or processed data either for short-term staging or long-term persistent storage. Though the term of *data sink* is commonly used in real-time data processing, there is no specific harm in calling any storage layer where ingested data lands a data sink. Just like data sources, there are also different types of data sinks. You will learn about a few of the most common ones in the following sections.

Ingesting into data warehouses

Data warehouses are a specific type of persistent data storage most prominent in Business Intelligence type workloads. There is an entire field of study dedicated to Business Intelligence and data warehousing. Typically, a data warehouse uses an RDBMS as its data store. However, a data warehouse is different from a traditional database in that it follows a specific type of data modeling technique, called **dimensional modeling**. Dimensional models are very intuitive for representing real-world business attributes and are conducive for Business Intelligence types of queries used in building business reports and dashboards. A data warehouse could be built on any commodity RDBMS or using specialist hardware and software.

Let's use PySpark to save a DataFrame to an RDBMS table, as shown in the following code block:

```
wordcount_df = spark.createDataFrame(
    [("data", 10), ("parallel", 2), ("Processing", 30),
    ("Spark", 50), ("Apache", 10)], ("word", "count"))
```

In the previous block of code, we programmatically create a DataFrame with two columns from a Python List object. Then, we save the Spark DataFrame to a MySQL table using the spark.write() function, as shown in the following code snippet:

```
wordcount_df.write.format("jdbc").options(
    url="jdbc:mysql://localhost:3306/pysparkdb",
    driver = "org.mariadb.jdbc.Driver",
    dbtable = "word_counts",
    user="######",
    password="@@@@@@").save()
```

The preceding snippet of code to write data to an RDBMS is almost the same as the one to read data from an RDBMS. We still need to use the MySQL JDBC driver and specify the *hostname, port number, database name*, and *database credentials*. The only difference is that here, we need to use the `spark.write()` function instead of `spark.read()`.

Ingesting into data lakes

Data warehouses are excellent for intuitively representing real-world business data and storing highly structured relational data in a way that is conducive for Business Intelligence types of workloads. However, data warehouses fall short when handling unstructured data that is required by data science and machine learning types of workloads. Data warehouses are not good at handling the high *Volume* and *Velocity* of big data. That's where data lakes step in to fill the gap left by data warehouses.

By design, data lakes are highly scalable and flexible when it comes to storing various types of data, including highly structured relational data and unstructured data such as images, text, social media, videos, and audio. Data lakes are also adept at handling data in batches as well as in streams. With the emergence of the cloud, data lakes have become very common these days, and they seem to be the future of persistent storage for all big data analytics workloads. A few examples of data lakes include Hadoop HDFS, AWS S3, Azure Blob or ADLS storage, and Google Cloud Storage.

Cloud-based data lakes have a few advantages over their on-premises counterparts:

- They are on-demand and infinitely scalable.
- They are pay-per-use, thus saving you on upfront investments.
- They are completely independent of computing resources; so, storage can scale independently of computing resources.
- They support both structured and unstructured data, along with simultaneous batch and streaming, allowing the same storage layer to be used by multiple workloads.

Because of the preceding advantages, cloud-based data lakes have become prominent over the past few years. Apache Spark treats these data lakes as yet another file-based data storage. Therefore, working with data lakes using Spark is as simple as working with any other file-based data storage layer.

Let's take a look at how easy it is to save data to a data lake using PySpark, as shown in the following code example:

```
(wordcount_df
        .write
```

```
        .option("header", "true")
        .mode("overwrite")
        .save("/tmp/data-lake/wordcount.csv")
)
```

In the preceding code block, we take the `wordcount_df` DataFrame that we created in the previous section and save it to the data lake in CSV format using the DataFrame's `write()` function. The `mode` option instructs `DataFrameWriter` to overwrite any existing data in the specified file location; note that you could also use `append` mode.

Ingesting into NoSQL and in-memory data stores

Data warehouses have always been the traditional persistent storage layer of choice for data analytics use cases, and data lakes are emerging as the new choice to cater to a wider range of workloads. However, there are other big data analytics use cases involving ultra-low latency query response times that require special types of storage layers. Two such types of storage layers are NoSQL databases and in-memory databases, which we will explore in this section.

NoSQL databases for operational analytics at scale

NoSQL databases are an alternative to traditional relational databases, where there is a requirement for handling messy and unstructured data. NoSQL databases are very good at storing large amounts of unstructured data in the form of **Key-Value** pairs and very efficient at retrieving the **Value** for any given **Key** in constant time, at high concurrency.

Let's consider a use case where a business wants to provide precalculated, hyper-personalized content to their individual customers using millisecond query response times in a highly concurrent manner. A NoSQL database such as Apache Cassandra or MongoDB would be an ideal candidate for the use case.

> **Note**
> Apache Spark doesn't come out of the box with any connectors for NoSQL databases. However, they are built and maintained by the respective database provider and can be downloaded for the respective provider and then configured with Apache Spark.

In-memory database for ultra-low latency analytics

In-memory databases store data purely in memory only, and persistent storage such as disks are not involved. This property of in-memory databases makes them faster in terms of data access speeds compared to their disk-based counterparts. A few examples of in-memory databases include **Redis** and **Memcached**. Since system memory is limited and data stored in memory is not durable over power cycles, in-memory databases are not suitable for the persistent storage of large amounts of historical data, which is typical for big data analytics systems. They do have their use in real-time analytics involving ultra-low latency response times.

Let's consider the example of an online retailer wanting to show the estimated shipment delivery time of a product to a customer at the time of checkout on their online portal. Most of the parameters that are needed to estimate delivery lead time can be precalculated. However, certain parameters, such as customer Zip Code and location, are only available when the customer provides them during checkout. Here, data needs to be instantly collected from the web portal, processed using an ultra-fast event processing system, and the results need to be calculated and stored in an ultra-low latency storage layer to be accessed and served back to the customer via the web app. All this processing should happen in a matter of seconds, and an in-memory database such as Redis or Memcached would serve the purpose of an ultra-low latency data storage layer.

So far, you have learned about accessing data from a few different data sources and ingesting them into various data sinks. Additionally, you have learned that you do not have much control over the data source. However, you do have complete control of your data sinks. Choosing the right data storage layer for certain high concurrency, ultra-low latency use cases is important. However, for most big data analytics use cases, data lakes are becoming the de facto standard as the preferred persistent data storage layer.

Another key factor for optimal data storage is the actual format of the data. In the following section, we will explore a few data storage formats and their relative merits.

Using file formats for data storage in data lakes

The file format you choose to store data in a data lake is key in determining the ease of data storage and retrieval, query performance, and storage space. So, it is vital that you choose the optimal data format that can balance these factors. Data storage formats can be broadly classified into structured, unstructured, and semi-structured formats. In this section, we will explore each of these types with the help of code examples.

Unstructured data storage formats

Unstructured data is any data that is not represented by a predefined data model and can be either human or machine-generated. For instance, unstructured data could be data stored in plain text documents, PDF documents, sensor data, log files, video files, images, audio files, social media feeds, and more.

Unstructured data might contain important patterns, and extracting these patterns could lead to valuable insights. However, storing data in unstructured format is not very useful due to the following reasons:

- Unstructured data might not always have an inherent compression mechanism and can take up large amounts of storage space.

- Externally compressing unstructured files saves space but expends the processing power for the compression and decompression of files.

- Storing and accessing unstructured files is somewhat difficult because they inherently lack any schema information.

Given the preceding reasons, it makes sense to ingest unstructured data and convert it into a structured format before storing it inside the data lake. This makes the downstream processing of data easier and more efficient. Let's take a look at an example where we take a set of unstructured image files and convert them into a DataFrame of image attributes. Then, we store them using the CSV file format, as shown in the following code snippet:

```
Raw_df = spark.read.format("image").load("/FileStore/FileStore/
shared_uploads/images/")
```
```
raw_df.printSchema()
```
```
image_df = raw_df.select("image.origin", "image.height",
"image.width", "image.nChannels", "image.mode", "image.data")
```
```
image_df.write.option("header", "true").mode("overwrite").
csv("/tmp/data-lake/images.csv")
```

In the previous code block, the following occurs:

- We load a set of images files using Spark's built-in image format; the result is a Spark DataFrame of image attributes.

- We use the printSchema() function to take a look at the DataFrame's schema and discover that the DataFrame has a single nested column named image with origin, height, width, nChannels, and more, as its inner attributes.

- Then, we bring up the inner attributes to the top level using the `image` prefix with each inner attribute, such as `image.origin`, and create a new DataFrame named `image_df` with all of the image's individual attributes as top-level columns.

- Now that we have our final DataFrame, we write it out to the data lake using the CSV format.

- Upon browsing the data lake, you can see that the process writes a few CSV files to the data lake with file sizes of, approximately, 127 bytes.

> **Tip**
> The number of files written out to storage depends on the number of partitions of the DataFrame. The number of DataFrame partitions depends on the number of executors cores and the `spark.sql.shuffle.partitions` Spark configuration. This number also changes every time the DataFrame undergoes a shuffle operation. In Spark 3.0, **Adaptive Query Execution** automatically manages the optimal number of shuffle partitions.

Along with file sizes, query performance is also an important factor when considering the file format. So, let's run a quick test where we perform a moderately complex operation on the DataFrame, as shown in the following block of code:

```
from pyspark.sql.functions import max, lit
temp_df = final_df.withColumn("max_width", lit(final_
df.agg(max("width")).first()[0]))
temp_df.where("width == max_width").show()
```

The previous block of code, first, creates a new column with every row value as the maximum width among all rows. Then, it filters out the row that has this maximum value for the `width` column. The query is moderately complex and typical of the kind of queries used in data analytics. In our sample test case, the query running on an unstructured binary file took, approximately, *5.03 seconds*. In the following sections, we will look at the same query on other file formats and compare query performances.

Semi-structured data storage formats

In the preceding example, we were able to take a binary image file, extract its attributes, and store them in CSV format, which makes the data structured but still keeps it in a human-readable format. CSV format is another type of data storage format called semi-structured data format. Semi-structured data formats, like unstructured data formats, do not have a predefined data model. However, they organize data in a way that makes it easier to infer schema information from the files themselves, without any external metadata being supplied. They are a popular data format for the exchange of data between distinct data processing systems. Examples of semi-structured data formats include CSV, XML, and JSON.

Let's take a look an example of how we can use PySpark to handle semi-structured data, as shown in the following code block:

```
csv_df = spark.read.options(header="true", inferSchema="true").
csv("/tmp/data-lake/images.csv")
csv_df.printSchema()
csv_df.show()
```

The previous code example takes the CSV files generated during the previous image processing example and loads them as a Spark DataFrame. We have enabled options to infer column names and data types from the actual data. The `printSchema()` function shows that Spark was able to infer column data types correctly for all columns except for the binary data column from the semi-structured files. The `show()` function shows that a DataFrame was correctly reconstructed from the CSV files along with column names.

Let's run a moderately complex query on the `csv_df` DataFrame, as shown in the following block of code:

```
from pyspark.sql.functions import max, lit
temp_df = csv_df.withColumn("max_width", lit(csv_
df.agg(max("width")).first()[0]))
temp_df.where("width == max_width").show()
```

In the preceding block of code, we perform a few DataFrame operations to get the row with the maximum value for the `width` column. The code took *1.24 seconds* to execute using CSV data format, compared to the similar code that we executed in the *Unstructured Data Storage Formats* section, which took, approximately, *5 seconds*. Thus, seemingly, semi-structured file formats are better than unstructured files for data storage, as it is relatively easier to infer schema information from this data storage format.

However, pay attention to the results of the show() function in the preceding code snippet. The data column containing binary data is inferred incorrectly as string type, and the column data is truncated. Therefore, it should be noted that semi-structured formats are not suitable for representing all data types, and they could also lose information with certain data types during the conversion from one data format into another.

Structured data storage formats

Structured data follows a predefined data model and has a tabular format with well-defined rows and named columns along with defined data types. A few examples of structured data formats are relational database tables and data generated by transactional systems. Note that there are also file formats that are fully structured data along with their data models, such as Apache Parquet, Apache Avro, and ORC files, that can be easily stored on data lakes.

Apache Parquet is a binary, compressed, and columnar storage format that was designed to be efficient at data storage as well as query performance. Parquet is a first-class citizen of the Apache Spark framework, and Spark's in-memory storage format, called **Tungsten**, was designed to take full advantage of the Parquet format. Therefore, you will get the best performance and efficiency out of Spark when your data is stored in Parquet format.

> **Note**
> A Parquet file is a binary file format, meaning that the contents of the file have a binary encoding. Therefore, they are not human-readable, unlike text-based file formats such as JSON or CSV. However, one advantage of this is that they are easily interpreted by machines without losing any time during the encoding and decoding processes.

Let's convert the image_df DataFrame, containing image attribute data from the *Unstructured data storage formats* section, into Parquet format, as shown in the following code block:

```
final_df.write.parquet("/tmp/data-lake/images.parquet")

parquet_df = spark.read.parquet("/tmp/data-lake/images.
parquet")

parquet_df.printSchema()

parquet_df.show()
```

The previous block of code loads binary image files into a Spark DataFrame and writes the data back into the data lake in Parquet format. The result of the show() function reveals that the binary data in the *data* column was not truncated and has been preserved from the source image files as-is.

Let's perform a moderately complex operation, as shown in the following block of code:

```
temp_df = parquet_df.withColumn("max_width", lit(parquet_
df.agg(max("width")).first()[0]))
temp_df.where("width == max_width").show()
```

The preceding code block extracts the row with the maximum value for the column named width. The query takes, approximately, *4.86 seconds* to execute, as compared to over *5 seconds* with the original unstructured image data. Therefore, this makes the structured Parquet file format the optimal format to be used to store data in data lakes with Apache Spark. Seemingly, the semi-structured CSV files took less time to execute the query, but they also truncated the data, making it not the right fit for every use case. As a general rule of thumb, the Parquet data format is recommended for almost all Apache Spark use cases, that is, unless a specific use case calls for another type of data storage format.

So far, you have seen that choosing the right data format can affect the correctness, ease of use, storage efficiency, query performance, and scalability of the data. Additionally, there is another factor that needs to be considered when storing data into data lakes no matter which data format you use. This technique is called **data partitioning** and can really make or break your downstream query performance.

Put simply, data partitioning is the process of physically dividing your data across multiple folders or partitions. Apache Spark uses this partition information to only read the relevant data files required by the query into memory. This mechanism is called **partition pruning**. You will learn more about data partitioning in *Chapter 3, Data Cleansing and Integration.*

So far, you have learned about the individual components of an Enterprise DSS, namely, data sources, data sinks, and data storage formats. Additionally, you gained a certain level of familiarity with the Apache Spark Framework as a big data processing engine in the previous chapter. Now, let's put this knowledge to use and build an end-to-end data ingestion pipeline in the following section.

Building data ingestion pipelines in batch and real time

An end-to-end data ingestion pipeline involves reading data from data sources and ingesting it into a data sink. In the context of big data and data lakes, data ingestion involves a large number of data sources and, thus, requires a data processing engine that is highly scalable. There are specialist tools available in the market that are purpose-built for handling data ingestion at scale, such as StreamSets, Qlik, Fivetran, Infoworks, and more, from third-party vendors. In addition to this, cloud providers have their own native offerings such as AWS Data Migration Service, Microsoft Azure Data Factory, and Google Dataflow. There are also free and open source data ingestion tools available that you could consider such as Apache Sqoop, Apache Flume, Apache Nifi, to name a few.

> **Tip**
> Apache Spark is good enough for ad hoc data ingestion, but it is not a common industry practice to use Apache Spark as a dedicated data ingestion engine. Instead, you should consider a dedicated, purpose-built data ingestion tool for your dedicated data ingestion needs. You can either choose from third-party vendors or choose to manage one of the open source offerings by yourself.

In this section, we will explore Apache Spark's capabilities for data ingestion in both a batch and streams processing manner.

Data ingestion using batch processing

Batch processing refers to processing one group or batch of data at a time. Batch processes are scheduled to run at specified intervals without any user intervention. Customarily, batch processes are run at night, after business hours. The simple reason for this is that batch processes tend to read a large number of transactions from the operational systems, which adds a lot of load to the operational systems. This is undesirable because operational systems are critical for the day-to-day operations of a business, and we do not want to unnecessarily burden the transactional system with workloads that are non-critical to daily business operations.

Additionally, batch processing jobs tend to be repetitive as they run at regular intervals, bringing in the new set of data generated after the last successful batch process has been run. Batch processing can be of two types, namely, **full data load** and **incremental data load**.

Full data loads

A full data load involves completely overwriting an existing dataset. This is useful for datasets that are relatively small in size and that do not change often. It is also an easier process to implement, as we just have to scan the entire source dataset and completely overwrite the destination dataset. There is no need to maintain any state information regarding the previous data ingestion job. Let's take an example of a dimensional table from a data warehouse, such as a calendar table or a table containing the data of all the physical stores of a retailer. These tables do not change often and are relatively small, making them ideal candidates for full data loads. Though easy to implement, full data loads have their drawbacks when it comes to dealing with very large source datasets that change regularly.

Let's consider the transactional data of a large retailer with more than a thousand stores all over the country, generating about 500 transactions per month per store. This translates to, approximately, 15,000 transactions ingested into the data lake per day. This number quickly adds up when we also consider historical data. Let's say that we just started building our data lake, and so far, we have only about 6 months of transactional data ingested. Even at this scale, we already have 3 million transactional records in our dataset, and completely truncating and loading the dataset is not a trivial task.

Another important factor to consider here is that typically, operational systems only retain historical data for small time intervals. Here, a full load means losing history from the data lake as well. At this point, you should consider an incremental load for data ingestion.

Incremental data loads

During an incremental data load, we only ingest the new set of data that was created in the data source after the previous case of successful data ingestion. This incremental dataset is generally referred to as the delta. An incremental load ingests datasets that are smaller in size compared to a full load, and since we already maintain the full historical data in our delta lake, incremental doesn't need to depend on the data source maintaining a full history.

Building on the same retailer example from earlier, let's assume that we run our incremental batch load once per night. In this scenario, we only need to ingest 15,000 transactions into the data lake per day, which is pretty easy to manage.

Designing an incremental data ingestion pipeline is not as simple compared to a full load pipeline. State information about the previous run of the incremental job needs to be maintained so that we can identify all of the new records from the data source that have not already been ingested into the data lake. This state information is stored in a special data structure, called a *watermark* table. This watermark table needs to be updated and maintained by the data ingestion job. A typical data ingestion pipeline is illustrated as follows:

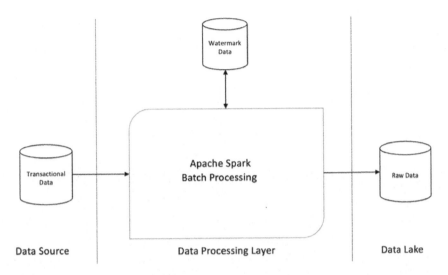

Figure 2.2 – Data ingestion

The preceding diagram shows a typical data ingestion pipeline using Apache Spark, along with the watermark table for incremental loads. Here, we ingest raw transactional data from source systems using Spark's built-in data sources, process them using DataFrame operations and then send the data back to a data lake.

Expanding on the retail example from the previous section, let's build an end-to-end data ingestion pipeline with batch processing using PySpark. One of the prerequisites for building a data pipeline is, of course, data, and for this example, we will make use of the *Online Retail* dataset made available by *UC Irvine Machine Learning Repository*. The dataset is available in CSV format in the GitHub repository mentioned in the *Technical requirements* section of this chapter. The *Online Retail* dataset contains transactional data for an online retailer.

We will download the dataset, consisting of two CSV files, and upload them to the *Databricks Community Edition* notebook environment via the upload interface that is present within the notebook's file menu. Once the dataset has been uploaded, we will make a note of the file location.

> **Note**
>
> If you are using your own Spark environment, make sure that you have the datasets available at a location that is accessible for your Spark cluster.

Now we can get started with the actual code for the data ingestion pipeline, as shown in the following code example:

```
retail_df = (spark
                .read
                .option("header", "true")
                .option("inferSchema", "true")
                .csv("/FileStore/shared_uploads/online_retail/
online_retail.csv")
            )
```

In the preceding code block, we loaded the CSV files with the `header` and `inferSchema` options enabled. This creates a Spark DataFrame with eight columns along with their respective data types and column names. Now, let's ingest this data into the data lake in Parquet format, as shown in the following code block:

```
(retail_df
        .write
        .mode("overwrite")
        .parquet("/tmp/data-lake/online_retail.parquet")
)
```

Here, we save the `retail_df` Spark DataFrame, containing raw retail transactions, to the data lake in Parquet format using the DataFrameWriter's `write()` function. We also specify the `mode` option to `overwrite` and, essentially, implement a full data load.

One thing to note here is that the entire data ingestion job is a mere **10** lines of code, and this can easily be scaled up to tens of millions of records, processing up to many petabytes of data. This is the power and simplicity of Apache Spark, which has made it the de facto standard for big data processing in a very short period of time. Now, how would you actually scale the preceding data ingestion batch job and then, eventually, productionize it?

Apache Spark was built from the ground up to be scalable, and its scalability is entirely dependent on the number of cores available to a job on the cluster. So, to scale your Spark job, all you need to do is to allocate more processing cores to the job. Most commercially available Spark-as-a-managed-service offerings provide a nifty **Autoscaling** functionality. With this autoscaling functionality, you just need to specify the minimum and the maximum number of nodes for your cluster, and **Cluster Manager** dynamically figures out the optimal number of cores for your job.

Most commercial Spark offerings also come with a built-in **Job Scheduler** and support directly scheduling notebooks as jobs. External schedulers, ranging from the rudimentary **crontab** to sophisticated job orchestrators such as **Apache Airflow**, can also be used to productionize your Spark jobs. This really makes the process of cluster capacity planning easier for you, freeing up your time to focus on actual data analytics rather than spending your time and energy on capacity planning, tuning, and maintaining Spark clusters.

So far, in this section, you have viewed an example of a full load batch ingestion job that loads the entire data from the data source and then overwrites the dataset in the data lake. You would need to add a little more business logic to maintain the ingestion job's state in a watermark data structure and then calculate the delta to perform an incremental load. You could build all this logic by yourself, or, alternatively, you could simply use Spark's structured streaming engine to do the heavy lifting for you, as discussed in the following section.

Data ingestion in real time using structured streaming

Often, businesses need to make tactical decisions in real time along with strategic decision-making in order to stay competitive. Therefore, the need to ingest data into a data lake arises in real time. However, keeping up with the fast data *Velocity* of big data requires a robust and scalable streams processing engine. Apache Spark has one such streams processing engine, called **Structured Streaming**, which we will explore next.

Structured Streaming primer

Structured Streaming is a Spark streams processing engine based on the Spark SQL engine. Just like all other components of Spark, Structured Streaming is also scalable and fault-tolerant. Since Structured Streaming is based on the Spark SQL engine, you can use the same Spark DataFrame API that you have already been using for batch processing for streams processing, too. Structured Streaming supports all of the functions and constructs supported by the DataFrame API.

Structured Streaming treats each incoming stream of data just like tiny a batch of data, called a *micro-batch,* and keeps appending each micro-batch to the target dataset. Structured Streaming's programming model continuously processes micro-batches, treating each micro-batch just like a batch job. So, an existing Spark batch job can be easily converted into a streaming job with a few minor changes. Structured Streaming is designed to provide maximum throughput, which means that a Structured Streaming job can scale out to multiple nodes on a cluster and process very large amounts of incoming data in a distributed fashion.

Structured Streaming comes with additional fault tolerance to failures and guarantees exactly once semantics. To achieve this, Structured Streaming keeps track of the data processing progress. It keeps track of the offsets or events processed at any point in time using concepts such as **checkpointing** and **write-ahead logs**. Write-ahead logging is a concept from relational databases and is used to provide atomicity and durability to databases. In this technique, records are first written to the log before any changes are written to the final database. Checkpointing is another technique in Structured Streaming, where the position of the current offset being read is recorded on a persistent storage system.

Together, these techniques enable Structured Streaming to keep a record of the position of the last offset processed within the stream, giving it the ability to resume processing the stream exactly where it left off, just in case the streaming job fails.

> **Note**
> We recommended that checkpoints are stored in persistent storage with high availability and partition tolerance support, such as a cloud-based data lake.

These techniques of checkpointing, write-ahead logs, and repayable streaming data sources, along with streaming data sinks that support the reprocessing of data, enable Structured Streaming to guarantee that every event of the stream is processed exactly once.

> **Note**
>
> Structured Streaming's micro-batch processing model is not suitable for processing an event as soon as it occurs at the source. There are other streams processing engines such as Apache Flink or Kafka Streams that are more suitable for ultra-low latency streams processing.

Loading data incrementally

Since Structured Streaming has built-in mechanisms to help you to easily maintain the state information that is required for an incremental load, you can simply choose Structured Streaming for all your incremental loads and really simplify your architectural complexity. Let's build a pipeline to perform incremental loads in a real-time streaming fashion.

Typically, our data ingestion starts with data already loaded onto a data source such as a data lake or a message queue such as Kafka. Here, we, first, need to load some data into a Kafka topic. You can start with an existing Kafka cluster with some data already in a topic, or you can set up a quick Kafka server and load the *Online Retail* dataset using the code provided at `https://github.com/PacktPublishing/Essential-PySpark-for-Data-Analytics/blob/main/Chapter02/utils/kafka-setup.ipynb`.

Let's take a look at how to perform real-time data ingestion from Kafka into a data lake using Structured Streaming, as shown in the following snippets of code:

```python
from pyspark.sql.types import StructType, StructField,
StringType, IntegerType, TimestampType, DoubleType
eventSchema = ( StructType()
  .add('InvoiceNo', StringType())
  .add('StockCode', StringType())
  .add('Description', StringType())
  .add('Quantity', IntegerType())
  .add('InvoiceDate', StringType())
  .add('UnitPrice', DoubleType())
  .add('CustomerID', IntegerType())
  .add('Country', StringType())
)
```

In the preceding block of code, we declare all the columns that we intend to read from a Kafka event along with their data types. Structured Streaming requires that the data schema be declared upfront. Once the schema has been defined, we can start reading data from a Kafka topic and load it into a Spark DataFrame, as shown in the following block of code:

```
kafka_df = (spark
                .readStream
                 .format("kafka")
                  .option("kafka.bootstrap.servers",
                       "localhost:9092")
                    .option("subscribe", "retail_events")
                     .option("startingOffsets", "earliest")
                  .load()
            )
```

In the preceding code block, we start reading a stream of events from a Kafka topic, called `retail_events`, and tell Kafka that we want to start loading the events from the beginning of the stream using the `startingOffsets` option. The events in a Kafka topic follow a key-value pattern. This means that our actual data is encoded within a JSON object in the `value` column that we need to extract, as shown in the following code block:

```
from pyspark.sql.functions import col, from_json, to_date
retail_df = (kafka_df
                 .select(from_json(col("value").
cast(StringType()), eventSchema).alias("message"),
col("timestamp").alias("EventTime"))
                 .select("message.*", "EventTime")
            )
```

In the preceding code block, we extract the data using the `from_json()` function by passing in the data schema object that we defined earlier. This results in a `retail_df` DataFrame that has all of the columns of the event that we require. Additionally, we append an `EventTime` column from the Kafka topic, which shows when the event actually arrived in Kafka. This could be of some use later, during further data processing. Since this DataFrame was created using the `readStream()` function, Spark inherently knows this is a Streaming DataFrame and makes Structured Streaming APIs available to this DataFrame.

Once we have extracted the raw event data from the Kafka stream, we can persist it to the data lake, as shown in the following block of code:

```
base_path = "/tmp/data-lake/retail_events.parquet"
(retail_df
   .withColumn("EventDate", to_date(retail_df.EventTime))
     .writeStream
       .format('parquet')
       .outputMode("append")
       .trigger(once=True)
       .option('checkpointLocation', base_path + '/_checkpoint')
     .start(base_path)
 )
```

In the preceding code block, we make use of the `writeStream()` function that is available to Streaming DataFrames to save data to the data lake in a streaming fashion. Here, we write data in Parquet format, and the resultant data on the data lake will be a set of `.parquet` files. Once saved, these Parquet files are no different from any other Parquet files, whether created by batch processing or streams processing.

Additionally, we use `outputMode` as `append` to indicate that we will treat this as an unbounded dataset and will keep appending new Parquet files. The `checkpointLocation` option stores the Structured Streaming write-ahead log and other checkpointing information. This makes it an incremental data load job as the stream only picks up new and unprocessed events based on the offset information stored at the checkpoint location.

Note

Structured Streaming supports `complete` and `update` modes in addition to `append` mode. A description of these modes and when to use them can be found in Apache Spark's official documentation at `https://spark.apache.org/docs/latest/structured-streaming-programming-guide.html#output-modes`.

But what if you need to run the incremental data load job as a less frequent batch process instead of running it in a continuous streaming manner?

Well, Structured Streaming supports this too via the `trigger` option. We can use `once=True` for this option, and the streaming job will process all new and unprocessed events when the job is externally triggered and then stop the stream when there are no new events to be processed. We can schedule this job to run periodically based on a time interval and it will just behave like a batch job but with all the benefits of an incremental load.

In summary, the Spark SQL engine's DataFrame API is both powerful and easy to use for batch data processing and streams processing. There are slight differences between the functions and utilities provided between a static DataFrame and streaming DataFrame. However, for the most part, the programming models between batch processing and streams processing that use DataFrames are very similar. This minimizes the learning curve and helps to unify batch and streams processing using Apache Spark's unified analytics engine.

Now, in the next section, let's examine how to implement a unified data processing architecture with Apache Spark using a concept called **Lambda Architecture**.

Unifying batch and real time using Lambda Architecture

Both batch and real-time data processing are important elements of any modern Enterprise DSS, and an architecture that seamlessly implements both these data processing techniques can help increase throughput, minimize latency, and allow you to get to fresh data much more quickly. One such architecture is called **Lambda Architecture**, which we will examine next.

Lambda Architecture

Lambda Architecture is a data processing technique that is used to ingest, process, and query both historical and real-time data with a single architecture. Here, the goal is to increase throughput, data freshness, and fault tolerance while maintaining a single view of both historical and real-time data for end users. The following diagram illustrates a typical Lambda Architecture:

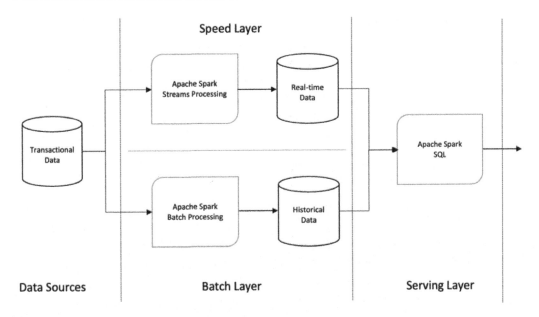

Figure 2.3 – Lambda Architecture

As shown in the preceding diagram, a Lambda Architecture consists of three main components, namely, the **Batch Layer**, the **Speed Layer**, and the **Serving Layer**. We will discuss each of these layers in the following sections.

The Batch layer

The Batch layer is like any typical ETL layer involving the batch processing of data from the source system. This layer usually involves scheduled jobs that run periodically, typically, at night.

Apache Spark can be used to build batch processing jobs or Structured Streaming jobs that get triggered on a schedule, and it can also be used for the batch layer to build historical data in the data lake.

The Speed layer

The Speed layer continuously ingests data from the same data source as the Batch layer from the data lake into real-time views. The Speed layer continuously delivers the latest data that the Batch layer cannot provide yet due to its inherent latency. Spark Structured Steaming can be used to implement low latency streaming jobs to continuously ingest the latest data from the source system.

The Serving layer

The Serving layer combines the historical data from the Batch layer and the latest data from the Speed layer into a single view to support ad hoc queries by end users. Spark SQL makes a good candidate for the Serving layer as it can help users query historical data from the Batch layer, as well as the latest data from the Speed layer, and present the user with a unified view of data for low-latency, ad hoc queries.

In the previous sections, you implemented data ingestion jobs for batch as well as streaming using Apache Spark. Now, let's explore how you can combine the two views to give users a single unified view, as shown in the following code snippet:

```
batch_df = spark.read.parquet("/tmp/data-lake/online_retail.
parquet")
speed_df = spark.read.parquet("/tmp/data-lake/retail_events.
parquet").drop("EventDate").drop("EventTime")
serving_df = batch_df.union(speed_df)
serving_df.createOrReplaceGlobalTempView("serving_layer")
```

In the preceding code block, we create two DataFrames, one from the **Batch Layer** location and the other from the **Speed Layer** location on the data lake. We call the `union` function to unite these two DataFrames and then create a **Spark Global Temp View** using the combined DataFrame. The result is a view that is accessible across all **Spark Sessions** across the cluster, which gives you a unified view of data across both the batch and speed layers, as shown in the following line of code:

```
%sql
SELECT count(*) FROM global_temp.serving_layer;
```

The preceding line of code is a SQL query that queries data from the Spark global view, which acts as the **Serving Layer** and can be presented to end users for ad hoc queries across both the latest data and historical data.

In this way, you can make use of Apache Spark's SQL engine's DataFrame, Structured Streaming, and SQL APIs to build a Lambda Architecture that improves data freshness, throughput, and provides a unified view of data. However, the Lambda Architecture is somewhat complex to maintain because there are two separate data ingestion pipelines for batch and real-time processing along with two separate data sinks. Indeed, there is an easier way to unify the batch and speed layers using an open source storage layer called **Delta Lake**. You will learn about this in *Chapter 3, Data Cleansing and Integration*.

Summary

In this chapter, you learned about Enterprise DSS in the context of big data analytics and its components. You learned about various types of data sources such as RDBMS-based operational systems, message queues, and file sources, and data sinks, such as data warehouses and data lakes, and their relative merits.

Additionally, you explored different types of data storage formats such as unstructured, structured, and semistructured and learned about the benefits of using structured formats such as Apache Parquet with Spark. You were introduced to data ingestion in a batch and real-time manner and learned how to implement them using Spark DataFrame APIs. We also introduced Spark's Structured Streaming framework for real-time streams processing, and you learned how to use Structured Streaming to implement incremental data loads using minimal programming overheads. Finally, you explored the Lambda Architecture to unify batch and real-time data processing and its implementation using Apache Spark. The skills learned in this chapter will help you to implement scalable and performant distributed data ingestion pipelines via Apache Spark using both batch and streams processing models.

In the next chapter, you will learn about the techniques to process, cleanse, and integrate the raw data that was ingested into a data lake in this chapter into clean, consolidated, and meaningful datasets that are ready for end users to perform business analytics on and generate meaningful insights.

3
Data Cleansing and Integration

In the previous chapter, you were introduced to the first step of the data analytics process – that is, ingesting raw, transactional data from various source systems into a cloud-based data lake. Once we have the raw data available, we need to process, clean, and transform it into a format that helps with extracting meaningful, actionable business insights. This process of cleaning, processing, and transforming raw data is known as data cleansing and integration. This is what you will learn about in this chapter.

Raw data sourced from operational systems is not conducive for data analytics in its raw format. In this chapter, you will learn about various data integration techniques, which are useful in consolidating raw, transactional data from disparate source systems and joining them to enrich them and present the end user with a single, consolidated version of the truth. Then, you will learn how to clean and transform the form and structure of raw data into a format that is ready for data analytics using data cleansing techniques. Data cleansing broadly deals with fixing inconsistencies within data, dealing with bad and corrupt data, eliminating any duplicates within data, and standardizing data to meet the enterprise data standards and conventions. You will also learn about the challenges involved in using a cloud data lake as an analytics data store. Finally, you will be introduced to a modern data storage layer called Delta Lake to overcome these challenges.

This chapter will equip you with essential skills for consolidating, cleaning, and transforming raw data into a structure that is ready for analytics, as well as provide you with useful techniques for building scalable, reliable, and analytics-ready data lakes in the cloud. As a developer, the topics included in this chapter will help you give your business users access to all of their data at all times, allowing them to draw actionable insights from their raw data much faster and easier.

In this chapter, the following main topics will be covered:

- Transforming raw data into enriched meaningful data

- Building analytical data stores using cloud data lakes

- Consolidating data using data integration

- Making raw data analytics-ready using data cleansing

Technical requirements

In this chapter, we will be using the Databricks Community Edition to run our code (`https://community.cloud.databricks.com`). Sign-up instructions can be found at `https://databricks.com/try-databricks`.

The code in this chapter can be downloaded from `https://github.com/PacktPublishing/Essential-PySpark-for-Data-Analytics/tree/main/Chapter03`.

The datasets for this chapter can be found at `https://github.com/PacktPublishing/Essential-PySpark-for-Data-Analytics/tree/main/data`.

Transforming raw data into enriched meaningful data

Every data analytics system consists of a few key stages, including data ingestion, data transformation, and loading into a data warehouse or a data lake. Only after the data passes through these stages does it become ready for consumption by end users for descriptive and predictive analytics. There are two common industry practices for undertaking this process, widely known as **Extract, Transform, Load** (**ETL**) and **Extract, Load, Transform** (**ELT**). In this section, you will explore both these methods of data processing and understand their key differences. You will also learn about the key advantages ELT has to offer over ETL in the context of big data analytics in the cloud.

Extracting, transforming, and loading data

This is the typical data processing methodology that's followed by almost all data warehousing systems. In this methodology, data is extracted from the source systems and stored in a temporary storage location such as a relational database, called the staging area. Then, the data in the staging area is integrated, cleansed, and transformed before being loaded into the data warehouse. The following diagram illustrates a typical ETL process:

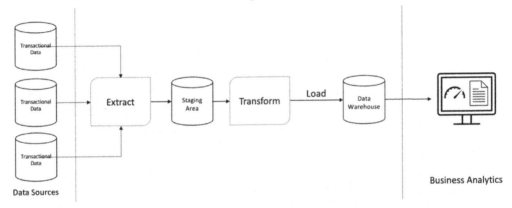

Figure 3.1 – Extract, transform, and load

As shown in the previous diagram, the ETL process consists of three main stages. We will discuss these in the following sections.

Extracting data from operational systems

The ETL stage involves extracting selective, raw, transactional data from multiple source systems and staging it at a temporary storage location. This step is equivalent to the data ingestion process, which you learned about in *Chapter 2, Data Ingestion*. The ETL process typically processes large volumes of data, though running it directly on the source systems might put excessive load on them. Operational systems are critical to the functionality of day-to-day business functions and it is not advisable to unnecessarily tax them. Thus, the **Extract** process extracts data from source systems during off-business hours and stores it in a staging area. Furthermore, ETL processing can happen on the data in the staging area, leaving operational systems to handle their core functions.

Transforming, cleaning, and integrating data

This stage involves various data transformation processes such as data integration, data cleansing, joining, filtering, splitting, standardization, validation, and more. This step converts raw transactional data into a clean, integrated, and enriched version that is ready for business analytics. We will dive deeper into this stage in the *Consolidating data using data integration* and *Making raw data analytics ready using data cleansing* sections of this chapter.

Loading data into a data warehouse

This is the final stage of the ETL process, where the transformed data is finally loaded into a persistent, historical data storage layer, such as a data warehouse. Typically, ETL processing systems accomplish the **Transform** and **Load** steps in a single flow, where raw data from the staging area is cleansed, integrated, and transformed according to the business rules and loaded into a warehouse, all in a single flow.

Pros and cons of ETL and data warehousing

Some advantages of the ETL methodology are that data is transformed and loaded into a structured analytical data store such as a data warehouse, which allows for efficient and performant analysis of the data. Since the ETL paradigm has been in existence for a few decades now, there are sophisticated platforms and tools on the market that can perform ETL in a very efficient manner in a single, unified flow.

Another advantage of ETL is that since data is processed before being loaded into its final storage, there is the opportunity to either omit unwanted data or obscure sensitive data. This greatly helps with data regulatory and compliance requirements.

However, ETL processes run in a batch processing manner and typically run once every night. Thus, new data is only available to end users once the ETL batch process has finished successfully. This creates a dependency on data engineers to efficiently run the ETL processes, and there is a considerable delay before end users can get access to the latest data.

The data in the staging area is almost entirely cleared every time before the start of the next scheduled ETL load. Also, operational systems do not typically keep a historical record of the transactional data for more than a few years. This means that end users cease to have any access to historical raw data, other than the processed data in the data warehouse. This historical raw data could prove to be very useful for certain types of data analytics such as predictive analytics, but data warehouses generally do not retain it.

The ETL process evolved around data warehousing concepts and is more suited for business intelligence workloads, in an on-premises type of setting. The highly structured and somewhat rigid nature of data warehouses makes ETL not very conducive for data science and machine learning, both of which deal with a lot of unstructured data. Moreover, the batch nature of the ETL process makes it unfit for real-time analytics. Also, ETL and data warehouses do not take full advantage of the cloud and cloud-based data lakes. That's why a new methodology for data processing has emerged called **Extract, Load, and Transform**, or **ELT**, which we will take a look at in the following section.

Extracting, loading, and transforming data

In the ELT methodology, transactional data from source systems is ingested into a data lake in its original, raw format. The ingested, raw data in the data lake is then transformed either on-demand or in a scheduled manner. In the ELT process, raw data is directly staged on the data lake and is typically never purged. As a result, data can grow enormously in size and require virtually unlimited storage and compute capacity. On-premises data warehouses and data lakes were not designed to handle data at such an enormous scale. Thus, the ELT methodology is only made possible by modern cloud technologies that offer highly scalable and elastic compute and storage resources. The following diagram depicts a typical ELT process:

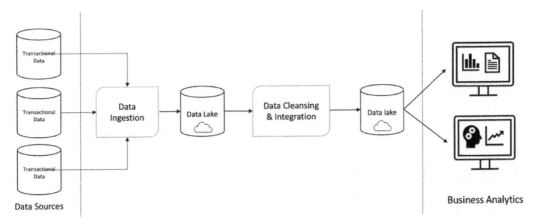

Figure 3.2 – Extract, load, and transform

In the preceding diagram, raw data is either continuously or periodically ingested from multiple source systems into a data lake. Then, the raw data in the data lake is integrated, cleaned, and transformed before being stored back inside it. The clean and aggregated data in the data lake serves as a single source of truth for all types of downstream analytics.

With ELT, virtually any amount of history can be maintained, and data can be made available as soon as it is created in the source systems. There is no requirement to pre-process data before ingesting it and since data lakes do not impose any strict requirements on the format or structure of data, ELT can ingest and store all kinds of structured, unstructured, and semi-structured data. Thus, the ETL process makes all the historical raw data available so that data transformation can become completely on demand.

Advantages of choosing ELT over ETL

Some of the advantages of the ELT methodology are that data can be ingested at much faster speeds since no pre-processing steps are required. It is much more flexible with the kinds of data that can be ingested, helping unlock new analytics use cases such as data science and machine learning. ETL leverages elastic storage provided by cloud data lakes, helping organizations maintain a replica of transactional data, along with virtually unlimited history. ELT, typically being cloud-based, takes away the hassle of managing data replication and archiving as most cloud providers have managed services for these and guarantee **Service-Level Agreements (SLAs)**.

The ELT methodology is quickly becoming the de facto standard for big data processing in the cloud for organizations with huge amounts of transactional data. The ELT methodology of data processing is recommended for organizations that are already in the cloud or with a future cloud strategy.

However, the ELT methodology in the cloud is still very nascent, and cloud data lakes do not offer any of the transactional or reliability guarantees that their data warehousing counterparts already offer. In the next section, you will explore some of the challenges involved in building cloud-based data lakes and some ways to overcome them.

Building analytical data stores using cloud data lakes

In this section, you will explore the advantages afforded by cloud-based data lakes for big data analytics systems, and then understand some of the challenges facing big data analytics systems while leveraging cloud-based data analytics systems. You will also write a few **PySpark** code examples to experience these challenges first-hand.

Challenges with cloud data lakes

Cloud-based data lakes offer unlimited, scalable, and relatively inexpensive data storage. They are offered as managed services by the individual cloud providers and offer availability, scalability, efficiency, and lower **total cost of ownership**. This helps organizations accelerate their digital innovation and achieve faster time to market. However, cloud data lakes are object storages that evolved primarily to solve the problem of storage scalability. They weren't designed to store highly structured, strongly typed, analytical data. Given this, there are a few challenges in using cloud-based data lakes as analytical storage systems.

Data reliability challenges with data lakes

Data lakes are not based on any underlying filesystem but on the object storage mechanism, which manages data as objects. Object storage represents data as objects with a unique identifier and its associated metadata. Object storages weren't designed to manage frequently changing transactional data. Thus, they have a few limitations regarding analytical data stores and data processing, such as eventual consistency, lack of transactional guarantees, and more. We will look at these in the following sections.

Eventual consistency of data

Cloud-based data lakes are distributed storage systems where data storage happens across multiple machines instead of a single machine. Distributed storage systems are governed by a theorem referred to as the CAP theorem. The **CAP theorem** states that a distributed storage system can be tuned for only two of the three parameters of CAP; that is, consistency, availability, and partition tolerance. Not guaranteeing strong availability and partition tolerance can lead to data loss or errors, so cloud-based data lakes prioritize these two so that they're made eventually consistent.

Eventual consistency means that data written to a cloud data lake might not be available instantly. This could lead to `FileNotFound` errors in a data analytics system, where downstream business analytics processes try to read data from the data lake while it is being written by an ELT process.

Lack of transactional guarantees

A typical relational database provides transactional guarantees when data is being written. This simply means that a database operation either completely succeeds or completely fails, and that any consumer trying to read the data simultaneously doesn't get any inconsistent or incorrect data because of a database operation failure.

Data lakes do not provide any such atomic transactional or durability guarantees. This means that it's up to the developer to clean up and manually roll back half-written, incomplete data from any failed jobs and reprocess the data all over again.

Consider the following code snippet, where we are ingesting CSV data, converting it into Parquet format, and saving it to the data lake:

```
(spark
  .read
    .csv("/FileStore/shared_uploads/online_retail/")
  .write
    .mode("overwrite")
    .format("parquet")
```

```
       .save("/tmp/retail.parquet")
)
```

Here, let's try and interrupt the job halfway through to simulate a Spark job failure. Upon browsing the data lake at /tmp/retail.parquet, you will notice a few half-written Parquet files. Let's try and read those Parquet files via another Spark job, as shown in the following code:

```
(spark
  .read
    .format("parquet")
      .load("dbfs:/tmp/retail.parquet/part-00006-tid-
6775149024880509486-a83d662e-809e-4fb7-beef-208d983f0323-212-
1-c000.snappy.parquet")
      .count()
)
```

In the preceding code block, we have read a Parquet file that was the result of a data ingestion job that failed halfway through. The expected result, when we try to read this data on a data store that supports atomic transactions, is that either the query yields no results or it just fails because the data is incorrect. However, in the case of the preceding Spark job, we do get a few thousand records, which is incorrect. This is because of the lack of atomic transaction guarantees on the part of Apache Spark, as well as the data lake.

Lack of schema enforcement

Data lakes, being object stores, are not concerned with the structure and schema of data and are happy to store all and any data without performing any checks to make sure that data is consistent. Apache Spark also doesn't have any built-in mechanism to enforce a user-defined schema. This results in corrupt and bad data, with mismatched data types ending up in your data lake. This reduces data quality, which is critical for end user analytical applications.

Take a look at the following code example, where we have written an initial DataFrame with a few columns. The first column is of IntegerType, while the second column is of StringType. We wrote the first DataFrame to the data lake in Parquet format. Then, we generated a second DataFrame where both columns are of IntegerType. Then, we tried to append the second DataFrame to the original Parquet dataset already in the data lake, as shown in the following code:

```
from pyspark.sql.functions import lit
df1 = spark.range(3).withColumn("customer_id", lit("1"))
```

```
(df1
    .write
      .format("parquet")
      .mode("overwrite")
    .save("/tmp/customer")
)
df2 = spark.range(2).withColumn("customer_id", lit(2))
(df2
    .write
      .format("parquet")
      .mode("append")
    .save("/tmp/customer"))
```

The expected result on a strongly typed analytical data store such as a data warehouse should be a data type mismatch error. However, neither Apache Spark nor the data lake or the Parquet data format itself, throw an error while we try to perform this operation, and the transaction seems to complete successfully. This is undesirable as we have allowed inconsistent data to enter our data lake. However, performing a read operation on the Parquet dataset would fail with a type mismatch, which could be confusing and quite difficult to debug. This error could have easily been caught during the data loading process if data lakes or Apache Spark came with data validation support. It is important to always validate the data's correctness and consistency before making it available for business analytics because business decision-makers depend on it.

Unifying batch and streaming

One of the key requirements of modern big data analytics systems is getting access to the latest data and insights in real time. Apache Spark comes with structured streaming to handle all real-time analytics requirements. Despite stream processing, batch processing remains a key aspect of big data analytics, and Apache Spark has done quite a good job of unifying both real-time and batch analytics via its Spark SQL Engine, which acts as the core abstraction layer for both batch and streaming Spark jobs.

However, data lakes do not support any level of atomic transactions or isolation between different transactions on the same table or dataset. So, something like the **Lambda Architecture**, which you learned about in *Chapter 2, Data Ingestion*, would need to be employed to unify batch and stream processing pipelines. This results in separate data processing pipelines, separate code bases, and separate tables being maintained, one for batch processing and another stream processing. This architecture of your big data analytics system is very complex to design and maintain.

Updating and deleting data

In the ELT methodology, you are continuously ingesting new data into the data lake and maintaining a replica of your source transactions inside it, along with history over a certain period. Operational systems are constantly generating transactions. However, from time to time, you must update and delete records.

Consider the example of an order that's been placed by a customer at an online retailer. The transaction goes through different phases, starting with the order being placed, the order being processed, the order getting ready for shipment, the order getting shipped, the order in transit, and the order being delivered. This change in the state of the transaction must be reflected in the data lake.

This process of capturing the change in the state of data is known as **change data capture** (**CDC**) and is an essential process for maintaining a replica of the operating system in the data lake. CDC requires multiple UPDATE and DELETE operations in the data lake. Data lakes are append-only systems and not designed to handle a large number of arbitrary updates and deletes. Thus, implementing arbitrary updates and deletes increases the complexity of your ELT application.

Rolling back incorrect data

Earlier, you learned that data lakes do not support any atomic transactional guarantees on write operations. It is up to the data engineer to identify the incorrect records, clean them up, and reprocess the data again for failed jobs. For smaller datasets, this cleanup process could be as simple as truncating and loading the entire dataset. However, for larger datasets at a big data scale with petabytes of data, truncating and loading data is not at all feasible. Neither data lakes nor Apache Spark has an easy rollback option, requiring the data engineer to build complex mechanisms to handle failed jobs.

A new class of modern data storage formats has emerged that tries to overcome the data lake challenges mentioned in the previous section. Some examples of these technologies are Apache Hudi, Apache Iceberg, and Delta Lake. In the following section, we will explore Delta Lake and see how it can help in overcoming various data lake challenges.

Overcoming data lake challenges with Delta Lake

In this section, you will be introduced to Delta Lake and understand how it helps overcome some of the challenges of data lakes. You will also write a few code examples to see Delta Lake in action.

Introduction to Delta Lake

Delta Lake is an open source data storage layer that helps bring reliability, ACID transactional guarantees, schema validation, and evolution to cloud-based data lakes. Delta Lake also helps in unifying batch and stream processing. Delta Lake was created by Databricks, the original creators of Apache Spark, and it was designed to be completely compatible with all Apache Spark APIs.

Delta Lake is made up of a set of versioned Parquet files, along with a write-ahead log called the **transaction log**. The Delta Transaction Log helps enable all the features of Delta Lake. Let's dive deeper into the inner workings of Delta Transaction Log to gain a better understanding of how Delta Lake operates.

Delta Lake transaction log

The **Delta transaction log** is based on a popular technique that's performed on relational databases known as **write-ahead logging (WAL)**. This technique guarantees the atomicity and durability of write operations on a database. This is achieved by recording each write operation as a transaction in the write-ahead log before any data is written to the database. The Delta Transaction Log is based on the same technique as WAL, but here, WAL, as well as the data that's been written, is in files on the data lake.

Let's try to understand the Delta Transaction Log using a simple Spark job that ingests CSV data into the data lake in Delta format, as shown in the following code block:

```
(spark
  .read
    .option("header", True)
    .option("inferSchema", True)
    .csv("/FileStore/shared_uploads/online_retail/")
  .write
    .format("delta")
    .save("/FileStore/shared_uploads/delta/online_retail")
)
```

The preceding code reads CSV files from the data lake, infers the schema of the underlying data, along with the header, converts the data into Delta format, and saves the data in a different location on the data lake. Now, let's explore the Delta file's location on the data lake using the following command:

```
%fs ls /FileStore/shared_uploads/delta/online_retail
```

After you execute the preceding command, you will notice the folder structure of the Delta location, as shown in the following screenshot:

	path	▲
1	dbfs:/FileStore/shared_uploads/delta/online_retail/_delta_log/	
2	dbfs:/FileStore/shared_uploads/delta/online_retail/part-00000-02b5cb40-205e-490d-bb30-21b6581c176c-c000.snappy.parquet	
3	dbfs:/FileStore/shared_uploads/delta/online_retail/part-00001-c4fc297f-22a4-4083-9ae8-40095daa249e-c000.snappy.parquet	
4	dbfs:/FileStore/shared_uploads/delta/online_retail/part-00002-f2da06cf-31bd-465c-8187-dd8057156fbd-c000.snappy.parquet	
	dbfs:/FileStore/shared_uploads/delta/online_retail/part-00003-aab693bb-6fcd-41eb-9dbe-bd4066ddf943-c000.snappy.parquet	

Figure 3.3 – Delta folder structure

In the preceding screenshot, you can see that a Delta Lake location contains two parts: a folder named _delta_log and a set of Parquet files. The _delta_log folder contains the Delta Transaction Log's files. Let's explore the transaction log using the following command:

```
%fs ls dbfs:/FileStore/shared_uploads/delta/online_retail/_
delta_log/
```

The preceding command displays the contents of the _delta_log folder, as shown in the following screenshot:

	path	▲
1	dbfs:/FileStore/shared_uploads/delta/online_retail/_delta_log/00000000000000000000.json	
2	dbfs:/FileStore/shared_uploads/delta/online_retail/_delta_log/00000000000000000000.crc	

Figure 3.4 – Delta transaction log

In the preceding screenshot, we can see that the folder contains a few different types of files. There are also a few files with the .json extension. These JSON files are actual Delta Transaction Log files and contain an ordered record of all the successful transactions that are performed on the Delta table.

> **Note**
> The previously used %fs filesystem commands are only available on the Databricks platform. You will need to use the appropriate command to browse the data lake that's appropriate for your Spark and data lake distribution.

Delta Lake transactions can be any operations that are performed on the Delta table, such as inserts, updates, and deletes, or even metadata operations such as renaming the table, changing the table schema, and so on. Every time an operation takes place, a new record is appended to the Delta Transaction Log with actions such as **Add file**, **Remove file**, **Update metadata**, and so on. These actions are atomic units and are recorded in the order that they took place. They are called **commits**.

After every 10 commits, Delta Lake generates a checkpoint file in Parquet format that contains all the transactions until that point in time. These periodic Parquet checkpoint files make it fast and easy for a Spark job to read and reconstruct the table's state. This can easily be illustrated with the help of the following Spark code:

```
spark.read.json("/FileStore/shared_uploads/delta/online_
retail/_delta_log/").show()
```

In the preceding line of code, we read the Delta Transaction Log just like any other JSON file by using a `spark.read()` function and created a Spark DataFrame. Every time a `spark.read()` command is run on a Delta Lake table, a small Spark job is executed to read the table's state, making metadata operations on Delta Lake completely scalable.

> **Note**
>
> The `%fs` filesystem command to explore files on a data lake is only available on the Databricks platform. You would need to choose a mechanism appropriate for your Spark environment and data lake.

Now that you have an understanding of the components of Delta Lake and the inner workings of the Delta Transaction Log, let's see how Delta Lake can help solve the challenges that data lakes face.

Improving data lake reliability with Delta Lake

Delta Lake, along with its transaction log, guarantees the atomicity and durability of data written to the data lake. Delta Lake only commits a transaction to the transaction log when all the data of the operation is completely written to the data lake. Any Delta-aware consumer reading data from a Delta table will always parse the Delta Transaction Log first to get the latest state of the Delta table.

This way, if the data ingestion job fails midway, a Delta Transaction Log-aware consumer will parse the transaction log, get the last stable state of the table, and only read the data that has commits in the transaction log. Any half-written, dirty data that might be in the data lake will be completely ignored because such data will not have any commits in the transaction log. Thus, Delta Lake, coupled with its transaction log, makes data lakes more reliable by providing transactional atomicity and durability guarantees.

> **Tip**
>
> Both data readers and data writers need to be *Delta Transaction Log aware* to get the ACID transaction guarantees of Delta Lake. Any reader or writer using Apache Spark can be made fully *Delta Transaction Log aware* by just including the appropriate version of the Delta Lake library on the Spark cluster. Delta Lake also has connectors to external data processing systems such as Presto, Athena, Hive, Redshift, and Snowflake.

Enabling schema validation with Delta Lake

Clean and consistent data is an essential requirement for any kind of business analytics application. One of the easier ways to ensure that only clean data enters the data lake is to make sure the schema is validated during the data ingestion process. Delta Lake comes with a built-in schema validation mechanism and ensures that any data being written to Delta Lake conforms to the user-defined schema of the Delta table. Let's explore this feature by creating a new Delta table and trying to insert data with mismatching data types into it, as shown in the following code:

```
from pyspark.sql.functions import lit
df1 = spark.range(3).withColumn("customer_id", lit("1"))
(df1
    .write
        .format("delta")
        .mode("overwrite")
    .save("/tmp/delta/customer"))
df2 = spark.range(2).withColumn("customer_id", lit(2))
(df2
    .write
        .format("delta")
        .mode("append")
    .save("/tmp/delta/customer"))
```

In the previous code snippet, we created a Spark DataFrame named `df1` with two columns, with `StringType` as the data type for both columns. We wrote this DataFrame to the data lake using the Delta Lake format. Then, we created another Spark DataFrame named `df2`, also with two columns, but their data types were set to `LongType` and `IntegerType`.

Next, we tried to append the second DataFrame to the original Delta table. As expected, Delta Lake fails the operation and throws a *Failed to merge incompatible data types StringType and IntegerType* exception. This way, Delta Lake ensures data quality in data lakes by providing schema validation and enforcement during data ingestion.

Schema evolution support with Delta Lake

Another common use case during data ingestion and the ELT process is that the source schema might evolve from time to time and that it needs to be handled in the data lake. One such scenario is that new columns could be added to the source system tables. It is desirable to bring those new columns into our data lake table, without it affecting our already existing data. This process is generally known as **schema evolution**, and Delta Lake has built-in support for this. Let's explore schema evolution in Delta Lake with the following code example:

```python
from pyspark.sql.functions import lit
df1 = spark.range(3)
(df1
    .write
        .format("delta")
        .mode("overwrite")
    .save("/tmp/delta/customer"))
df2 = spark.range(2).withColumn("customer_id", lit(2))
(df2
    .write
        .format("delta")
        .option("mergeSchema", True)
        .mode("append")
    .save("/tmp/delta/customer"))
```

In the preceding code snippet, we created a Spark DataFrame named `df1` that has just one column labeled `id`. Then, we saved this DataFrame to the data lake in Delta Lake format. Then, we created a second Spark DataFrame named `df2` with two columns called `id` and `customer_id`. After, we appended the second DataFrame to the original Delta table that was created from `df1`. This time, we used the `mergeSchema` option. This `mergeSchema` option specifies that we are expecting new columns to be written to Delta Lake, and these need to be appended to the existing table. We can easily verify this by running the following command on the Delta table:

```
spark.read.format("delta").load("/tmp/delta/customer").show()
```

In the previous code block, we are loading the data in the Delta table into a Spark DataFrame and calling the `show()` action to display the contents of the DataFrame, as shown in the following figure:

```
+---+-----------+
| id|customer_id|
+---+-----------+
|  0|          2|
|  1|          2|
|  0|       null|
|  1|       null|
|  2|       null|
+---+-----------+
```

Figure 3.5 – Delta Lake schema evolution

As you can see, new **id** column values, along with their corresponding **customer_id** column values, were inserted into the Delta table, and all the old **id** values with no previous **column_id** values were marked as null. With `mergeSchema` enabled, Delta Lake automatically adds the new column to the existing table and marks the values of the rows that did not exist previously as `null` values.

Arbitrary updates and deletes in data lakes with Delta Lake

Transactions not only get inserted into operating systems – they are also updated and deleted from time to time. In the ELT process, a replica of the source system data is maintained in the data lake. Thus, it becomes necessary to be able to not only insert data into data lakes but also update and delete it. However, data lakes are append-only storage systems with minimal or no support for any updates or deletes. Delta Lake, however, has full support for inserting, updating, and deleting records.

Let's take a look at an example of how we can update and delete arbitrary data from Delta Lake, as shown in the following block of code:

```
from pyspark.sql.functions import lit
df1 = spark.range(5).withColumn("customer_id", lit(2))
df1.write.format("delta").mode("overwrite").save("/tmp/df1")
```

In the preceding block of code, we created a Spark DataFrame with two columns labeled id and customer_id. id has values ranging from 1 through 5. We saved this table to the data lake using the Delta Lake format. Now, let's update the customer_id column where values of the id column are greater than 2, as shown in the following code block:

```
%sql
UPDATE delta.`/tmp/df1` SET customer_id = 5 WHERE id > 2;
SELECT * FROM delta.`/tmp/df1`;
```

In the preceding code block, we updated the customer_id column using an UPDATE SQL clause and specified the condition via a WHERE clause, just as you would do on any RDBMS.

> **Tip**
> The %sql magic command specifies that we intend to execute SQL queries in the current notebook cell. Even though we did not explicitly create a table, we can still refer to the Delta Lake location as a table using the delta.`path-to-delta-table` syntax.

The second SQL query reads the data back from the Delta table and displays it using the SELECT SQL clause, as shown in the following screenshot:

	id	▲	customer_id	▲
1	0		2	
2	1		2	
3	2		2	
4	3		5	
5	4		5	

Figure 3.6 – Updates with Delta Lake

Here, we can verify that all the rows of the Delta table with the value of the `id` column greater than 2 were successfully updated. Thus, Delta Lake has full support for updating multiple arbitrary records at scale with a simple SQL-like syntax.

> **Tip**
>
> A Delta table's metadata is entirely stored in the Delta Transaction Log itself. This makes registering Delta tables with an external **metastore** such as **Hive** completely optional. This makes it easier to just save the Delta table to the data lake and use it via Spark's DataFrame and SQL APIs seamlessly.

Now, let's see how Delta supports deletes with the help of the following block of code:

```sql
%sql
DELETE FROM delta.`/tmp/df1` WHERE id = 4;
SELECT * FROM delta.`/tmp/df1`;
```

In the preceding code snippet, we used the `DELETE` command to delete all the records that have an `id` of value 4. The second query, where we used the `SELECT` clause, displays the contents of the Delta table after the `DELETE` operation, as shown in the following screenshot:

	id	customer_id
1	0	2
2	1	2
3	2	2
4	3	5

Figure 3.7 – Deletes with Delta Lake

Here, we can easily verify that we no longer have any rows with an `id` value of 4. Thus, Delta Lake also supports deleting arbitrary records at scale.

> **Tip**
>
> Delta Lake supports both SQL and DataFrame syntax for DELETES, UPDATES, and UPSERTS. A syntax reference can be found in the open source documentation, which is maintained at `https://docs.delta.io/latest/delta-update.html#table-deletes-updates-and-merges`.

Even DELETE and UPDATE operations on Delta Lake support the same transactional guarantees of atomicity and durability as write operations. However, an interesting thing to note is that every time a DELETE or UPDATE operation takes place, instead of updating or deleting any data in place, Delta Lake generates a brand-new file with the updated or deleted records and appends these new files to the existing Delta table. Then, Delta Lake creates a new **commit** for this write transaction in the transaction log and marks the older **commits** of the deleted or updated records as invalid.

Thus, Delta Lake is never actually deleting or updating the actual data files in the data lake; it is just appending new files for any operation and updating the transaction log. Updating a smaller set of transaction log files is much faster and more efficient than updating a large number of very large data files. This process of updating and deleting records with Delta Lake is ultra-efficient and can be scaled to petabytes of data. This feature is very useful for use cases where customer arbitrary records need to be identified and deleted, such as in GDPR compliance use cases.

One more interesting side effect of this technique of always appending data files and never deleting them is that Delta Lake maintains a historical audit record of all the changes that happen to the data. This audit log is maintained in the **Delta transaction log** and with its help, Delta Lake can travel back in time to reproduce a snapshot of a Delta table at that point. We will explore this feature in the next section.

Time travel and rollbacks with Delta Lake

Delta Lake keeps an audit log of how data has changed over time in its transaction log. It also maintains older versions of Parquet data files every time data changes. This gives Delta Lake the ability to reproduce a snapshot of the entire Delta table at that point. This feature is called **Time Travel**.

You can easily explore the audit trail of a Delta table using the following SQL query:

```
%sql DESCRIBE HISTORY delta.`/tmp/df1`
```

In the preceding Spark SQL query, we used the `DESCRIBE HISTORY` command to reproduce the entire audit log of the changes that happened to the Delta table, as shown here:

	version	timestamp	userId	userName	operation
1	2	2021-01-15T11:38:52.000+0000	4803548200198498	snudurupati@outlook.com	DELETE
2	1	2021-01-15T11:10:09.000+0000	4803548200198498	snudurupati@outlook.com	UPDATE
3	0	2021-01-15T10:59:17.000+0000	4803548200198498	snudurupati@outlook.com	WRITE

Figure 3.8 – Time Travel with Delta Lake

In the preceding screenshot, you can see that this Delta table changed three times. First, data was inserted into the table, then the table was updated, and then records were deleted from the table. Delta Lake records all these events as transactions called **commits**. The timestamp of the commit event version number is also recorded in the change audit log. The timestamp or the table version number can be used to travel back in time to a particular snapshot of the Delta table using a SQL query, as follows:

```
%sql SELECT * from delta.`/tmp/delta/df1` VERSION AS OF 0
```

In the preceding SQL query, we performed a Delta Time Travel to the original version of the table. Time Travel is very useful during data engineering and ELT processing for performing rollbacks on tables if a data ingestion process fails. Delta Time Travel can be used to restore a Delta table to a previous state, as shown here:

```
%sql
INSERT OVERWRITE delta.`/tmp/df1`
SELECT * from delta.`/tmp/df1` VERSION AS OF 0
```

In the preceding SQL query, we overwrote the Delta table using a snapshot from a previous version of the table, all while making use of the **Delta Time Travel** feature.

Another scenario where Delta Time Travel comes in handy is in data science and machine learning use cases. Data scientists often conduct multiple machine learning experiments by modifying the dataset that's used for experimentation. In the process, they end up maintaining multiple physical versions of the same dataset or table. Delta Lake can help eliminate these physical versions of tables with the help of Time Travel, since Delta has built-in data versioning. You will explore this technique in more detail in *Chapter 9, Machine Learning Life Cycle Management*.

> **Tip**
> Delta continues to maintain versions of Parquet data files with every operation that mutates data. This means that older versions of data files get accumulated and Delta Lake doesn't automatically delete them. This could lead to a considerable increase in the size of the data lake over a while. To overcome this scenario, Delta Lake provides a VACUUM command to permanently remove older files that are no longer referenced by the Delta table. More information regarding the VACUUM command can be found at `https://docs.delta.io/latest/delta-utility.html#vacuum`.

Unifying batch and stream processing using Delta Lake

Batch and real-time stream processing are essential components of any modern big data architecture. In *Chapter 2, Data Ingestion*, you learned how to use Apache Spark for batch and real-time data ingestion. You also learned about the Lambda Architecture, which you can use to implement simultaneous batch and stream processing. An implementation of the Lambda Architecture with Apache Spark is still relatively complex as two separate data processing pipelines need to be implemented for batch and real-time processing.

This complexity arises from the limitation of data lakes as they inherently do not provide any transactional, atomicity, or durability guarantees on write operations. Thus, batch and streaming processes cannot write data to the same table or location on the data lake. Since Delta Lake already solves this challenge of data lakes, a single Delta Lake can be used in conjunction with multiple batch and real-time pipelines, further simplifying the Lambda Architecture. You will explore this in more detail in *Chapter 4, Real-Time Data Analytics*.

In summary, in this section, you learned that data lakes are instrumental in enabling truly scalable big data processing systems. However, they weren't built to be data analytics storage systems and have a few shortcomings, such as a lack of ACID transactional guarantees, as well as the ability to support the process of updating or deleting records, preserving data quality schema enforcement, or unification of batch and stream processing. You also learned how modern data storage layers such as Delta Lake can help overcome the challenges of data lakes and bring them closer to being true data analytics storage systems.

Now that you have an understanding of how to make cloud-based data lakes more reliable and conducive for data analytics, you are ready to learn about the process of transforming raw transactional data into meaningful business insights. We will start by consolidating data from various disparate sources and creating a single, unified view of data.

Consolidating data using data integration

Data integration is an important step in both the ETL and ELT modes of data processing. Data integration is the process of combining and blending data from different data sources to create enriched data that happens to represent a single version of the truth. Data integration is different from data ingestion because data ingestion simply collects data from disparate sources and brings it to a central location, such as a data warehouse. On the other hand, data integration combines those disparate data sources to create a meaningful unified version of the data that represents all the dimensions of the data. There are multiple ways to perform data integration, and a few of them will be explored in this section.

Data consolidation via ETL and data warehousing

Extracting, transforming, and loading data into data warehouses has been the best technique of data integration over the last few decades. One of the primary goals of data consolidation is to reduce the number of storage locations where the data resides. The ETL process extracts data from various source systems and then joins, filters, cleanses, and transforms the data according to user-specified business rules and then loads it into a central data warehouse.

This way, ETL and data warehousing techniques, as well as the tools and technologies that have been purposely built for this, support data consolidation and data integration. Although ELT is a slightly different process than ETL and with Apache Spark, we intend to build a data lake, the techniques of data integration and data consolidation remain the same, even with ETL.

Let's implement a data integration process using PySpark. As a first step, upload all the datasets provided with this chapter to a location where they can be accessed by your Spark cluster. In the case of Databricks Community Edition, the datasets can be directly uploaded to the data lake from within the **File** menu of the notebook. The links for the datasets and code files can be found in the *Technical requirements* section at the beginning of this chapter.

Let's explore the schema of the two transactional datasets labeled `online_retail.csv` and `online_retail_II.csv` using the following block of code:

```
from pyspark.sql.types import StructType, StructField,
IntegerType, TimestampType, StringType, DoubleType
schema = (StructType()
            .add("InvoiceNo", StringType(), True)
            .add("StockCode", StringType(), True)
```

```
        .add("Description", StringType(), True)
        .add("Quantity", StringType(), True)
        .add("InvoiceDate", StringType(), True)
        .add("UnitPrice", StringType(), True)
        .add("CustomerID", StringType(), True)
        .add("Country", StringType(), True))
df1 = spark.read.schema(schema).option("header", True).
csv("dbfs:/FileStore/shared_uploads/online_retail/online_
retail.csv")
df2 = spark.read.schema(schema).option("header", True).
csv("dbfs:/FileStore/shared_uploads/online_retail/online_
retail_II.csv")
df1.printSchema()
df2.printSchema()
```

In the preceding code snippet, we did the following:

1. We defined the schema of a Spark DataFrame as a `StructType` consisting of multiple StructFields. PySpark comes with these built-in structures to programmatically define the schema of a DataFrame.

2. Then, we loaded the two CSV files into separate Spark DataFrames while using the `schema` option to specify the data schema we created during *Step 1*. We still specified the header option as `True` because the first line of the CSV file has a header defined and we need to ignore it.

3. Finally, we printed the schema information of the two Spark DataFrames we created in *Step 2*.

Now that we have the retail datasets from the CSV files loaded into Spark DataFrames, let's integrate them into a single dataset, as shown in the following lines of code:

```
retail_df = df1.union(df2)
retail_df.show()
```

In the preceding code, we simply combined the two Spark DataFrames containing online retail transactional data to create a single Spark DataFrame by using the `union()` function. The union operation combines the two distinct DataFrames into a single DataFrame. The resultant consolidated dataset is labeled `retail_df`. We can verify the results using the `show()` function.

> **Tip**
>
> The `union()` function is a transformation and thus lazily evaluated. This means that as soon as you call a `union()` on two Spark DataFrames, Spark checks to see if the two DataFrames have the same number of columns and that their data types match. It doesn't manifest the DataFrames into memory yet. The `show()` function is an action, so Spark processes the transformations and manifests data in memory. However, the `show()` function only works on a small number of the DataFrame partitions and returns a sample set of the results to Spark Driver. Thus, this action helps verify our code quickly.

Next, we have some data describing country codes and names stored in the `country_codes.csv` file. Let's integrate it with the `retail_df` DataFrame we created in the previous step by using the following block of code:

```
df3 = spark.read.option("header", True).option("delimiter",
";").csv("/FileStore/shared_uploads/countries_codes.csv")
country_df = (df3
    .withColumnRenamed("OFFICIAL LANG CODE", "CountryCode")
    .withColumnRenamed("ISO2 CODE", "ISO2Code")
    .withColumnRenamed("ISO3 CODE", "ISO3Code")
    .withColumnRenamed("LABEL EN", "CountryName")
    .withColumnRenamed("Geo Shape", "GeoShape")
    .drop("ONU CODE")
    .drop("IS ILOMEMBER")
    .drop("IS RECEIVING QUEST")
    .drop("LABEL FR")
    .drop("LABEL SP")
    .drop("geo_point_2d")
)
integrated_df = retail_df.join(country_df, retail_df.Country ==
country_df.CountryName, "left_outer")
```

In the previous code snippet, we did the following:

1. We loaded the `country_codes.csv` file into a Spark DataFrame, with the header option set to `True` and the file delimiter specified as `";"`.

2. We renamed a few column names to follow standard naming conventions using the `withColumnRenamed()` function. We dropped a few other columns that we thought were not necessary for any of our business use cases. This resulted in a DataFrame labeled `country_df` that contains the country code and other descriptive columns.

3. Then, we joined this DataFrame to the `retail_df` DataFrame from the previous step. We used a **left outer join** here because we wanted to preserve all the rows from the `retail_df` DataFrame, irrespective of whether they have a matching record in the `country_df` DataFrame.

4. The resultant `integrated_df` DataFrame contains online retail transactional data that's been enriched with descriptive columns from the `country_codes.csv` dataset.

We also have another dataset named `adult.data` that contains the income dataset from the US census. Let's integrate this dataset with the already integrated and enriched retail transactional dataset, as shown in the following lines of code:

```
from pyspark.sql.functions import monotonically_increasing_id
income_df = spark.read.schema(schema).csv("/FileStore/
shared_uploads/adult.data").withColumn("idx", monotonically_
increasing_id())
retail_dfx = retail_df.withColumn("CustomerIDx", monotonically_
increasing_id())
income_dfx = income_df.withColumn("CustomerIDx", monotonically_
increasing_id())
income_df = spark.read.schema(schema).csv("/FileStore/
shared_uploads/adult.data").withColumn("idx", monotonically_
increasing_id())
retail_dfx = integrated_df.withColumn("RetailIDx",
monotonically_increasing_id())
income_dfx = income_df.withColumn("IncomeIDx", monotonically_
increasing_id())
retail_enriched_df = retail_dfx.join(income_dfx, retail_dfx.
RetailIDx == income_dfx.IncomeIDx, "left_outer")
```

In the previous code snippet, we did the following:

1. We created a Spark DataFrame from the income dataset using the `spark.read.csv()` function. This is a comma-delimited file with a header, so we used the appropriate options. As a result, we have a DataFrame called `income_df`, with a few columns related to consumer demographics and their income levels.

2. Then, we added two **surrogate key** columns to both the `income_df` and `integrated_df` DataFrames so that they can be joined. We achieved this using the `monotonically_increasing_id()` function, which generates unique incremental numbers.

3. The two DataFrames were then joined based on the newly generated **surrogate key** columns. We used a **left outer join** as we intended to preserve all the rows of the `integrated_df` DataFrame, regardless of whether they have corresponding matching rows in the `income_df` DataFrame. The result is integrated, enriched, retail transactional data, with the country and the customer demographic and income information in a single, unified dataset.

This intermediate dataset can be useful for performing **data cleansing** and producing further clean and consistent dataset. So, let's persist this dataset on the data lake using the Delta Lake format with the name `retail_enriched.delta`, as shown in the following code:

```
(retail_enriched_df
   .coalesce(1)
   .write
     .format("delta", True)
     .mode("overwrite")
     .save("/FileStore/shared_uploads/retail.delta"))
```

In the previous code block, we reduced the number of partitions of the `retailed_enriched_df` DataFrame to a single partition using the `coalesce()` function. This produces a single portable Parquet file.

> **Note**
>
> One of the biggest challenges with learning and experimenting with big data analytics is finding clean and useful datasets. In the preceding code example, we had to introduce a surrogate key to join two independent datasets. In real-world scenarios, you would never force a join between datasets unless the datasets are related and a common join key exists between them.

Thus, using Spark's DataFrame operations or using Spark SQL, you can integrate data from disparate sources and create an enriched and meaningful dataset that represents a single version of the truth.

Integrating data using data virtualization techniques

Data virtualization, as the name implies, is a virtual process where a data virtualization layer acts as a logical layer on top of all the disparate data sources. This virtual layer acts as a conduit for business users to seamlessly access the required data in real time. The advantage data virtualization has over the traditional **ETL** and **ELT** processes is that it doesn't require any data movement, and just exposes an integrated view of data to business users. When business users try to access the data, the data virtualization layer queries the underlying datasets and retrieves data in real time.

The advantage of the data virtualization layer is that it completely bypasses any data movement, saving any time and resources that would typically be invested in this process. It can present data in real time with minimal to no latency as it directly fetches data from the source systems.

The disadvantage of data virtualization is that it is not a widely adopted technique and the products that do offer it come at a premium price. Apache Spark doesn't support data virtualization in its purest sense. However, Spark does support a type of data virtualization technique called **data federation**, which you will learn about in the next section.

Data integration through data federation

Data federation is a type of data virtualization technique that uses a virtual database, also called a federated database, to provide a consolidated and homogeneous view of heterogeneous data sources. The idea here is to access any data anywhere from a single data processing and metadata layer. Apache Spark SQL Engine supports data federation, where Spark data sources can be used to define external data sources for seamless access from within Spark SQL. With Spark SQL, multiple data sources can be used with a single SQL query, without you having to consolidate and transform the datasets first.

Let's take a look at a code example to learn how to achieve data federation with Spark SQL:

```
%sql
CREATE TABLE mysql_authors IF NOT EXISTS
USING org.apache.spark.sql.jdbc
OPTIONS (
  url "jdbc:mysql://localhost:3306/pysparkdb",
  dbtable "authors",
```

```
  user "@@@@@@",
  password "######"
);
```

In the previous block of code, we created a table with MySQL as the source. Here, the table we created with Spark is just a pointer to the actual table in MySQL. Every time this Spark table is queried, it fetches data from the underlying MySQL table over a JDBC connection. Let's create another table from a Spark DataFrame and save it in CSV format, as follows:

```
from pyspark.sql.functions import rand, col
authors_df = spark.range(16).withColumn("salary",
rand(10)*col("id")*10000)
authors_df.write.format("csv").saveAsTable("author_salary")
```

In the preceding code block, we generated a Spark Dataframe with 16 rows and 2 columns. The first column, labeled `id`, is just an incremental number, while the second column, labeled `salary`, is a random number that was generated using the built-in `rand()` function. We saved the DataFrame to the data lake and registered it with Spark's built-in Hive metastore using the `saveAsTable()` function. Now that we have two tables, each residing in a separate data source, let's see how we can use them together in a federated query via Spark SQL, as shown in the following code:

```
%sql
SELECT
  m.last_name,
  m.first_name,
  s.salary
FROM
  author_salary s
  JOIN mysql_authors m ON m.uid = s.id
ORDER BY s.salary DESC
```

In the preceding SQL query, we joined the MySQL table to the CSV table residing on the data lake in the same query to produce an integrated view of data. This has demonstrated the data federation capabilities of Apache Spark.

> **Tip**
> Certain specialist data processing engines are designed purely to be federated databases, such as Presto. Presto is a distributed Massively Parallel Processing (MPP) query engine for big data that was designed to give very fast query performance on any data, anywhere. One advantage of using Apache Spark over Presto is that it supports data federation, along with other use cases such as batch and real-time analytics, data science, machine learning, and interactive SQL analytics, all with a single unified engine. This makes the user experience much more seamless. However, it is also very common for organizations to leverage several big data technologies for different use cases.

To summarize, data integration is the process of consolidating and combining data from disparate data sources to produce meaningful data that gives a single version of the truth. There are several techniques surrounding data integration, including consolidating data using ETL or ELT techniques and data federation. In this section, you learned how to leverage these techniques using Apache Spark to achieve an integrated view of your data. The next step of your data analytics journey is to learn how to clean messy and dirty data via a process called **data cleansing**.

Making raw data analytics-ready using data cleansing

Raw transactional data can have many kinds of inconsistencies, either inherent to the data itself or developed during movement between various data processing systems, during the data ingestion process. The data integration process can also introduce inconsistencies in data. This is because data is being consolidated from disparate systems with their own mechanism for data representation. This data is not very clean, can have a few bad and corrupt records, and needs to be cleaned before it is ready to generate meaningful business insights using a process known as **data cleansing**.

Data cleansing is a part of the data analytics process and cleans data by fixing bad and corrupt data, removing duplicates, and selecting a set of data that's useful for a wide set of business use cases. When data is combined from disparate sources, there might be inconsistencies in the data types, including mislabeled or redundant data. Thus, data cleansing also incorporates data standardization to bring integrated data up to an enterprise's standards and conventions.

The goal of data cleansing is to produce clean, consistent, and pristine data that is ready for the final step of generating meaningful and actionable insights from raw transactional data. In this section, you will learn about the various steps involved in the data cleansing process.

Data selection to eliminate redundancies

Once data has been integrated from various sources, there might be redundancies in the integrated dataset. There might be fields that are not required by your business analytics teams. The first step of data cleansing is identifying these unnecessary data elements and removing them.

Let's perform data selection on the integrated dataset we produced in the *Data consolidation via ETL and data warehousing* section. We need to look at the table schema first to see what columns we have and what their data types are. We can do this using the following line of code:

```
retail_enriched_df.printSchema()
```

The result of the preceding line of code shows all columns, and we can easily spot that the Country and CountryName columns are redundant. We also have some columns that were introduced in the dataset for data integration, and they are not very useful for downstream analytics. Let's clean up the unwanted and redundant columns from the integrated dataset, as shown in the following block of code:

```
retail_clean_df = (retail_enriched_df
                   .drop("Country")
                   .drop("ISO2Code")
                   .drop("ISO3Code")
                   .drop("RetailIDx")
                   .drop("idx")
                   .drop("IncomeIDx")
                  )
```

In the preceding code snippet, we used the drop() DataFrame operation to eliminate unwanted columns. Now that we have selected the right data columns from the integrated dataset, the next step is to identify and eliminate any duplicate rows.

De-duplicating data

The first step of the deduplication process is to check if we have any duplicate rows to begin with. We can do this using a combination of DataFrame operations, as shown in the following block of code:

```
(retail_enriched_df
    .select("InvoiceNo", "InvoiceDate")
    .groupBy("InvoiceNo", "InvoiceDate")
```

```
    .count()
    .show())
```

The preceding lines of code show the count of all the rows after grouping the rows by the `InvoiceNo`, `InvoiceDate`, and `StockCode` columns. Here, we are assuming that the `InvoiceNo`, `InvoiceDate`, and `StockCode` column combination is unique and that they form the **composite key** for the dataset. The expected result of the preceding query is that every row has a count of 1. However, in the results, we can see that some rows have counts greater than 1, which suggests that there might be duplicate rows in the dataset. This should be inspected manually, once you've sampled a few rows that show duplicates. This is to ensure they are duplicate rows. We can do this using the following block of code:

```
(retail_enriched_df.where("InvoiceNo in ('536373', '536382',
'536387') AND StockCode in ('85123A', '22798', '21731')")
    .display()
)
```

In the preceding query, we checked a sample of the `InvoiceNo` and `StockCode` values to see if the returned data contains duplicates. Just eyeballing the results, we can see that there are duplicates in the dataset. We need to eliminate these duplicates. Fortunately, PySpark comes with a handy function called `drop_duplicates()` to just do that, as shown in the following line of code:

```
retail_nodupe = retail_clean_df.drop_duplicates(["InvoiceNo",
"InvoiceDate", "StockCode"])
```

In the preceding line of code, we used the `drop_duplicates()` function to eliminate duplicates based on a subset of columns. Let's see if it eliminated the duplicate rows by using the following line of code:

```
(retail_nodupe
    .select("InvoiceNo", "InvoiceDate", "StockCode")
    .groupBy("InvoiceNo", "InvoiceDate", "StockCode")
    .count()
    .where("count > 1")
    .show())
```

The previous code groups the rows based on the **composite key** and checks the count of each group. The result is an empty dataset, meaning that all the duplicates have been successfully eliminated.

So far, we have dropped unwanted columns from the integrated dataset and eliminated duplicates. During the data selection step, we noticed that all the columns were of the string type and that the column's names were following different naming conventions. This can be rectified using the data standardization process.

Standardizing data

Data standardization refers to where we make sure all the columns adhere to their proper data types. This is also where we bring all the column names up to our enterprise naming standards and conventions. This can be achieved in PySpark using the following DataFrame operation:

```
retail_final_df = (retail_nodupe.selectExpr(
    "InvoiceNo AS invoice_num", "StockCode AS stock_code",
    "description AS description", "Quantity AS quantity",
    "CAST(InvoiceDate AS TIMESTAMP) AS invoice_date",
    "CAST(UnitPrice AS DOUBLE) AS unit_price",
    "CustomerID AS customer_id",
    "CountryCode AS country_code",
    "CountryName AS country_name", "GeoShape AS geo_shape",
    "age", "workclass AS work_class",
    "fnlwgt AS final_weight", "education",
    "CAST('education-num' AS NUMERIC) AS education_num",
    "'marital-status' AS marital_status", "occupation",
    "relationship", "race", "gender",
    "CAST('capital-gain' AS DOUBLE) AS capital_gain",
    "CAST('capital-loss' AS DOUBLE) AS capital_loss",
    "CAST('hours-per-week' AS DOUBLE) AS hours_per_week",
    "'native-country' AS native_country")
)
```

In the preceding block of code, we essentially have a SQL SELECT query that casts columns to their proper data types and aliases column names so that they follow proper Pythonic naming standards. The result is a final dataset that contains data from various sources integrated into a cleansed, deduplicated, and standardized data format.

This final dataset, which is the result of the data integration and data cleansing phases of the data analytics process, is ready to be presented to business users for them to run their business analytics on. Thus, it makes sense to persist this dataset onto the data lake and make it available for end user consumption, as shown in the following line of code:

```
retail_final_df.write.format("delta").save("dbfs:/FileStore/
shared_uploads/delta/retail_silver.delta")
```

In the preceding line of code, we saved our final version of the pristine transactional data in the data lake in Delta Lake format.

> **Note**
>
> It is an industry convention to call transactional data that's been replicated straight from the source system **bronze** data, cleansed and integrated transactional data **silver** data, and aggregated and summarized data **gold** data. The data analytics process, in a nutshell, is a continuous process of ingesting bronze data and transforming it into silver and gold data, until it is ready to be converted into actionable business insights.

To summarize the data cleaning process, we took the result set of the data integration process, removed any redundant and unnecessary columns, eliminated duplicate rows, and brought the data columns up to enterprise standards and conventions. All these data processing steps were implemented using the DataFrame API, which is powered by Spark SQL Engine. It can easily scale out this process to terabytes and petabytes of data.

> **Tip**
>
> In this chapter, data integration and data cleansing have been presented as two independent and mutually exclusive processes. However, in real-life use cases, it is a very common practice to implement these two steps together as a single data processing pipeline.

The result of the data integration and data cleansing process is usable, clean, and meaningful data that is ready for consumption by business analytics users. Since we are working at a big data scale here, data must be structured and presented in a way that improves the performance of business analytics queries. You will learn about this in the following section.

Optimizing ELT processing performance with data partitioning

Data partitioning is a process where a large dataset is physically split into smaller parts. This way, when a query requires a portion of the larger dataset, it can scan and load a subset of the partitions. This technique of eliminating partitions that are not required by the query is called **partition pruning**.

Predicate pushdown is another technique where parts of a query that filter, slice, and dice data, called the **predicate**, are pushed down to the data storage layer. It then becomes the data storage layer's responsibility to filter out all the partitions not required by the query.

Traditional RDBMS and data warehouses have always supported data partitioning, partition pruning, and predicate pushdown. Semi-structured file formats such as CSV and JSON support data partitioning and partition pruning but do not support predicate pushdown. Apache Spark fully supports all three. With predicate pushdown, Spark can delegate the task of filtering out data to the underlying data storage layer, thus reducing the amount of data that needs to be loaded into Spark's memory and then processed.

Structured data formats such as Parquet, ORC, and Delta Lake fully support partitioning pruning and predicate pushdown. This helps Spark's Catalyst Optimizer generate the best possible query execution plan. This is a strong reason to favor structured file formats such as Apache Parquet with Spark over semi-structured data formats.

Consider that your data lake has historical data spanning several years and that your typical queries involve only a few months to a few years of data at a time. You can choose to store your data completely unpartitioned, with all the data in a single folder. Alternatively, you can partition your data by year and month attributes, as shown in the following diagram:

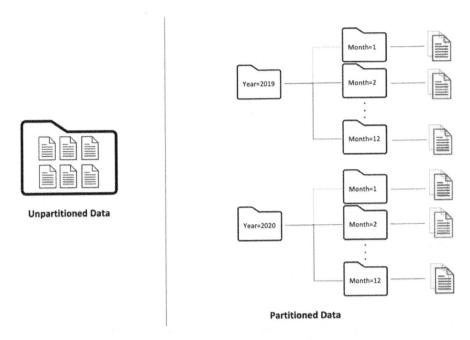

Unpartitioned Data

Partitioned Data

Figure 3.9 – Data partitioning

On the right-hand side of the preceding diagram, we have unpartitioned data. This pattern of data storage makes data storage a little easier because we just keep appending new data to the same folder over and over again. However, after a certain point, the data becomes unmanageable and makes it difficult to perform any updates or deletes. Moreover, Apache Spark would need to read the entire dataset into memory, losing any advantages that partition pruning and predicate pushdown could have offered.

On the right-hand side of the diagram, data is partitioned by year and then by month. This makes writing data a little more involved as the Spark application would need to choose the right partition every time before writing data. However, this is a small penalty compared to the efficiency and performance that's gained with updates and deletes, as well as downstream queries. Queries on such partitioned data will be orders of magnitude faster as they make full use of partition pruning and predicate pushdown. Thus, it is recommended to partition data with an appropriate partition key to get the best performance and efficiency out of your data lake.

Since data partitioning plays a crucial role in determining the performance of downstream analytical queries, it is important to choose the right partitioning column. As a general rule of thumb, choose a partition column with low cardinality. Partition sizes of at least one gigabyte are practical and typically, a date-based column makes for a good candidate for the partition key.

> **Note**
>
> Recursive file listing on cloud-based object storage is usually slow and expensive. So, using hierarchical partitioning on cloud-based object stores is not very efficient and thus not recommended. This could be a performance bottleneck when more than one partition key is required. Databricks's proprietary version of Delta Lake, along with their Delta Engine, supports techniques such as **dynamic file pruning** and **Z-order** multi-dimensional indexes to help solve the problems of hierarchical partitioning on cloud-based data lakes. You can read more about them at `https://docs.databricks.com/delta/optimizations/dynamic-file-pruning.html`. However, these techniques are not available in the open source version of Delta Lake yet.

Summary

In this chapter, you learned about two prominent methodologies of data processing known as **ETL** and **ELT** and saw the advantages of using ETL to unlock more analytics use cases than what's possible with ETL. By doing this, you understood the scalable storage and compute requirements of ETL and how modern cloud technologies help enable the ELT way of data processing. Then, you learned about the shortcomings of using cloud-based data lakes as analytics data stores, such as having a lack of atomic transactional and durability guarantees. After, you were introduced to Delta Lake as a modern data storage layer designed to overcome the shortcomings of cloud-based data lakes. You learned about the data integration and data cleansing techniques, which help consolidate raw transactional data from disparate sources to produce clean, pristine data that is ready to be presented to end users to generate meaningful insights. You also learned how to implement each of the techniques used in this chapter using DataFrame operations and Spark SQL. You gained skills that are essential for transforming raw transactional data into meaningful, enriched data using the ELT methodology for big data at scale.

Typically, the data cleansing and integration processes are performance-intensive and are implemented in a batch processing manner. However, in big data analytics, you must get the latest transactional data to the end users as soon as it is generated at the source. This is very helpful in tactical decision-making and is made possible by real-time data analytics, which you will learn about in the next chapter.

4

Real-Time Data Analytics

In the modern big data world, data is being generated at a tremendous pace, that is, faster than any of the past decade's technologies can handle, such as batch processing ETL tools, data warehouses, or business analytics systems. It is essential to process data and draw insights in real time for businesses to make tactical decisions that help them to stay competitive. Therefore, there is a need for real-time analytics systems that can process data in real or near real-time and help end users get to the latest data as quickly as possible.

In this chapter, you will explore the architecture and components of a real-time big data analytics processing system, including message queues as data sources, Delta as the data sink, and Spark's Structured Streaming as the stream processing engine. You will learn techniques to handle late-arriving data using stateful processing Structured Streaming. The techniques for maintaining an exact replica of source systems in a data lake using **Change Data Capture** (CDC) will also be presented. You will learn how to build multi-hop stream processing pipelines to progressively improve data quality from raw data to cleansed and enriched data that is ready for data analytics. You will gain the essential skills to implement a scalable, fault-tolerant, and near real-time analytics system using Apache Spark.

In this chapter, we will cover the following main topics:

- Real-time analytics systems architecture
- Stream processing engines
- Real-time analytics industry use cases
- Simplifying the Lambda Architecture using Delta Lake
- CDC
- Multi-hop streaming pipelines

Technical requirements

In this chapter, you will be using the Databricks Community Edition to run your code. This can be found at `https://community.cloud.databricks.com`:

- Sign-up instructions can be found at `https://databricks.com/try-databricks`.
- The code and data used in this chapter can be downloaded from `https://github.com/PacktPublishing/Essential-PySpark-for-Scalable-Data-Analytics/tree/main/Chapter04`.

Before we dive deeper into implementing real-time stream processing data pipelines with Apache Spark, first, we need to understand the general architecture of a real-time analytics pipeline and its various components, as described in the following section.

Real-time analytics systems architecture

A real-time data analytics system, as the name suggests, processes data in real time. This is because it is generated at the source, making it available for business users with the minimal latency possible. It consists of several important components, namely, streaming data sources, a stream processing engine, streaming data sinks, and the actual real-time data consumers, as illustrated in the following diagram:

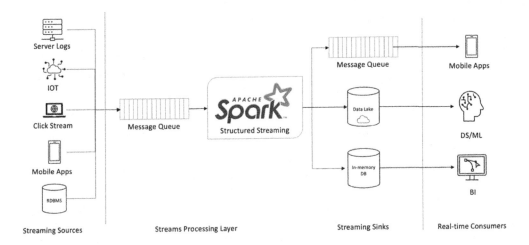

Figure 4.1 – Real-time data analytics

The preceding diagram depicts a typical real-time data analytics systems architecture. In the following sections, we will explore each of the components in more detail.

Streaming data sources

Similar to any of the other **enterprise decision support Systems**, a **real-time data analytics system** also starts with data sources. Businesses generate data continuously in real time; therefore, any data source used by a batch processing system is also a streaming data source. The only difference is in how often you ingest data from the data source. In batch processing mode, data is ingested periodically, whereas, in a real-time streaming system, data is continuously ingested from the same data source. However, there are a few considerations to bear in mind before continuously ingesting data from a data source. These can be described as follows:

- Can the data source keep up with the demands of a real-time streaming analytics engine? Or will the streaming engine end up taxing the data source?

- Can the data source communicate with the streaming engine asynchronously and replay events in any arbitrary order that the streaming engine requires?

- Can the data source replay events in the exact order that they occurred at the source?

The preceding three points bring up some important requirements regarding streaming data sources. A streaming data source should be distributed and scalable in order to keep up with the demands of a real-time streaming analytics system. Note that it must be able to replay events in any arbitrary order. This is so that the streaming engine has the flexibility to process events in any order or restart the process in the case of any failures. For certain real-time use cases, such as CDC, it is important that you replay events in the exact same order they occurred at the source in order to maintain data integrity.

Due to the previously mentioned reasons, no operating system is fit to be a streaming data source. In the cloud and big data works, it is recommended that you use a scalable, fault-tolerant, and asynchronous message queue such as Apache Kafka, AWS Kinesis, Google Pub/Sub, or Azure Event Hub. Cloud-based data lakes such as AWS S3, Azure Blob, and ADLS storage or Google Cloud Storage are also suitable as streaming data sources to a certain extent for certain use cases.

Now that we have an understanding of streaming data sources, let's take a look at how to ingest data from a data source such as a data lake in a streaming fashion, as shown in the flowing code snippet:

```
stream_df = (spark.readStream
                .format("csv")
                .option("header", "true")
                .schema(eventSchema)
                .option("maxFilesPerTrigger", 1)
                .load("/FileStore/shared_uploads/online_
retail/"))
```

In the previous code, we define a streaming DataFrame that reads one file at a time from a data lake location. The readStream() method of the DataStreamReader object is used to create the streaming DataFrame. The data format is specified as CSV, and the schema information is defined using the eventSchema object. Finally, the location of the CSV files within the data lake is specified using the load() function. The maxFilesPerTrigger option specifies that only one file must be read by the stream at a time. This is useful for throttling the rate of stream processing, if required, because of the compute resource constraints.

Once we have the streaming DataFrame created, it can be further processed using any of the available functions in the DataFrame API and persisted to a streaming data sink, such as a data lake. We will cover this in the following section.

Streaming data sinks

Once data streams are read from their respective streaming sources and processed, they need to be stored onto some form of persistent storage for further downstream consumption. Although any regular data sink could act as a streaming data sink, a number of considerations apply when choosing a streaming data sink. Some of these considerations include the following:

- What are the latency requirements for data consumption?
- What kind of data will consumers be consuming in the data stream?

Latency is an important factor when choosing the streaming data source, the data sink, and the actual streaming engine. Depending on the latency requirements, you might need to choose an entirely different end-to-end streaming architecture. Streaming use cases can be classified into two broad categories, depending on the latency requirements:

- Real-time transactional systems
- Near real-time analytics systems

Real-time transactional systems

Real-time transactional systems are operational systems that are, typically, interested in processing events pertaining to a single entity or transaction at a time. Let's consider an example of an online retail business where a customer visits an e-tailer's and browses through a few product categories in a given session. An operational system would be focused on capturing all of the events of that particular session and maybe display a discount coupon or make a specific recommendation to that user in real time. In this kind of scenario, the latency requirement is ultra-low and, usually, ranges in sub-seconds. These kinds of use cases require an ultra-low latency streaming engine along with an ultra-low latency streaming sink such as an in-memory database, such as **Redis** or **Memcached**, for instance.

Another example of a real-time transactional use case would be a CRM system where a customer service representative is trying to make an upsell or cross-sell recommendation to a live customer online. Here, the streaming engine needs to fetch certain precalculated metrics for a specific customer from a data store, which contains information about millions of customers. It also needs to fetch some real-time data points from the CRM system itself in order to generate a personalized recommendation for that specific customer. All of this needs to happen in a matter of seconds. A **NoSQL** database with constant seek times for arbitrary key records would be a good fit for the data source as well as a data sink to quickly fetch records for a particular key such as `CustomerID`.

> **Important note**
>
> Spark's Structured Streaming, with its micro-batch style of stream processing model, isn't well suited for real-time stream processing use cases where there is an ultra-low latency requirement to process events as they happen at the source. Structured Streaming has been designed for maximum throughput and scalability rather than for ultra-low latency. Apache Flink or another streaming engine that was purpose-built would be a good fit for real-time transactional use cases.

Now that you have gained an understanding of real-time analytics engines along with an example of a real-time analytics use case, in the following section, we will take a look at a more prominent and practical way of processing analytics in near real time.

Near real-time analytics systems

Near real-time analytics systems are analytics systems that process an aggregate of records in near real time and have a latency requirement ranging from a few seconds to a few minutes. These systems are not interested in processing events for a single entity or transaction but generate metrics or KPIs for an aggregate of transactions to depict the state of business in real time. Sometimes, these systems might also generate sessions of events for a single transaction or entity but for later offline consumption.

Since this type of real-time analytics system processes a very large volume of data, throughput and scalability are of key importance here. Additionally, since the processed output is either being fed into a Business Intelligence system for real-time reporting or into persistent storage for consumption in an asynchronous manner, a data lake or a data warehouse is an ideal streaming data sink for this kind of use case. Examples of near real-time analytics use cases are presented, in detail, in the *Real-time analytics industry use cases* section. Apache Spark was designed to handle near real-time analytics use cases that require maximum throughput for large volumes of data with scalability.

Now that you have an understanding of streaming data sources, data sinks, and the kind of real-time use cases that Spark's Structured Streaming is better suited to solve, let's take a deeper dive into the actual streaming engines.

Stream processing engines

A stream processing engine is the most critical component of any real-time data analytics system. The role of the stream processing engine is to continuously process events from a streaming data source and ingest them into a streaming data sink. The stream processing engine can process events as they arrive in a real real-time fashion or group a subset of events into a small batch and process one micro-batch at a time in

a near real-time manner. The choice of the engine greatly depends on the type of use case and the processing latency requirements. Some examples of modern streaming engines include Apache Storm, Apache Spark, Apache Flink, and Kafka Streams.

Apache Spark comes with a stream processing engine called **Structured Streaming**, which is based on Spark's SQL engine and DataFrame APIs. Structured Streaming uses the micro-batch style of processing and treats each incoming micro-batch as a small Spark DataFrame. It applies DataFrame operations to each micro-batch just like any other Spark DataFrame. The programming model for Structured Streaming treats the output dataset as an unbounded table and processes incoming events as a stream of continuous micro-batches. Structured Streaming generates a query plan for each micro-batch, processes them, and then appends them to the output dataset, treating it just like an unbounded table, as illustrated in the following diagram:

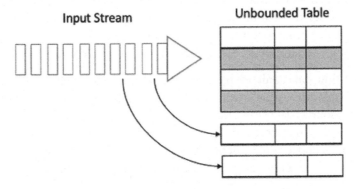

Figure 4.2 – The Structured Streaming programming model

As shown in the preceding diagram, Structured Streaming treats each incoming micro-batch of data like a small Spark DataFrame and appends it to the end of an existing Streaming DataFrame. An elaboration of Structured Streaming's programming model, with examples, was presented in the *Ingesting data in real time using Structured Streaming* section of *Chapter 2, Data Ingestion*.

Structured Streaming can simply process streaming events as they arrive in micro-batches and persist the output to a streaming data sink. However, in real-world scenarios, the simple model of stream processing might not be practical because of **Late-Arriving Data**. Structured Streaming also supports a stateful processing model to deal with data that is either arriving late or is out of order. You will learn more about handling late-arriving data in the *Handling late-arriving data* section.

Real-time data consumers

The final component of a real-time data analytics system is the actual data consumer. Data consumers can be actual business users that consume real-time data by the means of ad hoc Spark SQL queries, via interactive operational dashboards or other systems that take the output of a streaming engine and further process it. Real-time business dashboards are consumed by business users, and typically, these have slightly higher latency requirements as a human mind can only comprehend data at a given rate. Structured Streaming is a good fit for these use cases and can write the streaming output to a database where it can be further fed into a Business Intelligence system.

The output of a streaming engine can also be consumed by other business applications such as a mobile app or a web app. Here, the use case could be something such as hyper-personalized user recommendations, where the processed output of a streaming engine could be further passed on to something such as an online inference engine for generating personalized user recommendations. Structured Streaming can be used for these use cases as long as the latency requirements are in the range of a few seconds to a few minutes.

In summary, real-time data analytics has a few important components such as the streaming data sources and sinks, the actual streaming engine, and the final real-time data consumers. The choice of data source, data sink, and the actual engine in your architecture depends on your actual real-time data consumers, the use case that is being solved, the processing latency, and the throughput requirements. Now, in the following section, we'll take a look at some examples of real-world industry use cases that leverage real-time data analytics.

Real-time analytics industry use cases

There is an actual need for and an advantage to processing data in real time, so companies are quickly shifting from batch processing to real-time data processing. In this section, let's take a look at a few examples of real-time data analytics by industry verticals.

Real-time predictive analytics in manufacturing

With the advent of the **Internet of Things (IoT)**, manufacturing and other industries are generating a high volume of IoT data from their machines and heavy equipment. This data can be leveraged in few different ways to improve the way industries work and help them to save costs. One such example is predictive maintenance, where IoT data is continuously ingested from industrial equipment and machinery, data science, and machine learning techniques that have been applied to the data to identify patterns that can predict equipment or part failures. When this process is performed in real time, it can help to predict equipment and part failures before they actually happen. In this way, maintenance can be performed proactively, preventing downtime and thus preventing any lost revenue or missed manufacturing targets.

Another example is the construction industry where IoT data, such as equipment uptime, fuel consumption, and more, can be analyzed to identify any underutilized equipment and any equipment that can be redirected in real time for optimal utilization.

Connected vehicles in the automotive sector

Modern vehicles come with a plethora of connected features that definitely make the life of a consumer much easier and more convenient. Vehicle telematics, as well as user data generated by such vehicles, can be used for a variety of use cases or to further provide convenience features for the end user, such as real-time personalized in-vehicle content and services, advanced navigation and route guidance, and remote monitoring. Telematics data can be used by the manufacturer to unlock use cases such as predicting a vehicle's maintenance window or part failure and proactively alerting ancillary vendors and dealerships. Predicting part failures and better managing vehicle recalls helps automotive manufacturers with huge costs.

Financial fraud detection

Modern-day personal finance is rapidly moving from physical to digital, and with that comes the novel threat of digital financial threats such as fraud and identity theft. Therefore, there is a need for financial institutions to proactively assess millions of transactions in real time for fraud and to alert and protect the individual consumer of such fraud. Highly scalable, fault-tolerant real-time analytics systems are required to detect and prevent financial fraud at such a scale.

IT security threat detection

Consumer electronics manufactures of online connected devices, as well as corporations, have to continuously monitor their end users' devices for any malicious activity to safeguard the identity and assets of their end users. Monitoring petabytes of data requires real-time analytics systems that can process millions of records per second in real time.

Based on the previously described industry use cases, you might observe that real-time data analytics is becoming more and more prominent by the day. However, real-time data analytics systems don't necessarily negate the need for the batch processing of data. It is very much required for enriching real-time data streams with static data, generating lookups that add context to real-time data, and generating features that are required for real-time data science and machine learning use cases. In *Chapter 2, Data Ingestion*, you learned about an architecture that could efficiently unify batch and real-time processing, called the **Lambda Architecture**. In the following section, you will learn how to further simplify the Lambda Architecture using Structured Streaming in combination with Delta Lake.

Simplifying the Lambda Architecture using Delta Lake

A typical Lambda Architecture has three major components: a batch layer, a streaming layer, and a serving layer. In *Chapter 2, Data Ingestion*, you were able to view an implementation of the Lambda Architecture using Apache Spark's unified data processing framework. The Spark DataFrames API, Structured Streaming, and SQL engine help to make Lambda Architecture simpler. However, multiple data storage layers are still required to handle batch data and streaming data separately. These separate data storage layers could be easily consolidated by using the Spark SQL engine as the service layer. However, that might still lead to multiple copies of data and might require further consolidation of data using additional batch jobs in order to present the user with a single consistent and integrated view of data. This issue can be overcome by making use of Delta Lake as a persistent data storage layer for the Lambda Architecture.

Since Delta Lake comes built with ACID transactional and isolation properties for write operations, it can provide the seamless unification of batch and streaming data, further simplifying the Lambda Architecture. This is illustrated in the following diagram:

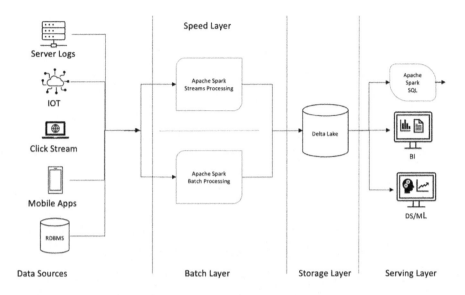

Figure 4.3 – A Lambda Architecture with Apache Spark and Delta Lake

In the preceding diagram, a simplified Lambda Architecture is presented. Here, batch data, as well as streaming data, is simultaneously ingested using batch processing with Apache Spark and Structured Streaming, respectively. Ingesting both batch and streaming data into a single Delta Lake table greatly simplifies the Lambda Architecture. Once the data has been ingested into Delta Lake, it is instantly available for further downstream use cases such as ad hoc data exploration via Spark SQL queries, near real-time Business Intelligence reports and dashboards, and data science and machine learning use cases. Since processed data is continuously streamed into Delta Lake, it can be consumed in both a streaming and batch manner:

1. Let's take a look at how this simplified Lambda Architecture can be implemented using Apache Spark and Delta Lake, as illustrated in the following block of code:

```
retail_batch_df = (spark
                   .read
                   .option("header", "true")
                   .option("inferSchema", "true")
                   .csv("/FileStore/shared_uploads/online_
retail/online_retail.csv"))
```

In the preceding code snippet, we create a Spark DataFrame by reading a CSV file stored on the data lake using the `read()` function. We specify the options to infer the headers and schema from the semi-structured CSV file itself. The result of this is a Spark DataFrame, named `retail_batch_df`, that is a pointer to the data and structure of the retail data stored in the CSV files.

2. Now, let's convert this CSV data into Delta Lake format and store it as a Delta table on the data lake, as shown in the following block of code:

```
(retail_batch_df
        .write
        .mode("overwrite")
        .format("delta")
        .option("path", "/tmp/data-lake/online_retail.
    delta")
        .saveAsTable("online_retail"))
```

In the preceding code snippet, we save the `retail_batch_df` Spark DataFrame to the data lake as a Delta table using the `write()` function along with the `saveAsTable()` function. The format is specified as `delta`, and a location for the table is specified using the `path` option. The result is a Delta table named `online_retail` with its data stored, in Delta Lake format, on the data lake.

> **Tip**
> When a Spark DataFrame is saved as a table, with a location specified, the table is called an external table. As a best practice, it is recommended that you always create external tables because the data of an external table is preserved even if the table definition is deleted.

In the preceding block of code, we performed an initial load of the data using Spark's batch processing:

*   Now, let's load some incremental data into the same Delta table defined previously, named `online_retail`, using Spark's Structured Streaming. This is illustrated in the following block of code:

```
retail_stream_df = (spark
                .readStream
```

```
                        .schema(retailSchema)
            .csv("/FileStore/shared_uploads/online_
  retail/"))
```

In the preceding code snippet, we read a set of CSV files stored on the data lake in a streaming fashion using the `readStream()` function. Structured Streaming requires the schema of data being read to be specified upfront, which we supply using the `schema` option. The result is a Structured Streaming DataFrame named `retail_stream_df`.

• Now, let's ingest this stream of data into the same Delta table, named `online_retail`, which was created earlier during the initial load. This is shown in the following block of code:

```
(retail_stream_df
        .writeStream
        .outputMode("append")
        .format("delta")
        .option("checkpointLocation", "/tmp/data-lake/
  online_retail.delta/")
        .start("/tmp/data-lake/online_retail.delta"))
```

In the preceding code block, the streaming `retail_stream_df` DataFrame is being ingested into the existing Delta table named `online_retail` using Structured Streaming's `writeStream()` function. The `outputMode` option is specified as `append`. This is because we want to continuously append new data to the existing Delta table. Since Structured Streaming guarantees **exactly-once semantics**, a `checkpointLocation` needs to be specified. This is so that Structured Streaming can track the progress of the processed data and restart exactly from the point where it left in the case of failures or if the streaming process restarts.

> **Note**
>
> A Delta table stores all the required schema information in the Delta Transaction Log. This makes registering Delta tables with a metastore completely optional, and it is only required while accessing Delta tables via external tools or via Spark SQL.

You can now observe from the previous blocks of code that the combination of Spark's unified batch and stream processing already simplifies Lambda Architecture by using a single unified analytics engine. With the addition of Delta Lake's transactional and isolation properties and batch and streaming unification, your Lambda Architecture can be further simplified, giving you a powerful and scalable platform that allows you to get to your freshest data in just a few seconds to a few minutes. One prominent use case of streaming data ingestion is maintaining a replica of the source transactional system data in the data lake. This replica should include all the delete, update, and insert operations that take place in the source system. Generally, this use case is termed CDC and follows a pattern similar to the one described in this section. In the following section, we will dive deeper into implementing CDC using Apache Spark and Delta Lake.

Change Data Capture

Generally, operational systems do not maintain historical data for extended periods of time. Therefore, it is essential that an exact replica of the transactional system data be maintained in the data lake along with its history. This has a few advantages, including providing you with a historical audit log of all your transactional data. Additionally, this huge wealth of data can help you to unlock novel business use cases and data patterns that could take your business to the next level.

Maintaining an exact replica of a transactional system in the data lake means capturing all of the changes to every transaction that takes place in the source system and replicating it in the data lake. This process is generally called CDC. CDC requires you to not only capture all the new transactions and append them to the data lake but also capture any deletes or updates to the transactions that happen in the source system. This is not an ordinary feat to achieve on data lakes, as data lakes have meager to no support at all for updating or deleting arbitrary records. However, CDC on data lakes is made possible with Delta Lake's full support to insert, update, and delete any number of arbitrary records. Additionally, the combination of Apache Spark and Delta Lake makes the architecture simple.

Let's implement a CDC process using Apache Spark and Delta Lake, as illustrated in the following block of code:

```
(spark
  .read
    .option("header", "true")
    .option("inferSchema", "true")
    .csv("/FileStore/shared_uploads/online_retail/online_
retail.csv")
```

```
    .write
      .mode("overwrite")
      .format("delta")
      .option("path", "/tmp/data-lake/online_retail.delta")
      .saveAsTable("online_retail"))
```

In the preceding code snippet, we perform an initial load of a static set of data into a Delta table using batch processing with Spark. We simply use Spark DataFrame's `read()` function to read a set of static CSV files and save them into a Delta table using the `saveAsTable()` function. Here, we use the `path` option to define the table as an external table. The result is a delta table with a static set of initial data from the source table.

Here, the question is how did we end up with transactional data from an operational system, which typically happens to be RDBMS, in the form of a set of text files in the data lake? The answer is a specialist set of tools that are purpose-built for reading CDC data from operational systems and converting and staging them onto either a data lake or a message queue or another database of choice. Some examples of such CDC tools include Oracle's Golden Gate and AWS Database Migration Service.

> **Note**
> Apache Spark can handle CDC data and ingest it seamlessly into Delta Lake; however, it is not suited for building end-to-end CDC pipelines, including ingesting from operational sources. There are open source and proprietary tools specifically built for this purpose, such as StreamSets, Fivetran, Apache Nifi, and more.

Now that we have an initial set of static transactional data loaded into a Delta table, let's ingest some real-time data into the same Delta table, as shown in the following block of code:

```
retail_stream_df = (spark
                    .readStream
                    .schema(retailSchema)
                    .csv("/FileStore/shared_uploads/online_
retail/"))
```

In the preceding code snippet, we define a streaming DataFrame from a location on the data lake. Here, the assumption is that a third-party CDC tool is constantly adding new files to the location on the data lake with the latest transactional data.

Now, we can merge the change data into the existing Delta table, as shown in the following block of code:

```
from delta.tables import *
deltaTable = DeltaTable.forPath(spark, "/tmp/data-lake/online_
retail.delta")
def upsertToDelta(microBatchOutputDF, batchId):
  deltaTable.alias("a").merge(
      microBatchOutputDF.dropDuplicates(["InvoiceNo",
"InvoiceDate"]).alias("b"),
      "a.InvoiceNo = b.InvoiceNo and a.InvoiceDate =
b.InvoiceDate") \
    .whenMatchedUpdateAll() \
    .whenNotMatchedInsertAll() \
    .execute()
```

In the preceding code block, the following happens:

1. We recreate a definition for the existing Delta table using the Delta Lake location and the `DeltaTable.forPath()` function. The result is a pointer to the Delta table in Spark's memory, named `deltaTable`.

2. Then, we define a function named `upsertToDelta()` that performs the actual `merge` or `upsert` operation into the existing Delta table.

3. The existing Delta table is aliased using the letter of a, and the Spark DataFrame containing new updates from each streaming micro-batch is aliased as letter b.

4. The incoming updates from the streaming micro-batch might actually contain duplicates. The reason for the duplicates is that a given transaction might have undergone multiple updates by the time its data reaches Structured Streaming. Therefore, there is a need to deduplicate the streaming micro-batch prior to merging into the Delta table. This is achieved by applying the `dropDuplicates()` function on the streaming micro-batch DataFrame.

5. The streaming updates are then merged into the Delta table by applying the `merge()` function on the existing Delta table. An equality condition is applied to the key columns of both the DataFrames, and all matching records from the streaming micro-batch updates are updated in the existing Delta table using the `whenMatchedUpdateAll()` function.

6. Any records from the streaming micro-batch that don't already exist in the target Delta table are inserted using the `whenNotMatchedInsertAll()` function.

> **Note**
>
> It is necessary to deduplicate the streaming updates coming in the form of micro-batches as a given transaction might have undergone multiple updates by the time our streaming job actually gets to process it. It is a common industry practice to select the latest update per transaction based on the key column and the latest timestamp. In the absence of such a timestamp column in the source table, most CDC tools have the functionality to scan records in the correct order that they were created or updated and insert their own timestamp column.

In this way, using a simple `merge()` function, change data can be easily merged into an existing Delta table stored on any data lake. This functionality greatly simplifies the architectural complexity of CDC use cases that are implemented in real-time analytics systems.

> **Important note**
>
> It is imperative that events arrive in the exact same order they were created at the source for CDC use cases. For instance, a delete operation cannot be applied prior to an insert operation. This would lead to incorrect data outright. Certain message queues do not preserve the order of events as they arrive in the queue, and care should be taken to preserve event ordering.

Behind the scenes, Spark automatically scales the merge process, making it scalable to even petabytes of data. In this way, Delta Lake brings data warehouse-like functionality to cloud-based data lakes that weren't actually designed to handle analytics types of use cases.

> **Tip**
>
> A Delta merge might progressively get slower as the data size in the target Delta table increases. A Delta merge's performance can be improved by using an appropriate data partitioning scheme and specifying data partition column(s) in the merge clause. In this way, a Delta merge will only select those partitions that actually need to be updated, thus greatly improving merge performance.

Another phenomenon that is unique to a real-time streaming analytics use case is late-arriving data. When an event or an update to an event arrives at the streaming engine a little later than expected, it is called late-arriving data. A capable streaming engine needs to be able to handle late-arriving data or data arriving out of order. In the following section, we will explore handling late-arriving data in more detail.

Handling late-arriving data

Late-arriving data is a situation that is unique to real-time streaming analytics, where events related to the same transaction do not arrive in time to be processed together, or they arrive out of order at the time of processing. Structured Streaming supports stateful stream processing to handle such scenarios. We will explore these concepts further next.

Stateful stream processing using windowing and watermarking

Let's consider the example of an online retail transaction where a user is browsing through the e-tailer's website. We would like to calculate the user session based on one of the two following events taking place: either the users exit the e-tailer's portal or a timeout occurs. Another example is that a user places an order and then subsequently updates the order, and due to the network or some other delay, we receive the update first and then the original order creation event. Here, we would want to wait to receive any late or out-of-order data before we go ahead and save the data to the final storage location.

In both of the previously mentioned scenarios, the streaming engine needs to be able to store and manage certain state information pertaining to each transaction in order to account for late-arriving data. Spark's Structured Streaming can automatically handle late-arriving data by implementing stateful processing using the concept of **Windowing**.

Before we dive deeper into the concept of windowing in Structured Screaming, you need to understand the concept of event time. **Event time** is the timestamp at which an event of a transaction is generated at the source. For instance, the timestamp at which an order is placed becomes the event time for the order creation event. Similarly, if the same transaction is updated at the source, then the update timestamp becomes the event time for the update event of the transaction. Event time is an important parameter for any stateful processing engine in order to determine which event took place first.

Using windowing, Structured Steaming maintains a state for each key and updates the state for a given key if a new event for the same key arrives, as illustrated in the following diagram:

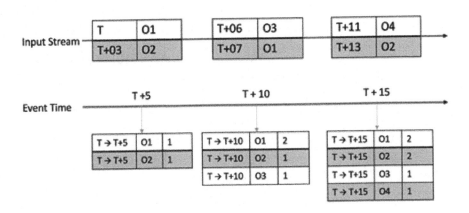

Figure 4.4 – Stateful stream processing

In the preceding illustration, we have a stream of transactional events of orders being placed. Each of **O1, O2,** and **O3,** indicates the order numbers, and **T, T+03,** and so on, indicates timestamps at which orders were created. The input stream has a steady stream of order-related events being generated. We define a stateful window of **10** minutes with a sliding interval of every **5** minutes. What we are trying to achieve here in the window is to update the count of each unique order placed. As you can see, at each **5**-minute interval, any new events of the same order get an updated count. This simple illustration depicts how stateful processing works in a stream processing scenario.

However, there is one problem with this type of stateful processing; that is, the state seems to be perpetually maintained, and over a period of time, the state data itself might grow to be too huge to fit into the cluster memory. It is also not practical to maintain the state perpetually. This is because real-world scenarios rarely ever require the state to be maintained for extended periods of time. Therefore, we need a mechanism to expire the state after a certain time interval. Structured Streaming has the ability to define a watermark that governs for how long the individual state is maintained per key, and it drops the state as soon as the watermark expires for a given key.

> **Note**
> In spite of defining a watermark, the state could still grow to be quite large, and Structured Streaming has the ability to spill the state data onto the executor's local disk when needed. Structured Streaming can also be configured to use an external state store such as RocksDB in order to maintain state data for a very large number of keys ranging in the millions.

The following code blocks show the implementation details of arbitrary stateful processing with Spark's Structured Streaming using the event time, windowing, and watermarking:

1. Let's implement the concepts of **windowing** and **watermarking** using Structured Streaming, as shown in the following code example:

```
from pyspark.sql.functions import window, max, count,
current_timestamp, to_timestamp
raw_stream_df = (spark
                 .readStream
                 .schema(retailSchema)
                 .option("header", True)
                 .csv("/FileStore/shared_uploads/online_
retail/")
                 .withColumn("InvoiceTime", to_
timestamp("InvoiceDate", 'dd/M/yy HH:mm')))
```

In the preceding code block, we define a streaming DataFrame using a location on the data lake. Additionally, we append a new column to the DataFrame named `InvoiceTime` by converting the `InvoiceDate` column from `StringType` into `TimestampType`.

2. Next, we will perform some stateful processing on the `raw_stream_df` Streaming DataFrame by defining windowing and watermarking functions on it, as shown in the following block of code:

```
aggregated_df = (
    raw_stream_df.withWatermark("InvoiceTime",
                                "1 minutes")
    .groupBy("InvoiceNo", window("InvoiceDate",
                                "30 seconds",
                                "10 seconds",
                                "0 seconds"))
    .agg(max("InvoiceDate").alias("event_time"),
         count("InvoiceNo").alias("order_count"))
)
```

The following observations can be drawn from the preceding code snippet:

A. We define a watermark on the `raw_stream_df` streaming DataFrame for 1 minute. This specifies that Structured Streaming should accumulate a state for each key for only a duration of 1 minute. The watermark duration depends entirely on your use case and how late your data is expected to arrive.

B. We define a group by function on the key column, named `InvoiceNo`, and define the desired window for our stateful operation as 30 seconds with a sliding window of every 10 seconds. This means that our keys will be aggregated every 10 seconds after the initial 30-second window.

C. We define the aggregation functions to be `max` on the timestamp column and `count` on the key column.

D. The streaming process will write data to the streaming sink as soon as the watermark expires for each key.

3. Once the stateful stream has been defined using windowing and watermarking functions, we can quickly verify whether the stream is working as expected, as shown in the following code snippet:

```
(aggregated_df
    .writeStream
    .queryName("aggregated_df")
    .format("memory")
    .outputMode("complete")
    .start())
```

The previous code block writes the output of the stateful processing streaming DataFrame to a memory sink and specifies a `queryName` property. The stream gets registered as an in-memory table with the specified query name, and it can be easily queried using Spark SQL to quickly verify the correctness of the code.

In this way, making use of windowing and watermarking functionalities provided by Structured Streaming, stateful stream processing can be implemented using Structured Streaming and late-arriving data can be easily handled. Another aspect to pay attention to in all of the previous code examples presented in this chapter, so far, is how the streaming data progressively gets transformed from its raw state into a processed state and further into an aggregated state. This methodology of progressively transforming data using multiple streaming processes is generally called a **multi-hop architecture**. In the following section, we will explore this methodology further.

Multi-hop pipelines

A multi-hop pipeline is an architecture for building a series of streaming jobs chained together so that each job in the pipeline processes the data and improves the quality of the data progressively. A typical data analytics pipeline consists of multiple stages, including data ingestion, data cleansing and integration, and data aggregation. Later on, it consists of data science and machine learning-related steps, including feature engineering and machine learning training and scoring. This process progressively improves the quality of data until it is finally ready for end user consumption.

With Structured Streaming, all these stages of the data analytics pipelines can be chained together into a **Directed Acyclic Graph (DAG)** of streaming jobs. In this way, new raw data continuously enters one end of the pipeline and gets progressively processed by each stage of the pipeline. Finally, end user ready data exits from the tail end of the pipeline. A typical multi-hop architecture is presented in the following diagram:

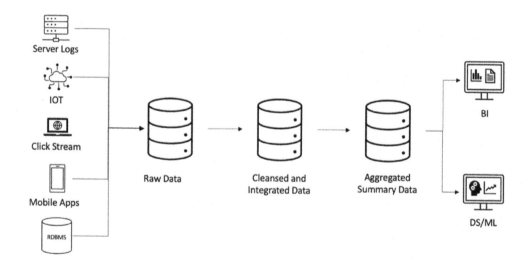

Figure 4.5 – The Multi-hop pipeline architecture

The previous diagram represents a multi-hop pipeline architecture, where raw data is ingested into the data lake and is processed in order to improve its quality through each stage of the data analytics pipeline until it is finally ready for end user use cases. End user use cases could be Business Intelligence and reporting, or they can be for further processing into predictive analytics use cases using data science and machine learning techniques.

Although it seems like a simple architecture to implement, a few key prerequisites have to be met for the seamless implementation of multi-hop pipelines, without frequent developer intervention. The prerequisites are as follows:

1. For the stages of the pipelines to be chained together seamlessly, the data processing engine needs to support exactly-once data processing guarantees resiliency to data loss upon failures.

2. The data processing engine needs to have capabilities to maintain watermark data. This is so that it is aware of the progress of data processed at a given point in time and can seamlessly pick up new data arriving in a streaming manner and process it.

3. The underlying data storage layer needs to support transactional and isolation guarantees so that there is no need for any developer intervention of any bad or incorrect data clean-up upon job failures.

Apache Spark's Structured Streaming solves the previously mentioned points, *1* and *2*, as it guarantees exactly-once data processing semantics and has built-in support for checkpointing. This is to keep track of the data processing progress and also to help with restarting a failed job exactly at the point where it left off. Point *3* is supported by Delta Lake with its ACID transactional guarantees and support for simultaneous batch and streaming jobs.

1. Let's implement an example multi-hop pipeline using Structured Streaming and Delta Lake, as shown in the following blocks of code:

```
raw_stream_df = (spark
                    .readStream
                    .schema(retailSchema)
                    .option("header", True)
                    .csv("/FileStore/shared_uploads/online_
retail/"))
(raw_stream_df
    .writeStream
      .format("delta")
      .option("checkpointLocation",
              "/tmp/delta/raw_stream.delta/checkpoint")
    .start("/tmp/delta/raw_stream.delta/"))
```

In the preceding code block, we create a raw streaming DataFrame by ingesting source data from its raw format into the data lake in Delta Lake format. The `checkpointLocation` provides the streaming job with resiliency to failures whereas Delta Lake for the target location provides transactional and isolation guarantees for `write` operations.

2. Now we can further process the raw ingested data using another job to further improve the quality of data, as shown in the following code block:

```
integrated_stream_df = (raw_stream_df
                            .withColumn("InvoiceTime", to_
timestamp("InvoiceDate", 'dd/M/yy HH:mm')))
(integrated_stream_df
    .writeStream
        .format("delta")
        .option("checkpointLocation", "/tmp/delta/int_
stream.delta/checkpoint")
        .start("/tmp/delta/int_stream.delta/"))
```

In the preceding block of code, we convert a string column into a timestamp column and persist the cleansed data into Delta Lake. This is the second stage of our multi-hop pipeline, and typically, this stage reads from the Delta table generated by the previous raw data ingestion stage. Again, the use of a checkpoint location here helps to perform the incremental processing of data, processing any new records added to the raw Delta table as they arrive.

3. Now we can define the final stage of the pipeline where we aggregate the data to create highly summarized data that is ready for end user consumption, as shown in the following code snippet:

```
aggregated_stream_df = (integrated_stream_df
.withWatermark("InvoiceTime", "1 minutes")
.groupBy("InvoiceNo", window("InvoiceTime",
        "30 seconds", "10 seconds", "0 seconds"))
.agg(max("InvoiceTime").alias("event_time"),
        count("InvoiceNo").alias("order_count")))

(aggregated_stream_df
    .writeStream
```

```
.format("delta")
.option("checkpointLocation",
        "/tmp/delta/agg_stream.delta/checkpoint")
.start("/tmp/delta/agg_stream.delta/"))
```

In the preceding code block, integrated and cleansed data is aggregated into the highest level of summary data. This can be further consumed by Business Intelligence or data science and machine learning use cases. This stage of the pipeline also makes use of the checkpoint location and Delta table for resiliency to job failures and keep the tracking of new data that needs to be processed when it arrives.

Therefore, with the combination of Apache Spark's Structured Streaming and Delta Lake, implementing multi-hop architecture becomes seamless and efficient. The different stages of a multi-hop could be implemented as a single monolithic job containing multiple streaming processes. As a best practice, the individual streaming processes for each stage of the pipeline are broken down into multiple independent streaming jobs, which can be further chained together into a DAG using an external orchestrator such as Apache Airflow. The advantage of the latter is easier maintenance of the individual streaming jobs and the minimized downtime of the overall pipeline when an individual stage of the pipeline needs to be updated or upgraded.

Summary

In this chapter, you were introduced to the need for real-time data analytics systems and the advantages they have to offer in terms of getting the freshest data to business users, helping businesses improve their time to market, and minimizing any lost opportunity costs. The architecture of a typical real-time analytics system was presented, and the major components were described. A real-time analytics architecture using Apache Spark's Structured Streaming was also depicted. A few examples of prominent industry use cases of real-time data analytics were described. Also, you were introduced to a simplified Lambda Architecture using the combination of Structured Streaming and Delta Lake. The use case for CDC, including its requirements and benefits, was presented, and techniques for ingesting CDC data into Delta Lake were presented along with working examples leveraging Structured Streaming for implementing a CDC use case.

Finally, you learned a technique for progressively improving data quality from data ingestion into highly aggregated and summarized data, in near real time, called multi-hop pipelines. You also examined a simple implementation of multi-hop pipelines using the powerful combination of Structured Streaming and Delta Lake.

This concludes the data engineering section of this book. The skills you have learned so far will help you to embark on a data analytics journey starting with raw transactional data from operational source systems, ingesting it into data lakes, cleansing the data, and integrating the data. Also, you should be familiar with building end-to-end data analytics pipelines that progressively improve the quality of data in a real-time streaming fashion and result in pristine, highest-level aggregated data that can be readily consumed by Business Intelligence and reporting use cases.

In the following chapters, you will build on the data engineering concepts learned thus far and delve into the realm of predictive analytics using Apache Spark's data science and machine learning capabilities. In the next chapter, we will begin with the concepts of exploratory data analysis and feature engineering.

Section 2: Data Science

Once we have clean data in a data lake, we can get started with performing data science and machine learning on the historical data. This section helps you understand the importance and need for scalable machine learning. The chapters in this section show how to perform exploratory data analysis, feature engineering, and machine learning model training in a scalable and distributed fashion using PySpark. This section also introduces MLflow, an open source machine learning life cycle management tool useful for tracking machine learning experiments and productionizing machine learning models. This section also introduces you to some techniques for scaling out single-machine machine learning libraries based on standard Python.

This section includes the following chapters:

Chapter 5, Scalable Machine Learning with PySpark

Chapter 6, Feature Engineering – Extraction, Transformation, and Selection

Chapter 7, Supervised Machine Learning

Chapter 8, Unsupervised Machine Learning

Chapter 9, Machine Learning Life Cycle Management

Chapter 10, Scaling Out Single-Node Machine Learning Using PySpark

5

Scalable Machine Learning with PySpark

In the previous chapters, we have established that modern-day data is growing at a rapid rate, with a volume, velocity, and veracity not possible for traditional systems to keep pace with. Thus, we learned about distributed computing to keep up with the ever-increasing data processing needs and saw practical examples of ingesting, cleansing, and integrating data to bring it to a level that is conducive to business analytics using the power and ease of use of Apache Spark's unified data analytics platform. This chapter, and the chapters that follow, will explore the data science and **machine learning (ML)** aspects of data analytics.

Today, the computer science disciplines of AI and ML have made a massive comeback and are pervasive. Businesses everywhere need to leverage these techniques to remain competitive, expand their customer base, introduce novel product lines, and stay profitable. However, traditional ML and data science techniques were designed to deal with limited samples of data and are not inherently scalable.

This chapter provides you with an overview of traditional ML algorithms, including supervised and unsupervised ML techniques and explores real-world use cases of ML in business applications. Then you will learn about the need for scalable ML. A few techniques for scaling out ML algorithms in a distributed fashion to handle very large data samples will be presented. Then, we will dive into the ML library of Apache Spark, called MLlib, along with code examples, to perform data wrangling using Apache Spark's MLlib to explore, clean, and manipulate data in order to get it ready for ML applications.

This chapter covers the following main topics:

- ML overview

- Scaling out machine learning

- Data wrangling with Apache Spark and MLlib

By the end of this chapter, you will have gained an appreciation for scalable ML and its business applications and acquired a basic understanding of Apache Spark's scalable ML library, named MLlib. You will have acquired the skills necessary to utilize MLlib to clean and transform data and get it ready for ML applications at scale, helping you to reduce the time taken for data cleansing tasks, and making your overall ML life cycle much more efficient.

Technical requirements

In this chapter, we will be using the Databricks Community Edition to run our code: `https://community.cloud.databricks.com`.

- Sign-up instructions can be found at `https://databricks.com/try-databricks`.

- The code and data used in this chapter can be downloaded from `https://github.com/PacktPublishing/Essential-PySpark-for-Scalable-Data-Analytics/tree/main/Chapter05`.

ML overview

Machine Learning is a field of AI and computer science that leverages statistical models and computer science algorithms for learning patterns inherent in data, without being explicitly programmed. ML consists of algorithms that automatically convert patterns within data into models. Where pure mathematical or rule-based models perform the same task over and over again, an ML model learns from data and its performance can be greatly improved by exposing it to vast amounts of data.

A typical ML process involves applying an ML algorithm to a known dataset called the training dataset, to generate a new ML model. This process is generally termed *model training* or *model fitting*. Some ML models are trained on datasets containing a known correct answer that we intend to predict in an unknown dataset. This known, correct value in the training dataset is termed the *label*.

Once the model is trained, the resultant model is applied to new data in order to predict the required values. This process is generally referred to as **model inference** or **model scoring**.

> Tip
> Instead of training a single model, it is a best practice to train multiple models using various different model parameters called **hyperparameters** and select the best model among all the trained models based on well-defined **accuracy metrics**. This process of training multiple models based on different parameters is generally referred to as hyperparameter **tuning** or **cross-validation**.

Examples of ML algorithms include classification, regression, clustering, collaborative filtering, and dimensionality reduction.

Types of ML algorithms

ML algorithms can be classified into three broad categories, namely, supervised learning, unsupervised learning, and reinforcement learning, as discussed in the following sections.

Supervised learning

Supervised learning is a type of ML where a model is trained on a dataset with a known value called the **label**. This label is tagged in the training dataset and represents the correct answer to the problem we are trying to solve. Our intention with supervised learning is to predict the label in an unknown dataset once the model is trained on a known dataset with the tagged label.

Examples of supervised learning algorithms include Linear Regression, Logistic Regression, Naive Bayes Classifiers, K-Nearest Neighbor, Decision Trees, Random Forest, Gradient Boosted Trees, and Support Vector Machine.

Supervised learning can be divided into two main classes, namely, regression and classification problems. While regression deals with predicting an unknown label, classification tries to classify the training dataset into known categories. Detailed implementation of supervised learning using **Apache Spark MLlib** will be introduced in *Chapter 6, Supervised Learning*.

Unsupervised learning

Unsupervised learning is a type of ML where the training data is unknown to the algorithm and is not already labeled with a correct answer. Unsupervised learning involves learning the structure of an unknown, unlabeled dataset, without any guidance from the user. Here, the task of the machine is to group data into cohorts or groups according to certain similarities or differences without any prior training.

Unsupervised learning can be further divided into **clustering** and **association** problems. Clustering deals with discovering cohorts within the training dataset, while association deals with discovering rules within the data that describe the relationship between entities. Examples of unsupervised learning include K-means clustering and collaborative filtering. Unsupervised learning will be explored at length with coding examples using Apache Spark MLlib in *Chapter 7, Unsupervised Machine Learning*.

Reinforcement learning

Reinforcement learning is employed by software systems and machines to find the best possible behavior or path that should be taken in a given situation. Unlike supervised learning, which already holds the correct answer within the training dataset, in reinforcement learning, there is no correct answer, but the reinforcement agent employs trial and error to decide the outcome and is designed to learn from experience. The reinforcement agent is either rewarded or penalized depending on the path chosen and the goal here is to maximize the reward.

Reinforcement learning is used in applications such as self-driving cars, robotics, industrial automation, and natural language processing for chatbot agents. There aren't any out-of-the-box implementations of reinforcement learning within Apache Spark MLlib, so further exploration of this concept is beyond the scope of this book.

> **Note**
>
> Another branch of data science and ML is **deep learning**, which leverages advanced techniques for ML, such as neural networks, which are also becoming very prominent these days. Although Apache Spark does support certain deep learning algorithms, these concepts are too advanced to be included within the scope of this book.

Business use cases of ML

So far, we have discussed various categories of ML and briefly introduced you to the tasks the ML models can perform. In this section, you will learn about some real-life applications of ML algorithms that help solve actual business problems across various industry verticals.

Customer churn prevention

Building customer churn models using ML can be very useful in identifying all those customers who are likely to stop engaging with your business and also help you gain insight into the factors that might lead them to churn. A churn model can simply be a regression model that estimates the risk score of each individual. Customer churn models can be very useful in identifying customers at risk of churning, thereby allowing businesses to implement strategies for customer retention.

Customer lifetime value modeling

Retail businesses generate a huge share of their revenue from a small cohort of high-value customers who provide repeat business. Customer lifetime value models can estimate a customer's lifetime, a period after which they might churn. They can also predict the total revenue that a customer would probably generate over their lifetime. Thus, estimating the revenue that a potential high-value customer might bring over their lifetime could be essential in redirecting marketing dollars to attracting and retaining such customers.

Demand forecasting

Brick and mortar businesses, as well as online businesses, have limited storage space within their actual stores as well as at the warehouse. Hence, it is important to properly stock the available storage space with products that will actually be in demand. You could develop a simple model based on seasonality and the month of the year. However, building a sophisticated ML model that includes not just seasonality and historical data, but external data such as current trends on social media, weather forecast data, and customer sentiment on social media, could lead to better forecasting of demand and help maximize revenues as a result.

Shipment lead-time prediction

Any business that involves delivery and logistics operations, whether it be an online retailer or a food delivery aggregator, needs to be able to estimate the amount of time it would take for the order to reach the customer. Often, this shipment lead time is an essential decision-making factor by the customer in terms of doing business with you versus moving on to a competitor. Regression models can be used to accurately estimate the amount of time required to deliver the product to the customer's zip code, based on factors such as product origin and destination locations, weather, and other seasonal data.

Market basket analysis

Market basket analysis is a technique for making product recommendations to customers based on items already in their basket. ML can be used to discover association rules within product categories by leveraging the collaborative filtering algorithm in order to make product recommendations to online customers based on the items already in their cart and their past purchases. This is a prominent use case used by pretty much every e-tailer.

Financial fraud detection

ML has the inherent capability to detect patterns within data. Thus, ML can be leveraged to build models that can detect anomalies across financial transactions to flag certain transactions as being fraudulent. Traditionally, financial institutions have already been leveraging rule-based models for fraud detection, but incorporating ML models into the mix makes the fraud models even more potent, thereby helping to detect novel fraud patterns.

Information extraction using natural language processing

Pharma companies and businesses that generate a large corpus of knowledge are faced with a unique challenge specific to their industry. Trying to identify whether a certain piece of knowledge has already been created by another group within the vast organization is not a straightforward problem at organizations with tens of thousands of employees. ML's natural language processing techniques can be applied to sort, group, classify, and label a large corpus of documents so that users can easily search if a similar piece of knowledge already exists.

So far, you have explored the basics of ML, the different types of ML algorithms, and their applications in real-world business use cases. In the following section, we will discuss the need for scalable ML and a few techniques for scaling our ML algorithms, and get an introduction to Apache Spark's native, scalable ML library called **MLlib** and its application for performing data wrangling.

Scaling out machine learning

In the previous sections, we learned that ML is a set of algorithms that, instead of being explicitly programmed, automatically learn patterns hidden within data. Thus, an ML algorithm exposed to a larger dataset can potentially result in a better-performing model. However, traditional ML algorithms were designed to be trained on a limited data sample and on a single machine at a time. This means that the existing ML libraries are not inherently scalable. One solution to this problem is to down-sample a larger dataset to fit in the memory of a single machine, but this also potentially means that the resulting models aren't as accurate as they could be.

Also, typically, several ML models are built on the same dataset, simply varying the parameters supplied to the algorithm. Out of these several models, the best model is chosen for production purposes, using a technique called **hyperparameter tuning**. Building several models using a single machine, one model after another, in a linear manner takes a very long time to arrive at the best possible model, leading to a longer time to production and, hence, a longer time to market.

Given these scalability challenges with traditional ML algorithms, there is a need to either scale out existing ML algorithms or new scalable ML algorithms. We will explore some techniques for scaling out ML algorithms in the following section.

Techniques for scaling ML

Two of the prominent techniques for scaling out ML algorithms are described in the following sections.

Embarrassingly parallel processing

Embarrassingly parallel processing is a type of parallel computing technique where little to no effort is required to split a given computational problem into smaller parallel tasks. This is possible when the parallelized tasks do not have any interdependencies, and all tasks can execute completely independently of one another.

Now, let's try to apply this to the problem of scaling out single machine ML algorithms on very large datasets, and at the outset, this doesn't seem like a simple task at all. However, consider the problem of hyperparameter tuning or cross-validation. Here, we can run multiple parallel models, each with different model parameters, but on the same smaller dataset that can fit into a single machine's memory. Here, we can easily train multiple models on the same dataset by varying the model parameters. Thus, by leveraging the embarrassingly parallel processing technique, we can accelerate our model-building process by several orders of magnitude, helping us get to the best possible model within hours instead of several weeks or even months, and thereby accelerating your business time to value. You will learn more about applying this technique to scale out single-node Python ML libraries using Apache Spark in *Chapter 10, Scaling Out Single-Node Machine Learning Using PySpark*.

Scalable ML algorithms

While the embarrassingly parallel computing technique helps us get better models with greater accuracy in a faster time, it is still limited by smaller dataset sizes. This means that we might still be missing out on potential patterns of data because of down-sampling. To overcome this, we need ML algorithms that can inherently scale out across multiple machines and can train on a very large dataset in a distributed manner. Apache Spark's native ML library, called MLlib, consists of such inherently scalable ML algorithms, and we will explore MLlib further in the following section.

Introduction to Apache Spark's ML library

MLlib is Apache Spark's native ML library. Being a native library, MLlib has tight integration with the rest of Spark's APIs and libraries, including Spark SQL Engine, DataFrame APIs, Spark SQL API, and even Structured Streaming. This gives Apache Spark the unique advantage of being a truly unified data analytics platform that can perform all tasks pertaining to data analytics, starting from data ingestion to data transformation, the ad hoc analysis of data, building sophisticated ML models, and even leveraging those models for production use cases. In the following section, you will explore more of Spark MLlib and its core components.

Spark MLlib overview

In the early versions of Apache Spark, MLlib was based on Spark's RDD API. Starting with Spark version 2.0, a new ML library based on DataFrame APIs was introduced. Now, in Spark 3.0 and versions above this, the DataFrame API-based MLlib is standard, while the older RDD-based MLlib is in maintenance mode with no future enhancements planned.

The DataFrame-based MLlib closely mimics traditional single-machine Python-based ML libraries such as scikit-learn and consists of three major components, called transformers, estimators, and pipelines, as described in the following sections.

Transformers

A **transformer** is an algorithm that takes a DataFrame as input, performs processing on the DataFrame columns, and returns another DataFrame. An ML model trained using Spark MLlib is a transformer that takes a raw DataFrame and returns another DataFrame with the original raw data along with the new prediction columns. A typical transformer pipeline is shown in the following diagram:

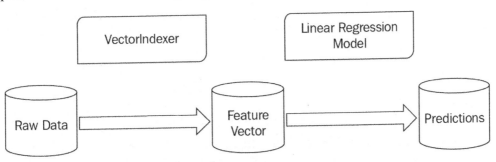

Transformer Pipeline

Figure 5.1 – A transformer pipeline

In the previous diagram, a typical transformer pipeline is depicted, where a series of transformer stages, including a **VectorIndexer** and an already trained **Linear Regression Model**, are applied to the raw DataFrame. The result is a new DataFrame with all the original columns, along with some new columns containing predicted values.

> **Note**
> The transformation DataFrame operation is a different concept compared to transformers within Spark's MLlib. While both transform one DataFrame into another DataFrame and are lazily evaluated, the former is an operation performed on a DataFrame, while the latter is an actual ML algorithm.

Estimators

An **estimator** is another algorithm that accepts a DataFrame as input and results in a transformer. Any ML algorithm is an estimator in that it transforms a DataFrame with raw data into a DataFrame with actual predictions. An estimator pipeline is depicted in the following diagram:

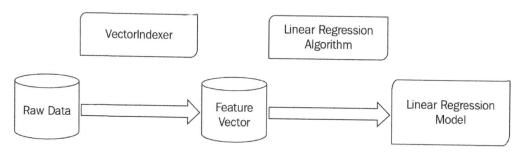

Estimator Pipeline

Figure 5.2 – An estimator pipeline

In the preceding diagram, a **Transformer** is first applied to a DataFrame with raw data to result in a **Feature Vector** DataFrame. An **Estimator** in the form of a **Linear Regression Algorithm** is then applied to the DataFrame containing **Feature Vectors** to result in a **Transformer** in the form of a newly trained **Linear Regression Model**.

> **Note**
>
> A feature vector is a special data structure within the Spark MLlib library. It is a DataFrame column consisting of actual vector objects of the floating-point type. Since ML is based on mathematics and statistics, all ML algorithms exclusively operate on vectors of floating-point values. Raw data is converted into feature vectors using feature extraction and feature engineering techniques.

Pipelines

An ML pipeline within Spark MLlib chains together several stages of transformers and estimators into a DAG that performs an end-to-end ML operation ranging from data cleansing, to feature engineering, to actual model training. A pipeline could be a transformer-only pipeline or an estimator-only pipeline or a mix of the two.

Using the available transformers and estimators within Spark MLlib, an entire end-to-end ML pipeline can be constructed. A typical ML pipeline consists of several stages, starting with data wrangling, feature engineering, model training, and model inferencing. You will learn more about data wrangling techniques in the following section.

Data wrangling with Apache Spark and MLlib

Data wrangling, also referred to within the data science community as **data munging**, or simply **data preparation**, is the first step in a typical data science process. Data wrangling involves sampling, exploring, selecting, manipulating, and cleansing data to make it ready for ML applications. Data wrangling takes up to 60 to 80 percent of the whole data science process and is the most crucial step in guaranteeing the accuracy of the ML model being built. The following sections explore the data wrangling process using Apache Spark and MLlib.

Data preprocessing

Data preprocessing is the first step in the data wrangling process and involves gathering, exploring, and selecting the data elements useful for solving the problem at hand. The data science process typically succeeds the data engineering process and the assumption here is that clean and integrated data is already available in the data lake. However, data that is clean enough for BI may not be good enough for data science. Also, data science applications require additional datasets, which may not be useful for other analytics use cases, and hence, may not yet be clean.

Before we start manipulating and wrangling our data, we need to load it into a Spark DataFrame and explore the data to gain some understanding of its structure. The following code example will make use of the integrated dataset produced toward the end of *Chapter 3*, *Data Cleansing and Integration*, named `retail_silver.delta`:

```
raw_data = spark.read.format("delta").load("dbfs:/FileStore/
shared_uploads/delta/retail_silver.delta")
raw_data.printSchema()
(select_data = raw_data.select("invoice_num", "stock_code",
                               "quantity", "invoice_date",
                               "unit_price","country_code",
                               "age", "work_class",
                               "final_weight")
select_data.describe().show()
```

In the preceding code snippet, we perform the following operations:

1. We load data from the data lake into a Spark DataFrame using the `spark.read()` function.

2. We print its schema to check the data types of the columns using the `printSchema()` function.

3. We display a few columns from the DataFrame to check their values using the `select()` operation.

4. We generate basic statistics on the DataFrame using the `describe()` operation.

Data cleansing

In the code example in the previous section, you must have noticed that most data types are just strings types. The dataset might also contain duplicates, and there are also NULL values in the data. Let's fix these inconsistencies in the dataset, as shown in the following code snippet:

```
dedupe_data = select_data.drop_duplicates(["invoice_num",
                                           "invoice_date",
                                           "stock_code"])
interim_data = (select_data
    .withColumn("invoice_time", to_timestamp("invoice_date",
                                             'dd/M/yy HH:mm'))
    .withColumn("cust_age", col("age").cast(FloatType()))
    .withColumn("working_class",
               col("work_class").cast(FloatType()))
    .withColumn("fin_wt",
               col("final_weight").cast(FloatType()))
)
clean_data = interim_data.na.fill(0)
```

In the preceding code snippet, we perform the following operations:

1. We de-duplicate data using the `dropduplicates()` operation using the key columns.

2. We then cast datetime columns into the proper timestamp type, using the `to_timestamp()` function, by supplying the correct format of the timestamp.

3. We change the data types of the DataFrame using the CAST() method.

4. We replace missing values and NULL values with 0 using the na.fill() operation.

This section showed you how to perform basic data cleansing at scale using PySpark. The following section will show you how to manipulate data steps such as filtering and renaming.

Data manipulation

Once you have a cleaner dataset, you can perform operations to filter out any data not required by your use case, rename columns to follow your naming conventions, and drop any unwanted data columns, as shown in the following code block:

```
final_data = (clean_data.where("year(invoice_time) = 2009")
                    .withColumnRenamed("working_class",
                                        "work_type")
                    .withColumnRenamed("fin_wt",
                                        "final_weight")
                    .drop("age")
                    .drop("work_class")
                    .drop("fn_wt"))
pd_data = final_data.toPandas()
```

In the preceding code snippet, we perform the following operations:

1. We filter, slice, and dice data using the where() function.

2. We rename columns using the withColumnsRenamed() function and drop unwanted columns using the drop() function.

3. We convert the Spark DataFrame to a PySpark DataFrame using the toPandas() function.

Sometimes, there is an ML algorithm that's not available in Spark MLlib, or there's a custom algorithm built using single-node Python libraries. For these use cases, you can convert your Spark DataFrame into a pandas DataFrame, as shown in *step 3* previously.

> **Note**
> Converting a Spark DataFrame to a pandas Dataframe involves collecting all the data from the Executors onto the Spark driver. Thus, care needs to be taken that this conversion is only applied to smaller datasets, otherwise this could lead to an `OutOfMemory` error on the Driver node.

Summary

In this chapter, you learned about the concept of ML and the different types of ML algorithms. You also learned about some of the real-world applications of ML to help businesses minimize losses and maximize revenues and accelerate their time to market. You were introduced to the necessity of scalable ML and two different techniques for scaling out ML algorithms. Apache Spark's native ML Library, MLlib, was introduced, along with its major components.

Finally, you learned a few techniques to perform data wrangling to clean, manipulate, and transform data to make it more suitable for the data science process. In the following chapter, you will learn about the send phase of the ML process, called feature extraction and feature engineering, where you will learn to apply various scalable algorithms to transform individual data fields to make them even more suitable for data science applications.

6
Feature Engineering – Extraction, Transformation, and Selection

In the previous chapter, you were introduced to Apache Spark's native, scalable machine learning library, called **MLlib**, and you were provided with an overview of its major architectural components, including transformers, estimators, and pipelines.

This chapter will take you to your first stage of the **scalable machine learning** journey, which is **feature engineering**. Feature engineering deals with the process of extracting machine learning features from preprocessed and clean data in order to make it conducive for machine learning. You will learn about the concepts of **feature extraction**, **feature transformation**, **feature scaling**, and **feature selection** and implement these techniques using the algorithms that exist within Spark MLlib and some code examples. Toward the end of this chapter, you will have learned the necessary techniques to implement scalable feature engineering pipelines that convert preprocessed data into a format that is suitable and ready for the machine learning model training process.

Particularly, in this chapter, you will learn the following:

- The machine learning process

- Feature extraction

- Feature transformation

- Feature selection

- Feature store as a central feature repository

- Delta as an offline feature store

Technical requirements

In this chapter, we will be using the Databricks Community Edition to run our code. This can be found at `https://community.cloud.databricks.com`.

- Sign-up instructions can be found at `https://databricks.com/try-databricks`. The code used in this chapter can be downloaded from `https://github.com/PacktPublishing/Essential-PySpark-for-Data-Analytics/tree/main/Chapter06`.

- The datasets used in this chapter can be found at `https://github.com/PacktPublishing/Essential-PySpark-for-Data-Analytics/tree/main/data`.

The machine learning process

A typical data analytics and data science process involves gathering raw data, cleaning data, consolidating data, and integrating data. Following this, we apply statistical and machine learning techniques to the preprocessed data in order to generate a machine learning model and, finally, summarize and communicate the results of the process to business stakeholders in the form of data products. A high-level overview of the machine learning process is presented in the following diagram:

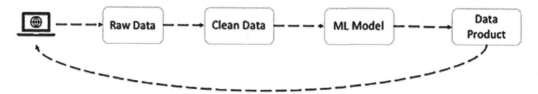

Figure 6.1 – The data analytics and data science process

As you can see from the preceding diagram, the actual machine learning process itself is just a small portion of the entire data analytics process. Data teams spend a good amount of time curating and preprocessing data, and just a portion of that time is devoted to building actual machine learning models.

The actual machine learning process involves stages that allow you to carry out steps such as data exploration, feature extraction, model training, model evaluation, and applying models for real-world business applications, as shown in the following diagram:

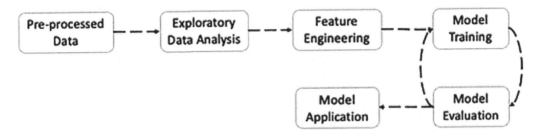

Figure 6.2 – The machine learning process

In this chapter, you will learn about the **Feature Engineering** phase of the machine learning process. The following sections will present a few of the prominent algorithms and utilities available in the **Spark MLlib** library that deal with the **Feature Extraction**, **Feature Transformation**, **Feature Scaling**, and **Feature Selection** steps of the **Feature Engineering** process.

Feature extraction

A machine learning model is equivalent to a function in mathematics or a method in computer programming. A machine learning model takes one or more parameters or variables as input and yields an output, called a prediction. In machine learning terminology, these input parameters or variables are called **features**. A feature is a column of the input dataset within a machine learning algorithm or model. A feature is a measurable data point, such as an individual's name, gender, or age, or it can be time-related data, weather, or some other piece of data that is useful for analysis.

Machine learning algorithms leverage linear algebra, a field of mathematics, and make use of mathematical structures such as matrices and vectors to represent data internally and also within the code level implementation of algorithms. Real-world data, even after undergoing the data engineering process, rarely occurs in the form of matrices and vectors. Therefore, the feature engineering process is applied to preprocessed data in order to convert it into a format that is suitable for machine learning algorithms.

The feature extraction process specifically deals with taking text, image, geospatial, or time series data and converting it into a feature vector. Apache Spark MLlib has a number of feature extractions available, such as TF-IDF, Word2Vec, CountVectorizer, and FeatureHasher.

Let's consider an example of a group of words and convert them into a feature vector using the CountVectorizer algorithm. In earlier chapters of this book, we looked at sample datasets for an online retailer and applied the data engineering process on those datasets to get a clean and consolidated dataset that was ready for analytics.

So, let's begin with the preprocessed and cleaned dataset produced toward the end of *Chapter 5, Scalable Machine Learning with PySpark*, named retail_ml.delta. This preprocessed dataset, which forms the input to the machine learning process, is also generally referred to as the **training dataset**:

1. As a first step, let's load the data from the data lake in Delta format into a Spark DataFrame. This is shown in the following code snippet:

```
preproc_data = spark.read.format("delta").load("dbfs:/
FileStore/shared_uploads/delta/retail_ml.delta")
preproc_data.show()
```

In the preceding code block, we load data stored in the data lake in Delta form into a Spark DataFrame and then display the data using the show() command.

2. The result of the display function is shown in the following diagram:

Figure 6.3 – Preprocessed data

In the preceding diagram, we have the preprocessed data as a result of the data engineering and data wrangling steps. Notice that there are 11 columns in the dataset with various data types, ranging from a string to a double, to a timestamp. In their current format, they are not suitable as inputs for a machine learning algorithm; therefore, we need to convert them into a suitable format via the feature engineering process.

3. Let's start with the `description` column, which is of the text type, and apply the `CountVectorizer` feature extraction algorithm to it in order to convert it into a feature vector, as shown in the following code block:

```
from pyspark.sql.functions import split, trim
from pyspark.ml.feature import CountVectorizer
cv_df = preproc_data.withColumn("desc_array",
split(trim("description"), " ")).where("description is
NOT NULL")
cv = CountVectorizer(inputCol="desc_array",
                     outputCol="description_vec",
                     vocabSize=2, minDF=2.0)
cv_model = cv.fit(cv_df)
train_df = model.transform(cv_df)
train_df.display()
```

In the previous code block, the following occurs:

A. We import `CountVectorizer` from the `pyspark.ml.feature` library.

B. `CountVectorizer` takes an `Array` object as input, so we use the `split()` function to split the description column into an `Array` object of words.

C. Then, we initialize a new `CountVectorizer` **estimator** by passing in the input column, defining the output column name, and then defining appropriate values for the **hyperparameters**.

D. Then, we call the `fit()` method using the previously defined estimator on the input dataset. The result is a trained model **transformer** object.

E. Finally, we call the `transform()` method on the input DataFrame, resulting in a new DataFrame with a new feature vector column for the description column.

In this way, by using the `CountVectorizer` feature extractor from Spark MLlib, we are able to extract a feature vector from a text type column.

4. Another feature extractor available within Spark MLlib, such as `Word2Vec`, can also be used, as shown in the following code snippet:

```
from pyspark.ml.feature import Word2Vec
w2v_df = preproc_data.withColumn("desc_array",
split(trim("description"), "\t")).where("description is
NOT NULL")
word2vec = Word2Vec(vectorSize=2, minCount=0,
                    inputCol="desc_array",
```

```
                          outputCol="desc_vec")
w2v_model = word2vec.fit(w2v_df)
train_df = w2v_model.transform(w2v_df)
```

In the preceding code block, the Word2Vec estimator is used in a similar fashion to the previously mentioned CountVectorizer. Here, we use it to extract a feature vector from a text-based data column. While both CountVectorizer and Word2Vec help to convert a corpus of words into a feature vector, there are differences in the internal implementations of each algorithm. They each have different uses depending on the problem scenario and input dataset and might produce different results under different circumstances.

Please note that discussing the nuances of these algorithms or making recommendations on when to use a specific feature extraction algorithm is beyond the scope of this book.

Now that you have learned a few techniques of feature extraction, in the next section, let's explore a few of Spark MLlib's algorithms for **feature transformation**.

Feature transformation

Feature transformation is the process of carefully reviewing the various variable types, such as categorical variables and continuous variables, present in the training data and determining the best type of transformation to achieve optimal model performance. This section will describe, with code examples, how to transform a few common types of variables found in machine learning datasets, such as text and numerical variables.

Transforming categorical variables

Categorical variables are pieces of data that have discrete values with a limited and finite range. They are usually text-based in nature, but they can also be numerical. Examples include country codes and the month of the year. We mentioned a few techniques regarding how to extract features from text variables in the previous section. In this section, we will explore a few other algorithms to transform categorical variables.

The tokenization of text into individual terms

The Tokenizer class can be used to break down text into its constituent terms, as shown in the following code example:

```
from pyspark.ml.feature import Tokenizer
tokenizer = Tokenizer(inputCol="description",
                      outputCol="desc_terms")
```

```
tokenized_df = tokenizer.transform(preproc_data)
tokenized_df.show()
```

In the preceding code block, we initialize the `Tokenizer` class by passing in the `inputCol` and `outputCol` parameters, which results in a transformer. Then, we transform the training dataset, resulting in a Spark DataFrame with a new column with an array of individual words from each sentence that have been converted into lowercase. This is shown in the following table:

description ▲	desc_terms
RED SPOT HEART HOT WATER BOTTLE	▶ ["red", "spot", "heart", "hot", "water", "bottle"]
PIZZA SLICE DISH	▶ ["pizza", "slice", "dish"]
BOYS ALPHABET IRON ON PATCHES	▶ ["boys", "alphabet", "iron", "on", "patches"]
SMALL RETRO SPOT MUG IN BOX WHITE	▶ ["small", "retro", "spot", "mug", "in", "box", "", "white"]
RED SPOTTY WASHBAG	▶ ["red", "spotty", "washbag"]
HOME SWEET HOME METAL SIGN	▶ ["home", "sweet", "home", "metal", "sign"]
RED SPOTTY CHARLOTTE BAG	▶ ["red", "spotty", "charlotte", "bag"]

Figure 6.4 – Tokenizing the text using Tokenizer

In the preceding table, you can see from the tokenized words that there are a few unwanted words, which we need to get rid of as they do not add any value.

Removing common words using StopWordsRemover

Every language contains common and frequently occurring words such as prepositions, articles, conjunctions, and interjections. These words do not carry any meaning in terms of the machine learning process and are better removed before training a machine learning algorithm. In Spark, this process can be achieved using the `StopWordsRemover` class, as shown in the following code snippet:

```
from pyspark.ml.feature import StopWordsRemover
stops_remover = StopWordsRemover(inputCol="desc_terms",
                                  outputCol="desc_nostops")
stops_df = stops_remover.transform(tokenized_df)
stops_df.select("desc_terms", "desc_nostops").show()
```

In the preceding code block, we initialize the `StopWordsRemover` class by passing in the `inputCol` and `outputCol` parameters, which results in a transformer. Then, we transform the training dataset, resulting in a Spark DataFrame with a new column that has an array of individual words with the stop words removed.

Once we have an array of strings with the stop words removed, a feature extraction technique such as `Word2Vec` or `CountVectorizer` is used to build a feature vector.

Encoding discrete, categorical variables

Now we have other types of string-type columns such as country codes that need to be converted into a numerical form for consumption by a machine learning algorithm. You cannot simply assign arbitrary numerical values to such discrete, categorical variables, as this could introduce a pattern that might not necessarily exist within the data.

Let's consider an example where we monotonically assign increasing values to categorical variables in alphabetical order. However, this might introduce ranking to those variables where one didn't exist in the first place. This would skew our machine learning model and is not desirable. To overcome this problem, we can use a number of Spark MLlib algorithms in which to encode these categorical variables.

Encoding string variables using StringIndexer

In our training dataset, we have string types, or categorical variables, with discrete values such as `country_code`. These variables can be assigned label indices using `StringIndexer`, as shown in the following code example:

```
from pyspark.ml.feature import StringIndexer
string_indexer = StringIndexer(inputCol="country_code",
                               outputCol="country_indexed",
                               handleInvalid="skip" )
indexed_df = string_indexer.fit(stops_df).transform(stops_df)
indexed_df.select("country_code", "country_indexed").show()
```

In the preceding code snippet, we initialize the `StringIndexer` class with input and output column names. Then, we set `handleInvalid` to `skip` in order to skip `NULL`s and invalid values. This results in an estimator that can be applied to the training DataFrame, which, in turn, results in a transformer. The transformer can be applied to the training dataset. This results in a DataFrame with a new Spark DataFrame along with a new column that contains label indices for the input categorical variable.

Transforming a categorical variable into a vector using OneHotEncoder

Once we have our categorical variables encoded into label indices, they can finally be converted into a binary vector, using the `OneHotEncoder` class, as shown in the following code snippet:

```
from pyspark.ml.feature import OneHotEncoder
ohe = OneHotEncoder(inputCol="country_indexed",
                    outputCol="country_ohe")
ohe_df = ohe.fit(indexed_df).transform(indexed_df)
ohe_df.select("country_code", "country_ohe").show()
```

In the preceding code snippet, we initialize the `OneHotEncoder` class with input and output column names. This results in an estimator that can be applied to the training DataFrame, which, in turn, results in a transformer. The transformer can be applied to the training dataset. This results in a DataFrame with a new Spark DataFrame along with a new column that contains a feature vector representing the original categorical variable.

Transforming continuous variables

Continuous variables represent data in the form of measurements or observations. Typically, they are numerical in nature and can virtually have an infinite range. Here, the data is continuous and not discrete, and a few examples include age, quantity, and unit price. They seem straightforward enough and can be directly fed into a machine learning algorithm. However, they still need to be engineered into features, as continuous variables might have just far too many values to be handled by the machine learning algorithm. There are multiple ways in which to handle continuous variables, such as binning, normalization, applying custom business logic, and more, and an appropriate method should be chosen depending on the problem being solved and the business domain.

One such technique to feature engineer continuous variables is binarization, where the continuous numerical values are converted into binary values based on a user-defined threshold, as shown in the following code example:

```
from pyspark.ml.feature import Binarizer
binarizer = Binarizer(threshold=10, inputCol="unit_price",
                      outputCol="binarized_price")
binarized_df = binarizer.transform(ohe_df)
binarized_df.select("quantity", "binarized_price").show()
```

In the preceding code block, we initialize the `Binarizer` class with the input and output column parameters, which results in a transformer. The transformer can then be applied to the training DataFrame, which, in turn, results in a new DataFrame along with a new column representing the binary values for the continuous variable.

Transforming the date and time variables

A date or timestamp type of column in itself doesn't add much value to a machine learning model training process. However, there might be patterns within the components of a date such as month, year, or day of the week. Therefore, it would be useful to choose a part of the datetime column and transform it into an appropriate feature.

In the following code example, we extract the month value from a datetime column and transform it into a feature, treating it like a categorical variable:

```python
from pyspark.sql.functions import month
month_df = binarized_df.withColumn("invoice_month",
                                    month("invoice_time"))
month_indexer = StringIndexer(inputCol="invoice_month",
                                    outputCol="month_indexed",
                                    handleInvalid="skip" )
month_df = month_indexer.fit(month_df).transform(month_df)
month_df.select("invoice_month", "month_indexed").show()
```

In the preceding code block, first, we extract the month from the timestamp column using the `month()` function and append it to the DataFrame. Then, we run the new column through the `StringIndexer` estimator and transform the month numeric column into a label index.

Assembling individual features into a feature vector

Most machine learning algorithms accept a single feature vector as input. Therefore, it would be useful to combine the individual features that you have extracted and transformed into a single feature vector. This can be accomplished using Spark MLlib's `VectorAssembler` transformer, as shown in the following code example:

```python
from pyspark.ml.feature import VectorAssembler
vec_assembler = VectorAssembler(
    inputCols=["desc_vec", "country_ohe",
                "binarized_price", "month_indexed",
                "quantity_indexed"],
```

```
        outputCol="features")
features_df = vec_assembler.transform(month_df)
features_df.select("features").show()
```

In the preceding block of code, we initialize the `VectorAssembler` class with input and output parameters, which results in a transformer object. We make use of the transformer to combine the individual features into a single feature vector. This results in a new column of the vector type being appended to the training DataFrame.

Feature scaling

It is common for training datasets to have columns with different units of measurements. For instance, while one column uses the metric system of measurement, another column might be using the imperial system. It is also possible for certain columns to have a high range, such as a column representing dollar amounts than another column representing quantities, for instance. These differences might cause a machine learning model to unduly assign more weightage to a certain value compared to others, which is undesirable and might introduce bias or skew into the model. To overcome this issue, a technique called feature scaling can be utilized. Spark MLlib comes with a few feature scaler algorithms, such as `Normalizer`, `StandardScaler`, `RobustScaler`, `MinMaxScaler`, and `MaxAbsScaler`, built in.

In the following code example, we will make use of `StandardScaler` to demonstrate how feature scaling can be applied in Apache Spark. `StandardScaler` transforms a feature vector and normalizes each vector to have a unit of standard deviation:

```
from pyspark.ml.feature import StandardScaler
std_scaler = StandardScaler(inputCol="features",
                            outputCol="scaled_features")
scaled_df = std_scaler.fit(features_df).transform(features_df)
scaled_df.select("scaled_features").show()
```

In the preceding block of code, the `StandardScaler` class is initialized with the input and output column parameters. Then, the `StandardScaler` estimator is applied to the training dataset, resulting in a `StandardScaler` model transformer object. This, in turn, can be applied to the training DataFrame to yield a new DataFrame a new column that contains the normalized features.

So far, in this section, you have learned how to extract machine learning features from dataset columns. Additionally, you have learned a feature extraction technique to convert text-based columns into feature vectors. Feature transformation techniques for converting categorical, continuous, and date- and time-based variables were also explored. Techniques for combing multiple individual features into a single feature vector were introduced, and, finally, you were also introduced to a feature scaling technique to normalize features.

In the following section, you will learn techniques in which to reduce the number of features; this is referred to as **feature selection**.

Feature selection

Feature selection is a technique that involves reducing the number of features in the machine learning process while leveraging lesser data and also improving the accuracy of the trained model. Feature selection is the process of either automatically or manually selecting only those features that contribute the most to the prediction variable that you are interested in. Feature selection is an important aspect of machine learning, as irrelevant or semi-relevant features can gravely impact model accuracy.

Apache Spark MLlib comes packaged with a few feature selectors, including `VectorSlicer`, `ChiSqSelector`, `UnivariateFeatureSelector`, and `VarianceThresholdSelector`. Let's explore how to implement feature selection within Apache Spark using the following code example that utilizes `ChiSqSelector` to select the optimal features given the label column that we are trying to predict:

```python
from pyspark.ml.feature import ChiSqSelector
chisq_selector=ChiSqSelector(numTopFeatures=1,
                             featuresCol="scaled_features",
                             outputCol="selected_features",
                             labelCol="cust_age")
result_df = chisq_selector.fit(scaled_df).transform(scaled_df)
result_df.select("selected_features").show()
```

In the preceding code block, we initialize `ChiSqSelector` using the input and the output columns. We also specify the label column, as `ChiSqSelector` chooses the optimal features best suited for predicting the label columns. Then, the `ChiSqSelector` estimator is applied to the training dataset, resulting in a `ChiSqSelector` model transformer object. This, in turn, can be applied to the training DataFrame to yield a new DataFrame column that contains the newly selected features.

Similarly, we can also leverage `VectorSlicer` to select a subset of features from a given feature vector, as shown in the following code snippet:

```
from pyspark.ml.feature import VectorSlicer
vec_slicer = VectorSlicer(inputCol="scaled_features",
                          outputCol="selected_features",
                          indices=[1])
result_df = vec_slicer.transform(scaled_df)
result_df.select("scaled_features",
                 "selected_features").display()
```

The preceding code block also performs feature selection. However, unlike `ChiSqSelector`, `VectorSlicer` doesn't optimize feature selection for a given variable. Instead, `VectorSlicer` takes a vector column with specified indices. This results in a new vector column whose values are selected through the specified indices. Each feature selector has its own way of making feature selections, and the appropriate feature selector should be used for the given scenario and the problem being solved.

So far, you have learned how to perform feature extraction from text-based variables and how to perform feature transformation on categorical and continuous types of variables. Additionally, you have explored the techniques for feature slicing along with feature selection. You have acquired techniques to transform preprocessed raw data into feature vectors that are ready to be fed into a machine learning algorithm in order to build machine learning models.

However, it seems redundant and time-consuming to perform feature engineering for each and every machine learning problem. So, can you not just use some previously built features for a new model? The answer is yes, and you should reuse some of your previously built features for new machine learning problems. You should also be able to make use of the features of some of your other team members. This can be accomplished via a centralized feature store. We will explore this topic further in the following section.

Feature store as a central feature repository

A large percentage of the time spent on any machine learning problem is on data cleansing and data wrangling to ensure we build our models on clean and meaningful data. Feature engineering is another critical process of the machine learning process where data scientists spend a huge chunk of their time curating machine learning features, which happens to be a complex and time-consuming process. It appears counter-intuitive to have to create features again and again for each new machine learning problem.

Typically, feature engineering takes place on already existing historic data, and new features are perfectly reusable in different machine learning problems. In fact, data scientists spend a good amount of time searching for the right features for the problem at hand. So, it would be tremendously beneficial to have a centralized repository of features that is also searchable and has metadata to identify features. This central repository of searchable features is generally termed a **feature store**. A typical feature store architecture is depicted in the following diagram:

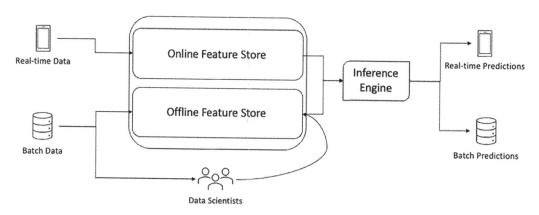

Figure 6.5 – The feature store architecture

Features are useful not only during the model training phase of the machine learning process, but they are also required during model inferencing. **Inferencing**, which is also referred to as **model scoring**, is the process of feeding an already built model with new and unseen features in order to generate predictions on the new data. Depending on whether the inferencing process takes place in batch mode or a streaming, real-time fashion, features can be very broadly classified into offline features and online features.

Batch inferencing using the offline feature store

Offline features, as the name suggests, are generated offline using a batch job. Their consumption also happens offline using either the model training process or model inferencing in a batch fashion, that is, using scheduled batch machine learning pipelines. These features can be time-consuming to create and are typically created using big data frameworks, such as Apache Spark, or by running scheduled queries off of a database or a data warehouse.

The storage mechanism used to generate offline features is referred to as an offline feature store. Historical datastores, RDBMS databases, data warehouse systems, and data lakes all make good candidates for offline feature stores. It is desirable for an offline feature store to be strongly typed, have a schema enforcement mechanism, and have the ability to store metadata along with the actual features. Any database or a data warehouse is adequate for an offline feature store; however, in the next section, we will explore Delta Lake as an offline feature store.

Delta Lake as an offline feature store

In *Chapter 3*, *Data Cleansing and Integration*, we established data lakes as the scalable and relatively inexpensive choice for the long-term storage of historical data. Some challenges with reliability and cloud-based data lakes were presented, and you learned how Delta Lake has been designed to overcome these challenges. The benefits of Delta Lake as an abstraction layer on top of cloud-based data lakes extend beyond just data engineering workloads to data science workloads as well, and we will explore those benefits in this section.

Delta Lake makes for an ideal candidate for an offline feature store on cloud-based data lakes because of the data reliability features and the novel time travel features that Delta Lake has to offer. We will discuss these in the following sections.

Structure and metadata with Delta tables

Delta Lake supports structured data with well-defined data types for columns. This makes Delta tables strongly typed, ensuring that all kinds of features of various data types can be stored in Delta tables. In comparison, the actual storage happens on relatively inexpensive and infinitely scalable cloud-based data lakes. This makes Delta Lake an ideal candidate offline feature store in the cloud.

Schema enforcement and evolution with Delta Lake

Delta Lake fully supports schema enforcement, which means that the data integrity of features inserted into a Delta Lake feature store is well maintained. This will help to ensure that only the correct data with proper data types will be used for the machine learning model building process, ensuring model performance. Delta Lake's support for schema evolution also means that new features could be easily added to a Delta Lake-based feature store.

Support for simultaneous batch and streaming workloads

Since Delta Lake fully supports unified batch and streaming workloads, data scientists can build near real-time, streaming feature engineering pipelines in addition to batch pipelines. This will help to train machine learning models with the freshest features and also generate predictions in a near real-time fashion. This will help to eliminate any operational overhead for use cases with relatively higher latency inferencing requirements by just leveraging Apache Spark's unified analytics engine.

Delta Lake time travel

Often, data scientists experiment with slight variations of data to improve model accuracy, and they often maintain several versions of the same physical data for this purpose. With Delta Lake's time travel functionality, a single Delta table can easily support multiple versions of data, thus eliminating the overhead for data scientists in maintaining several physical versions of data.

Integration with machine learning operations tools

Delta Lake also supports integration with the popular machine learning operations and workflow management tool called **MLflow**. We will explore MLOps and MLflow in *Chapter 9, Machine Learning Life Cycle Management*.

A code example of leveraging Delta Lake as an offline feature store is presented here:

```
spark.sql("CREATE DATABASE feature_store")
(result_df
    .write
    .format("delta")
    .mode("append")
    .option("location", "/FileStore/shared_uploads/delta/retail_
features.delta")
    .saveAsTable("feature_store.retail_features"))
```

First, we create a database named feature_store. Then, we save the DataFrame as a result of the *Feature selection* step in the previous section as a Delta table.

In this way, features can be searched for using simple SQL commands and can also be shared and used for other machine learning use cases via the shared Hive metastore. Delta Lake also supports common metadata such as column names and data types, and other metadata such as user notes and comments can be also included to add more context to the features in the feature store.

> **Tip**
>
> Most big data platforms, including Databricks, support the built-in Hive metastore for storing table metadata. Additionally, these platforms come with security mechanisms such as databases, tables, and, sometimes, even row- and column-level access control mechanisms. In this way, the feature store can be secured, and features can be selectively shared among data teams.

In this way, using Delta Lake can serve as an offline feature store on top of cloud-based data lakes. Once features are stored in Delta tables, they are accessible from all of Spark's APIs, including DataFrames and SQL APIs.

> **Note**
>
> All of the functions and methods present inside Spark MLlib have been designed to be natively scalable. Therefore, any machine learning operation performed using Spark MLlib is inherently scalable and can run Spark jobs with parallel and distributed tasks underneath.

Online feature store for real-time inferencing

Features that are used in online machine learning inferencing are called online features. Usually, these features have an ultra-low latency requirement, ranging from milliseconds to mere seconds. Some use cases of online features include real-time predictions in end user applications.

Let's consider the example of a customer browsing an e-tailer's web app. The customer adds a product to their cart, and based on the customer's zip code, the web app needs to provide an estimated delivery time within seconds. The machine learning model involved here requires a few features to estimate the delivery lead time, such as warehouse location, product availability, historical delivery times from this warehouse, and maybe even the weather and seasonal conditions, but most importantly, it needs the customer zip code. Most of the features could already be precalculated and available in an offline feature store. However, given the low latency requirement for this use case, the feature store must be able to deliver the features with the lowest latency possible. A data lake, or a database or data warehouse, is not an ideal candidate for this use case and requires an ultra-low latency, online feature store.

From the preceding example, we can conclude that online inferencing in real time requires a few critical components:

- An ultra-low latency, preferably, in-memory feature store.

- An event processing, low latency streaming engine

- RESTful APIs for integration with the end user web and mobile applications

An example of a real-time inferencing pipeline is presented in the following diagram:

Figure 6.6 – A real-time machine learning inferencing pipeline

In the preceding diagram, data arrives from the web or mobile apps onto a message queue such as Apache Kafka in real time. A low-latency event processing engine such as Apache Flink processes incoming features and stores them onto a NoSQL database such as Apache Cassandra or in-memory databases such as Redis for online feature stores. A machine learning inference engine fetches the features from the online feature store, generates predictions, and pushes them back to the web or mobile apps via REST APIs.

> **Note**
> Neither Apache Spark nor Delta Lake on cloud-based data lakes makes a good candidate for an online feature store. Spark's Structured Streaming has been designed to handle high throughput in favor of low latency or processing. Structured Streaming's micro-batch is not suitable to process an event as it arrives at the source. In general, cloud-based data lakes are designed for scalability and have latency specifications, and, therefore, Delta Lake cannot support the ultra-low latency requirements of online feature stores.

Summary

In this chapter, you learned about the concept of feature engineering and why it is an important part of the whole machine learning process. Additionally, you learned why it is required to create features and train machine learning models.

You explored various feature engineering techniques such as feature extraction and how they can be used to convert text-based data into features. Feature transformation techniques useful in dealing with categorical and continuous variables were introduced, and examples of how to convert them into features were presented. You also explored feature scaling techniques that are useful for normalizing features to help prevent some features from unduly biasing the trained model.

Finally, you were introduced to techniques for selecting the right features to optimize the model performance for the label being predicted via feature selection techniques. The skills learned in this chapter will help you to implement scalable and performant feature engineering pipelines using Apache Spark and leveraging Delta Lake as a central, sharable repository of features.

In the following chapter, you will learn about the various machine learning training algorithms that fall under the supervised learning category. Additionally, you will implement code examples that make use of the features generated in this chapter in order to train actual machine learning models using Apache Spark MLlib.

7
Supervised Machine Learning

In the previous two chapters, you were introduced to the machine learning process, the various stages involved, and the first step of the process, namely **feature engineering**. Equipped with the fundamental knowledge of the machine learning process and with a usable set of machine learning features, you are ready to move on to the core part of the machine learning process, namely **model training**.

In this chapter, you will be introduced to the **supervised learning** category of machine learning algorithms, where you will learn about **parametric** and **non-parametric** algorithms, as well as gain the knowledge required to solve **regression** and **classification** problems using machine learning. Finally, you will implement a few regression algorithms using the Spark machine learning library, such as **linear regression** and **decision trees**, and a few classification algorithms such as **logistic regression**, **naïve Bayes**, and **support vector machines**. **Tree ensemble** methods will also be presented, which can improve the performance and accuracy of decision trees. A few real-world applications of both regression and classification will also be presented to help you gain an appreciation of how machine learning can be leveraged in some day-to-day scenarios.

The following main topics will be covered in this chapter:

- Introduction to supervised machine learning
- Regression
- Classification
- Tree ensembles
- Real-world supervised learning applications

Toward the end of this chapter, you should have gained sufficient knowledge and the skills required for building your own regression and classification models at scale using Spark MLlib.

Technical requirements

In this chapter, we will be using Databricks Community Edition to run our code (`https://community.cloud.databricks.com`).

- Sign-up instructions can be found at `https://databricks.com/try-databricks`.
- The code for this chapter can be downloaded from `https://github.com/PacktPublishing/Essential-PySpark-for-Data-Analytics/tree/main/Chapter07`.
- The datasets for this chapter can be found at `https://github.com/PacktPublishing/Essential-PySpark-for-Data-Analytics/tree/main/data`.

Introduction to supervised machine learning

A machine learning problem can be considered as a process where an unknown variable is derived from a set of known variables using a mathematical or statistical function. The difference here is that a machine learning algorithm learns the mapping function from a given dataset.

Supervised learning is a class of machine learning algorithms where a model is trained on a dataset and the outcome for each set of inputs is already known. This is known as supervised learning as the algorithm here behaves like a teacher, guiding the training process until the desired level of model performance is achieved. Supervised learning requires data that is already labeled. Supervised learning algorithms can be further classified as parametric and non-parametric algorithms. We will look at these in the following sections.

Parametric machine learning

A machine learning algorithm that simplifies the learning process by summarizing the data with a fixed set of parameters is called a parametric learning algorithm. It achieves this by assuming a known form for the learning function and learning the coefficients of the linear function from the given dataset. The assumed form of the learning function is usually a linear function or an algebraic equation describing a straight line. Thus, parametric learning functions are also known as linear machine learning algorithms.

One important property of parametric learning algorithms is that the number of parameters needed for the linear learning function is independent of the input training dataset. This greatly simplifies the learning process and makes it relatively faster. One disadvantage here is that the underlying learning function for the given dataset might not necessarily be a straight line, hence oversimplifying the learned model. However, most practical machine learning algorithms are parametric learning algorithms, such as linear regression, logistic regression, and naïve Bayes.

Non-parametric machine learning

Non-parametric learning algorithms do not make any assumptions regarding the form of the learning function. These algorithms make the best use of the training dataset by learning a mapping function, while still maintaining the ability to conform to unseen data. This means that non-parametric learning algorithms can learn from a wider variety of learning functions. The advantage of these algorithms is that that they are flexible and yield better performing models, while the disadvantages are that they usually require more data to learn, have relatively slow training times, and may sometimes lead to model overfitting. Some examples of non-parametric learning algorithms include K-nearest neighbors, decision trees, and support vector machines.

Supervised learning algorithms have two major applications, namely regression and classification. We will explore these in the following sections.

Regression

Regression is a supervised learning technique that helps us learn the correlation between a continuous output parameter called **Label** and a set of input parameters called **Features**. Regression produces machine learning models that predict a continuous label, given a feature vector. The concept of regression can be best explained using the following diagram:

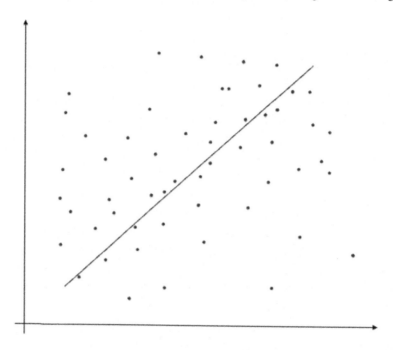

Figure 7.1 – Linear regression

In the preceding diagram, the scatterplot represents data points spread across a two-dimensional space. The linear regression algorithm, being a parametric learning algorithm, assumes that the learning function will have a linear form. Thus, it learns the coefficients that are required to represent a straight line that approximately fits the data points on the scatterplot.

Spark MLlib has distributed and scalable implementations of a few prominent regression algorithms, such as linear regression, decision trees, random forests, and gradient boosted trees. In the following sections, we will implement a few of these regression algorithms using Spark MLlib.

Linear regression

In the previous chapters, we cleaned, integrated, and curated a dataset containing online retail sales transactions by customers and captured their demographic information in the same integrated dataset. In *Chapter 6, Feature Engineering – Extraction, Transformation, and Selection*, we also converted the pre-processed data into a feature vector that's ready for machine learning training and stored it in **Delta Lake** as our offline **feature store**. Let's make use of this feature-engineered dataset to train a regression algorithm that can find out the age of a customer by providing other features as parameters, as shown in the following code block:

```
from pyspark.ml.regression import LinearRegression
retail_features = spark.read.table("retail_features")
train_df = retail_features.selectExpr("cust_age as label",
"selected_features as features")
lr = LinearRegression(maxIter=10, regParam=0.3,
                       elasticNetParam=0.8)
lr_model = lr.fit(train_df)
print("Coefficients: %s" % str(lr_model.coefficients))
print("Intercept: %s" % str(lr_model.intercept))
summary = lr_model.summary
print("RMSE: %f" % summary.rootMeanSquaredError)
print("r2: %f" % summary.r2)
```

In the preceding block of code, we have done the following:

1. First, we imported the `LinearRegression` algorithm from Spark MLlib.

2. The retail features were loaded from a Delta table and loaded into a Spark DataFrame.

3. We only needed the feature vector and the label column for training a `LinearRegression` model, so we only selected these two columns in the training DataFrame.

4. Then, we initialized a `LinearRegression` transformer by specifying the hyperparameters required by this algorithm.

5. After, we called the `fit` method on the training dataset to start the training process, which starts a Spark job behind the scenes that carries out the training task in a distributed manner.

6. Once the model has been successfully trained, we printed the model training summary, including the learned coefficients of the linear learning function and the intercept.

7. We also displayed the model accuracy metrics, such as the RMSE and R-squared metrics. It is generally desirable to get a model with as lower an RMSE as possible.

Thus, utilizing Spark MLlib's distributed implementation of linear regression, you can train a regression model in a distributed manner on a large dataset, without having to deal with any of the underlying complexities of distributed computing. The model can then be applied to a new set of data to generate predictions. Spark MLlib models can also be persisted to disk or a data lake using built-in methods and then reused later.

Now that we have trained a simple linear regression model using a parametric learning algorithm, let's look at using a non-parametric learning algorithm to solve the same regression problem.

Regression using decision trees

Decision trees are a popular form of non-parametric learning algorithm for solving both regression and classification machine learning problems. Decision trees are popular because they are easy to use, they can handle a wide variety of categorical as well as continuous features, and are also easy to interpret and explain.

Spark MLlib's implementation of decision trees allows for distributed training by partitioning data by rows. Since non-parametric learning algorithms typically require large amounts of data, Spark's implementation of decision trees can scale to a very large number of rows, even millions or billions.

Let's train a decision tree to predict the age of a customer while using other online retail transactional features as input, as shown in the following code block:

```
from pyspark.ml.evaluation import RegressionEvaluator
from pyspark.ml.regression import DecisionTreeRegressor
retail_features = spark.read.table("retail_features").
selectExpr("cust_age as label",
          "selected_features as features")
(train_df, test_df) = retail_features.randomSplit([0.8, 0.2])
dtree = DecisionTreeRegressor(featuresCol="features")
model = dtree.fit(train_df)
predictions = model.transform(test_df)
evaluator = RegressionEvaluator(
```

```
    labelCol="label", predictionCol="prediction",
    metricName="rmse")
rmse = evaluator.evaluate(predictions)
print("RMSE for test data = %g" % rmse)
print(model.toDebugString)
```

In the preceding code snippet, we have done the following:

1. First, we imported the DecisionTreeRegressor Spark ML library, along with a utility method to help evaluate the accuracy of the trained model.

2. We loaded our feature vector dataset from Delta Lake into a Spark DataFrame and only selected the feature and label columns.

3. To be able to evaluate our model accuracy after the training process, we needed a dataset that wouldn't be used for training. Thus, we split our dataset into two sets for training and testing, respectively. We used 80% of the data for model training while preserving 20% for model evaluation.

4. Then, we initialized the DecisionTreeRegressor class with the required hyperparameters, resulting in a Transformer object.

5. We fit the DecisionTreeRegressor transformer to our training dataset, which resulted in a decision tree model estimator.

6. We applied the model's Estimator object to the test dataset to produce actual predictions.

7. This prediction DataFrame was then used along with the RegressionEvaluator utility method to derive the RMSE of the model, which can be used to evaluate the accuracy of the trained model.

By using Spark MLlib's built-in decision tree regression algorithms, we can train regressions models in a distributed fashion on very large amounts of data, in a very fast and efficient manner. One thing to note is that the RMSE value of both regression models is about the same. These models can be tuned further using model tuning techniques, which help improve their accuracy. You will learn more about model tuning in *Chapter 9, Machine Learning Life Cycle Management*.

Classification

Classification is another type of supervised learning technique, where the task is to categorize a given dataset into different classes. Machine learning classifiers learn a mapping function from input parameters called **Features** that go to a discreet output parameter called **Label**. Here, the learning function tries to predict whether the label belongs to one of several known classes. The following diagram depicts the concept of classification:

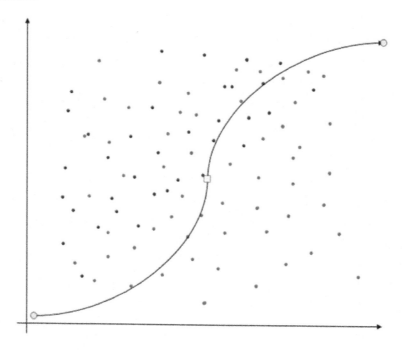

Figure 7.2 – Logistic regression

In the preceding diagram, a logistic regression algorithm is learning a mapping function that divides the data points in a two-dimensional space into two distinct classes. The learning algorithm learns the coefficients of a **Sigmoid function**, which classifies a set of input parameters into one of two possible classes. This type of classification can be split into two distinct classes. This is known as **binary classification** or **binomial classification**.

Logistic regression

Logistic regression is a popular classification algorithm that can learn a model from labeled data to predict the class of an output variable. Spark MLlib's implementation of logistic regression supports both binomial and multinomial classification problems.

Binomial classification

Binomial classification or binary classification is where the learning algorithm needs to classify whether the output variable belongs to one of two possible outcomes. Building on the example from previous sections, let's train a model using logistic regression that tries to predict the gender of a customer, given other features from an online retail transaction. Let's see how we can implement this using Spark MLlib, as shown in the following code example:

```python
from pyspark.ml import Pipeline
from pyspark.ml.feature import StringIndexer
from pyspark.ml.classification import LogisticRegression
train_df = spark.read.table("retail_features").
selectExpr("gender", "selected_features as features")
string_indexer = StringIndexer(inputCol="gender",
                               outputCol="label",
                               handleInvalid="skip" )
lr = LogisticRegression(maxIter=10, regParam=0.9,
                        elasticNetParam=0.6)
pipeline = Pipeline(stages=[string_indexer, lr])
model = pipeline.fit(train_df)
lr_model = model.stages[1]
print("Coefficients: " + str(lr_model.coefficientMatrix))
print("Intercepts: " + str(lr_model.interceptVector))
summary.roc.show()
print("areaUnderROC: " + str(summary.areaUnderROC))
```

In the preceding block of code, we have done the following:

1. The gender in our training dataset is a string data type, so it needs to be converted into numeric format first. For this, we made use of `StringIndexer` to convert it into a numeric label column.

2. Then, we initialized a `LogisticRegression` class by specifying the hyperparameters required by this algorithm.

3. Then, we stitched the `StringIndexer` and `LogisticRegression` stages together into a pipeline.

4. Then, we called the `fit` method on the training dataset to start the training process using the pipeline's `Transformer` object.

5. Once the model had been successfully trained, we printed the model's coefficients and intercepts, along with the receiver-operating characteristic and the area under the ROC curve metric, to measure the accuracy of the trained model.

With that, we have seen how, using the logistic regression algorithm from the Spark machine learning library, to implement binary classification in a scalable manner.

Multinomial classification

In **multinomial classification**, the learning algorithm needs to predict more than two possible outcomes. Let's extend the example from the previous section to build a model that, using logistic regression, tries to predict the country of origin of a customer, given other features from an online retail transaction, as shown in the following code snippet:

```
train_df = spark.read.table("retail_features").
selectExpr("country_indexed as label", "selected_features as
features")

mlr = LogisticRegression(maxIter=10, regParam=0.5,
                         elasticNetParam=0.3,
                         family="multinomial")

mlr_model = mlr.fit(train_df)

print("Coefficients: " + str(mlr_model.coefficientMatrix))

print("Intercepts: " + str(mlr_model.interceptVector))

print("areaUnderROC: " + str(summary.areaUnderROC))

summary.roc.show()
```

The previous code snippet is almost the same as the binary classification example, except the label column has more than two possible values and we specified the family parameter for the `LogisticRegression` class as `multinomial`. Once the model has been trained, the receiver-operating characteristics of the model and the area under the ROC curve metric can be displayed to measure the model's accuracy.

Classification using decision trees

Spark MLlib comes with a `DecsionTreeClassifier` class to solve classification problems as well. In the following code, we will implement binary classification using decision trees:

```
retail_df = spark.read.table("retail_features").
selectExpr("gender", "selected_features as features")
(train_df, test_df) = retail_df.randomSplit([0.8, 0.2])


string_indexer = StringIndexer(inputCol="gender",
                               outputCol="label",
                               handleInvalid="skip" )
dtree = DecisionTreeClassifier(labelCol="label",
                               featuresCol="features")
pipeline = Pipeline(stages=[string_indexer, dtree])
model = pipeline.fit(train_df)
predictions = model.transform(test_df)
evaluator = MulticlassClassificationEvaluator(
    labelCol="label", predictionCol="prediction",
    metricName="accuracy")
accuracy = evaluator.evaluate(predictions)
print("Accuracy = %g " % (accuracy))
dtree_model = model.stages[1]
#print(dtree_model.toDebugString)
```

In the previous block of code, we did the following:

1. First, we split our dataset into two sets for training and testing. This allows us to evaluate the model's accuracy once it has been trained.

2. Then, we made use of `StringIndexer` to convert the gender string column into a numeric label column.

3. After, we initialized a `DecsionTreeClassifier` class with the required hyperparameters.

4. Then, we combined the `StringIndexer` and `DecisionTreeClassifier` stages into a pipeline.

5. After, we called the `fit` method on the training dataset to start the model training process and applied the model's `Estimator` object on the test dataset to calculate predictions.

6. Finally, we used this DataFrame, along with the `MulticlassClassificationEvaluator` utility method, to derive the accuracy of the trained model.

This way, we have seen how the Spark machine learning library's decision trees can be used to solve classification problems at scale.

Naïve Bayes

Naïve Bayes is a family of probabilistic classification algorithms based on the Bayes' theorem, which assumes independence among features that are used as input to the learning algorithm. Bayes' theorem can be used to predict the probability of an event happening, given that another event has already taken place. The naïve Bayes algorithm calculates the probability of the given set of input features for all possible values of the category of the output label, and then it picks the output with the maximum probability. Naïve Bayes can used for binomial as well as multinomial classification problems. Let's see how naïve Bayes can be implemented using Spark MLlib, as shown in the following code example:

```
from pyspark.ml.classification import NaiveBayes
from pyspark.ml.evaluation import
MulticlassClassificationEvaluator
retail_df = spark.read.table("retail_features").
selectExpr("gender", "selected_features as features")
(train_df, test_df) = retail_df.randomSplit([0.8, 0.2])
string_indexer = StringIndexer(inputCol="gender",
                               outputCol="label",
                               handleInvalid="skip" )
nb = NaiveBayes(smoothing=0.9, modelType="gaussian")
pipeline = Pipeline(stages=[string_indexer, nb])
model = pipeline.fit(train_df)
predictions = model.transform(test_df)
evaluator = MulticlassClassificationEvaluator(
    labelCol="label",
    predictionCol="prediction",
    metricName="accuracy")
```

```
accuracy = evaluator.evaluate(predictions)
print("Model accuracy = %f" % accuracy)
```

In the preceding block of code, we did the following:

1. First, we split our dataset into two sets for training and testing, respectively.

2. Then, we made use of `StringIndexer` to convert the gender string column into a numeric label column.

3. After, we initialized a `NaiveBayes` class with the required hyperparameters.

4. Then we combined the `StringIndexer` and `NaiveBayes` stages into a pipeline.

5. After, we called the `fit` method on the training dataset to start the model training process, which applied the model's `Estimator` object to the test dataset to calculate predictions.

6. This DataFrame was then used with the `MulticlassClassificationEvaluator` utility method to derive the accuracy of the trained model.

> **Note**
>
> Multinomial and Bernoulli naïve Bayes models require non-negative features. Thus, it is recommended to select only features with positive values or to use another classification algorithm that can handle features with non-negative values.

Support vector machines

Support vector machines (SVM) is a class of classification algorithms that takes data points as input and outputs the hyperplane that best separates the given data points into two separate classes, represented on a two-dimensional plane. Thus, SVM supports binomial classification problems only. Let's implement binary classification using Spark MLlib's implementation of SVM, as shown in the following code block:

```
from pyspark.ml.classification import LinearSVC
train_df = spark.read.table("retail_features").
selectExpr("gender", "selected_features as features")
string_indexer = StringIndexer(inputCol="gender",
                               outputCol="label",
                               handleInvalid="skip" )
svm = LinearSVC(maxIter=10, regParam=0.1)
```

```
pipeline = Pipeline(stages=[string_indexer, svm])
model = pipeline.fit(train_df)
svm_model = model.stages[1]
# Print the coefficients and intercept for linear SVC
print("Coefficients: " + str(svm_model.coefficients))
print("Intercept: " + str(svm_model.intercept))
```

In the preceding code block, we did the following:

1. First, we made use of `StringIndexer` to convert the gender column into a numeric label column.

2. Then, we initialized a `LinearSVC` class by specifying the hyperparameters required by this algorithm.

3. Then, we combined the `StringIndexer` and `LinearSVC` stages into a pipeline.

4. After, we called the `fit` method on the training dataset to start the training process using the pipeline's `Transformer` object.

5. Once the model had been successfully trained, we printed the model coefficients and intercepts.

So far, you have learned about the most popular supervised learning algorithms for solving regression and classification problems and saw their implementation details in Spark MLlib using working code examples. In the following section, you will be introduced to the concept of tree ensembles and how they can be used to combine multiple decision tree models to arrive at the best possible model.

Tree ensembles

Non-parametric learning algorithms such as decision trees do not make any assumptions on the form of the learning function being learned and try to fit a model to the data at hand. However, decision trees run the risk of overfitting training data. Tree ensemble methods are a great way to leverage the benefits of decision trees while minimizing the risk of overfitting. Tree ensemble methods combine several decision trees to produce better-performing predictive models. Some popular tree ensemble methods include random forests and gradient boosted trees. We will explore how these ensemble methods can be used to build regression and classification models using Spark MLlib.

Regression using random forests

Random forests build multiple decision trees and merge them to produce a more accurate model and reduce the risk of overfitting. Random forests can be used to train regression models, as shown in the following code example:

```python
from pyspark.ml.regression import RandomForestRegressor
from pyspark.ml.evaluation import RegressionEvaluator
retail_features = spark.read.table("retail_features").
selectExpr("cust_age as label", "selected_features as
features")
(train_df, test_df) = retail_features.randomSplit([0.8, 0.2])
rf = RandomForestRegressor(labelCol="label",
                           featuresCol="features",
                           numTrees=5)
rf_model = rf.fit(train_df)
predictions = rf_model.transform(test_df)
evaluator = RegressionEvaluator(
    labelCol="label", predictionCol="prediction",
    metricName="rmse")
rmse = evaluator.evaluate(predictions)
print("RMSE for test data = %g" % rmse)
print(rf_model.toDebugString)
```

In the preceding code snippet, we did the following:

1. First, we split our dataset into two sets for training and testing, respectively.

2. Then, we initialized the `RandomForestRegressor` class with several trees to be trained. We set this to 5.

3. Next, we fit the `RandomForestRegressor` transformer to our training dataset to get a random forest model.

4. After, we applied the model's `Estimator` object to the test dataset to produce actual predictions.

5. This DataFrame was then used with the `RegressionEvaluator` utility method to derive the RMSE value.

6. Finally, we printed the trained random forest using the `toDebugString` attribute of the model object.

Classification using random forests

Just like decision trees, random forests also support training multi-class classification models, as shown in the following code block:

```
retail_df = spark.read.table("retail_features").
selectExpr("gender", "selected_features as features")
(train_df, test_df) = retail_df.randomSplit([0.8, 0.2])
string_indexer = StringIndexer(inputCol="gender",
                                outputCol="label",
                                handleInvalid="skip" )
rf = RandomForestClassifier(labelCol="label",
                             featuresCol="features",
                             numTrees=5)
pipeline = Pipeline(stages=[string_indexer, rf])
model = pipeline.fit(train_df)
predictions = model.transform(test_df)
evaluator = MulticlassClassificationEvaluator(
    labelCol="label", predictionCol="prediction",
    metricName="accuracy")
accuracy = evaluator.evaluate(predictions)
print("Accuracy = %g " % (accuracy))
rf_model = model.stages[1]
print(rf_model.toDebugString)
```

In the previous code snippet, we did the following:

1. First, we split our dataset into two sets for training and testing, respectively. This will allow us to evaluate the model's accuracy once it has been trained.

2. We made use of `StringIndexer` to convert the gender string column into a numeric label column.

3. Then, we initialized a `RandomForestClassifier` class with the required hyperparameters and specified the number of decision trees to be trained as 5.

4. Then, we joined the `StringIndexer` and `RandomForestClassifier` stages into a pipeline.

5. After, we called the `fit` method on the training dataset to start the model training process and applied the model's `Estimator` object to the test dataset to calculate predictions.

6. This DataFrame was then used with the
   `MulticlassClassificationEvaluator` utility method to derive the
   accuracy of the trained model.

7. The random forest model can also be printed using the `toDebugString` attribute,
   which is available on the model object.

This way, machine learning classification can be implemented at scale using the Spark
machine learning library.

Regression using gradient boosted trees

Gradient boosted trees (GBTs) is another type of ensemble method based on decision
trees that also improve the stability and accuracy of the trained model while minimizing
the risk of overfitting. GBTs iteratively train several decision trees while minimizing a loss
function through a process called gradient boosting. Let's explore an example of training
regression models using GBTs in Spark, as shown in the following code example:

```python
from pyspark.ml.regression import GBTRegressor
from pyspark.ml.evaluation import RegressionEvaluator
retail_features = spark.read.table("retail_features").
selectExpr("cust_age as label", "selected_features as
features")
(train_df, test_df) = retail_features.randomSplit([0.8, 0.2])
gbt = GBTRegressor(labelCol="label",featuresCol="features",
                   maxIter=5)
gbt_model = gbt.fit(train_df)
predictions = gbt_model.transform(test_df)
evaluator = RegressionEvaluator(
    labelCol="label", predictionCol="prediction",
    metricName="rmse")
rmse = evaluator.evaluate(predictions)
print("RMSE for test data = %g" % rmse)
print(gbt_model.toDebugString)
```

In the preceding code snippet, we did the following:

1. First, we split our dataset into two sets for training and testing, respectively.

2. Then, we initialized the `GBTRegressor` class with the max iterations set to 5.

3. Next, we fit the `RandomForestRegressor` transformer on our training dataset. This resulted in a random forest model estimator. After, we set the number of trees to be trained to 5.

4. After, we applied the model's `Estimator` object to the test dataset to produce actual predictions.

5. This DataFrame was then with the `RegressionEvaluator` utility method to derive the RMSE value.

6. The trained random forest can also be printed using the `toDebugString` attribute of the model object.

This way, the GBTs algorithm from the Spark MLlib can be used to implement regression at scale.

Classification using GBTs

GBTs can also be used to train classification models, as shown in the following code example:

```
retail_df = spark.read.table("retail_features").
selectExpr("gender", "selected_features as features")
(train_df, test_df) = retail_df.randomSplit([0.8, 0.2])
string_indexer = StringIndexer(inputCol="gender",
                                outputCol="label",
                                handleInvalid="skip" )
gbt = GBTClassifier(labelCol="label",
                    featuresCol="features",
                    maxIter=5)
pipeline = Pipeline(stages=[string_indexer, gbt])
model = pipeline.fit(train_df)
predictions = model.transform(test_df)
evaluator = MulticlassClassificationEvaluator(
    labelCol="label", predictionCol="prediction",
    metricName="accuracy")
accuracy = evaluator.evaluate(predictions)
print("Accuracy = %g " % (accuracy))
gbt_model = model.stages[1]
print(gbt_model.toDebugString)
```

In the previous code snippet, we did the following:

1. First, we made use of `StringIndexer` to convert the gender string column into a numeric label column.

2. Then, we initialized the `GBTClassifier` class and set the number of decision trees to be trained to 5.

3. Then, we joined the `StringIndexer` and `RandomForestClassifier` stages into a pipeline.

4. After, we called the `fit` method on the training dataset to start the model training process and applied the model's `Estimator` object to the test dataset to calculate predictions.

5. This DataFrame was then used with the `MulticlassClassificationEvaluator` utility method to derive the accuracy of the trained model.

So far, you have explored how to use tree ensemble methods to combine multiple decision trees to produce better and more accurate machine learning models for solving both regression and classification problems. In the following section, you will be introduced to some real-world applications of machine learning classification and regression models that can be applied to day-to-day scenarios.

Real-world supervised learning applications

In the past, data science and machine learning were used exclusively for academic research purposes. However, over the past decade, this field has found its use in actual business applications to help businesses find their competitive edge, improve overall business performance, and become profitable. In this section, we will look at some real-world applications of machine learning.

Regression applications

Some of the applications of machine learning regression models and how they help improve business performance will be presented in this section.

Customer lifetime value estimation

In any retail or CPG kind of business where customer churn is a huge factor, it is necessary to direct marketing spend at those customers who are profitable. In non-subscription kinds of businesses, typically 20% of the customer base generates up to 80% of revenue. Machine learning models can be leveraged to model and predict each customer's **lifetime value**. **Customer lifetime value (CLV)** models help predict an individual customer's **estimated lifetime**, which is an indicator of how much longer we can expect the customer to be profitable. CLV models can also be used to predict the amount of revenue that individual customers can be expected to generate over their expected lifetime. Thus, regression models can be used to estimate CLV and help direct marketing dollars toward promoting to and retaining profitable customers over their expected lifetimes.

Shipment lead time estimation

Retailers, logistics firms, food service aggregators, or any businesses that are in the business of delivering products to customers need to be able to predict the amount of time it will take them to ship a product to a customer. Regression models can be used to take factors such as origin and destination ZIP codes, the past performance of shipments between these locations, inventory availability, and also seasonality, weather conditions, and even local traffic into consideration to build models that can estimate the amount of time it would take for the product to reach the customer. This helps the business with inventory optimization, supply chain planning, and even improving overall customer satisfaction.

Dynamic price optimization

Dynamic price optimization, also known as **dynamic pricing**, is where you set a price for a product or service based on current product demand or market conditions. It is a common practice in many industries, ranging from transportation to travel and hospitality, e-commerce, entertainment, and digital aggregators to perform dynamic price optimization. Businesses can take advantage of the massive amounts of data that is generated in the digital economy by adjusting prices in real time. Although dynamic pricing is an **optimization** problem, regression models can be used to predict the price at a given point in time, current demand, market conditions, and competitor pricing.

Classification applications

A few examples of how classification models can be used to solve business scenarios will be discussed in this section.

Financial fraud detection

Financial fraud and identity theft are some of the biggest challenges facing the financial industry. Financial organizations have historically used statistical models and rules-based engines to detect financial fraud; however, fraudsters have managed to circumvent legacy fraud detection mechanisms using novel types of fraud. Classification models can be built using something rudimentary, such as naïve Bayes, or something much more robust, such as decision tree ensemble methods. These can be leveraged to keep up with emerging fraud patterns and flag financial transactions as fraudulent.

Email spam detection

This is a common scenario that anyone using email must have witnessed; that is, getting unwanted and soliciting or sometimes outright offensive content via email. Classification models are being used by email providers to classify and flag emails as spam and exclude them from user inboxes.

Industrial machinery and equipment and failure prediction

Heavy industries such as oil and construction companies have already installed or started installing IoT devices on their heavy industrial equipment, which sends out a constant stream of telemetry and diagnostic data to backend servers. Classification models that have been trained on the swath of telemetry and diagnostic data can help predict machine failures, help industries prevent downtime, flag problematic ancillary part vendors, and even save huge costs by preventing massive machinery recalls.

Object detection

Classification models have always been part of high-end cameras that have built-in object tracking and autofocus functions. Modern-day mobile phone applications also leverage classification models to isolate the subject of the photograph from the background, as well as to identify and tag individuals in photographs.

Summary

In this chapter, you were introduced to a class of machine learning algorithms called supervised learning algorithms, which can learn from well-labeled existing data. You explored the concepts of parametric and non-parametric learning algorithms and their pros and cons. Two major use cases of supervised learning algorithms called regression and classification were presented. Model training examples, along with code from Spark MLlib, were explored so that we could look at a few prominent types of regression and classification models. Tree ensemble methods, which improve the stability, accuracy, and performance of decision tree models by combining several models and preventing overfitting, were also presented.

Finally, you explored some real-world business applications of the various machine learning models presented in this chapter. We explained how supervised learning can be leveraged for business use cases, and working code samples were presented to help you train your models at scale using Spark MLlib and solve business problems efficiently.

In the next chapter, we will explore unsupervised machine learning algorithms, how they are different from supervised learning models, and their application in solving real-world business problems. We will also provide working code examples to showcase this.

8
Unsupervised Machine Learning

In the previous two chapters, you were introduced to the supervised learning class of machine learning algorithms, their real-world applications, and how to implement them at scale using Spark MLlib. In this chapter, you will be introduced to the unsupervised learning category of machine learning, where you will learn about parametric and non-parametric unsupervised algorithms. A few real-world applications of **clustering** and **association** algorithms will be presented to help you understand the applications of **unsupervised learning** to solve real-life problems. You will gain basic knowledge and understanding of clustering and association problems when using unsupervised machine learning. We will also look at the implementation details of a few clustering algorithms in Spark ML, such as **K-means clustering**, **hierarchical clustering**, **latent Dirichlet allocation**, and an association algorithm called **alternating least squares**.

In this chapter, we're going to cover the following main topics:

- Introduction to unsupervised learning
- Clustering using machine learning
- Building association using machine learning
- Real-world applications of unsupervised learning

By the end of this chapter, you should have gained sufficient knowledge and practical understanding of the clustering and association types of unsupervised machine learning algorithms, their practical applications, and skills to implement these types of algorithms at scale using Spark MLlib.

Technical requirements

In this chapter, we will be using Databricks Community Edition to run our code (`https://community.cloud.databricks.com`).

- Sign-up instructions can be found at `https://databricks.com/try-databricks`.

- The code for this chapter can be downloaded from `https://github.com/PacktPublishing/Essential-PySpark-for-Data-Analytics/tree/main/Chapter08`.

- The datasets for this chapter can be found at `https://github.com/PacktPublishing/Essential-PySpark-for-Data-Analytics/tree/main/data`.

Introduction to unsupervised machine learning

Unsupervised learning is a machine learning technique where no guidance is available to the learning algorithm in the form of known label values in the training data. Unsupervised learning is useful in categorizing unknown data points into groups based on patterns, similarities, or differences that are inherent within the data, without any prior knowledge of the data.

In supervised learning, a model is trained on known data, and then inferences are drawn from the model using new, unseen data. On the other hand, in unsupervised learning, the model training process in itself is the end goal, where patterns hidden within the training data are discovered during the model training process. Unsupervised learning is harder compared to supervised learning since it is difficult to ascertain if the results of an unsupervised learning algorithm are meaningful without any external evaluation, especially without access to any correctly labeled data.

One of the advantages of unsupervised learning is that it helps interpret very large datasets where labeling existing data would not be practical. Unsupervised learning is also useful for tasks such as predicting the number of classes within a dataset, or grouping and clustering data before applying a supervised learning algorithm. It is also very useful in solving classification problems as unsupervised learning can work well with unlabelled data, and there is no need for any manual intervention either. Unsupervised learning can be classified into two major learning techniques, known as clustering and association. These will be presented in the following sections.

Clustering using machine learning

In machine learning, clustering deals with identifying patterns or structures within uncategorized data without needing any external guidance. Clustering algorithms parse given data to identify clusters or groups with matching patterns that exist in the dataset. The result of clustering algorithms are clusters of data that can be defined as a collection of objects that are similar in a certain way. The following diagram illustrates how clustering works:

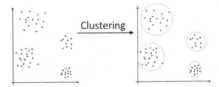

Figure 8.1 – Clustering

In the previous diagram, an uncategorized dataset is being passed through a clustering algorithm, resulting in the data being categorized into smaller clusters or groups of data, based on a data point's proximity to another data point in a two-dimensional Euclidian space.

Thus, the clustering algorithm groups data based on the Euclidean distance between the data on a two-dimensional plane. Clustering algorithms consider the Euclidean distance between data points in the training dataset in that, within a cluster, the distance between the data points should be small, while outside the cluster, the distance between the data points should be large. A few types of clustering techniques that are available in Spark MLlib will be presented in the following sections.

K-means clustering

K-means is the most popular clustering algorithm and one of the simplest of the unsupervised learning algorithms as well. The K-means clustering algorithm works iteratively on the provided dataset to categorize it into k groups. The larger the value of k, the smaller the size of the clusters, and vice versa. Thus, with K-means, the user can control the number of clusters that are identified within the given dataset.

In K-means clustering, each cluster is defined by creating a center for each cluster. These centroids are placed as far away as possible from each other. Then, K-means associates each data point with the given dataset to its nearest centroid, thus forming the first group of clusters. K-means then iteratively recalculates the centroids' position within the dataset so that it's as close to the center of the identified clusters. This process stops when the centroids don't need to be moved anymore.

The following code block illustrates how to implement K-means clustering using Spark MLlib:

```
from pyspark.ml.clustering import KMeans
from pyspark.ml.evaluation import ClusteringEvaluator
retail_features = spark.read.table("retail_features")
train_df = retail_features.selectExpr("selected_features as
features")
kmeans = KMeans(k=3, featuresCol='features')
kmeans_model = kmeans.fit(train_df)
predictions = kmeans_model.transform(train_df)
evaluator = ClusteringEvaluator()
silhouette = evaluator.evaluate(predictions)
print("Silhouette measure using squared Euclidean distance = "
+ str(silhouette))
cluster_centers = kmeans_model.clusterCenters()
print(cluster_centers)
```

In the preceding code snippet, we did the following:

1. First, we used `import` to import the appropriate MLlib packages related to clustering and clustering evaluation.

2. Then, we imported the already existing feature vector that we derived during the feature engineering process into a Spark DataFrame and stored it in the data lake in Delta format.

3. Next, a new `KMeans` object was initialized by us passing in the number of desired clusters and the column name for the feature vector.

4. The `fit()` method was called on the training DataFrame to kick off the learning process. A model object was generated as a result.

5. Predictions on the original training dataset were generated by calling the `transform()` method on the model object.

6. Next, we invoked Spark MLlib's `ClusteringEvaluator()` helper function, which is useful for evaluating clustering algorithms, and applied it to the predictions DataFrame we generated in the previous step. This resulted in a value referred to as `silhouette`, which is a measure of consistency within clusters and is calculated based on the Euclidean distance measure between data points. A `silhouette` value closer to 1 means that the points within a cluster are close together and that points outside the cluster are far apart. The closer the `silhouette` value is to 1, the more performant the learned model is.

7. Finally, we printed the centroids of each of the categorized clusters.

This way, using just a few lines of code, uncategorized data can easily be clustered using Spark's implementation of the K-means clustering algorithm.

Hierarchical clustering using bisecting K-means

Hierarchical clustering is a type of clustering technique where all the data points start within a single cluster. They are then recursively split into smaller clusters by moving them down a hierarchy. Spark ML implements this kind of divisive hierarchical clustering via the bisecting K-means algorithm. The following example illustrates how to implement bisecting K-means clustering using Spark MLlib:

```python
from pyspark.ml.clustering import BisectingKMeans
from pyspark.ml.evaluation import ClusteringEvaluator
retail_features = spark.read.table("retail_features")
train_df = retail_features.selectExpr("selected_features as
features")
bkmeans = BisectingKMeans(k=3, featuresCol='features')
bkmeans_model = kmeans.fit(train_df)
predictions = bkmeans_model.transform(train_df)
evaluator = ClusteringEvaluator()
silhouette = evaluator.evaluate(predictions)
print("Silhouette measure using squared euclidean distance = "
+ str(silhouette))
cluster_centers = kmeans_model.clusterCenters()
print(cluster_centers)
```

In the previous code snippet, we did the following:

1. First, we initialized a new `BisectingKMeans` object by passing in the number of desired clusters and the column name for the feature column.

2. The `fit()` method was called on the training DataFrame to start the learning process. A model object was generated as a result.

3. Next, predictions on the original training dataset were generated by calling the `transform()` method on the model object.

4. After, we invoked Spark MLlib's `ClusteringEvaluator()` helper function, which is useful for evaluating clustering algorithms, and applied it to the predictions DataFrame we generated in the previous step. This results in the `silhouette` value, which is a measure of consistency within clusters and is calculated based on the Euclidean distance measure between data points.

5. Finally, we printed the centroids of each of the clusters.

Now that we have learned a clustering technique, let's find out about a learning technique in the next section.

Topic modeling using latent Dirichlet allocation

Topic modeling is a learning technique where you categorize documents. Topic modeling is not the same as topic classification since topic classification is a supervised learning technique where the learning model tries to classify unseen documents based on some previously labeled data. On the other hand, topic modeling categorizes documents containing text or natural language in the same way as clustering groups categorize numeric data without any external guidance. Thus, topic modeling is an unsupervised learning problem.

Latent Dirichlet allocation (LDA) is a popular topic modeling technique. The goal of LDA is to associate a given document with a particular topic based on the keywords found within the document. Here, the topics are unknown and hidden within the documents, thus the latent part of LDA. LDA works by assuming each word within a document belongs to a different topic and assigns a probability score to each word. Once the probability of each word belonging to a particular topic is estimated, LDA tries to pick all the words belonging to a topic by setting a threshold and choosing every word that meets or exceeds that threshold value. LDA also considers each document to be just a bag of words, without placing any importance on the grammatical role played by the individual words. Also, stop words in a language such as articles, conjunctions, and interjections need to be removed before LDA is applied as these words do not carry any topic information.

The following code example illustrates how LDA can be implemented using Spark MLlib:

```
from pyspark.ml.clustering import LDA
train_df = spark.read.table("retail_features").
selectExpr("selected_features as features")
lda = LDA(k=3, maxIter=1)
lda_model = lda.fit(train_df)
topics = lda_model.describeTopics(3)
topics.show()
transformed = lda_model.transform(dataset)
transformed.show()
```

In the previous code snippet, we did the following:

1. First, we imported the appropriate MLlib packages related to LDA.

2. Next, we imported the already existing feature vector that had been derived during the feature engineering process into a Spark DataFrame and stored it in the data lake in Delta format.

3. After, we initialized a new LDA object by passing in the number of clusters and the maximum number of iterations.

4. Next, the `fit()` method was called on the training DataFrame to start the learning process. A model object was generated as a result.

5. The topics that were modeled by the LDA algorithm can be shown by using the `describeTopics()` method on the model object.

As we have seen, by using Apache Spark's implementation of the LDA algorithm, topic modeling can be implemented at scale.

Gaussian mixture model

One of the disadvantages of K-means clustering is that it will associate every data point with exactly one cluster. This way, it is not possible to get the probability of a data point belonging to a particular cluster. The **Gaussian mixture model** (**GSM**) attempts to solve this hard clustering problem of K-means clustering.

GSM is a probabilistic model for representing a subset of a sample within an overall sample of data points. A GSM represents a mixture of several Gaussian distributions of data points, where a data point is drawn from one of the *K* Gaussian distributions and has a probability score of it belonging to one of those distributions.

The following code example describes the implementation details of a GSM using Spark ML:

```
from pyspark.ml.clustering import GaussianMixture
train_df = spark.read.table("retail_features").
selectExpr("selected_features as features")
gmm = GaussianMixture(k=3, featuresCol='features')
gmm_model = gmm.fit(train_df)
gmm_model.gaussiansDF.display()
```

In the preceding code block, we initialized a new GaussianMixture object after importing the appropriate libraries from the pyspark.ml.clustering package. Then, we passed in some hyperparameters, including the number of clusters and the name of the column containing the feature vector. Then, we trained the model using the fit() method and displayed the results of the trained model using the model's gaussianDF attribute.

So far, you have seen different kinds of clustering and topic modeling techniques and their implementations when using Spark MLlib. In the following section, you will learn about another type of unsupervised learning algorithm called **association rules**.

Building association rules using machine learning

Association rules is a data mining technique where the goal is identifying relationships between various entities within a given dataset by identifying entities that occur frequently together. Association rules are useful in making new item recommendations based on the relationship between existing items that frequently appear together. In data mining association, rules are implemented using a series of if-then-else statements that help show the probability of relationships between entities. The association rules technique is widely used in recommender systems, market basket analysis, and affinity analysis problems.

Collaborative filtering using alternating least squares

In machine learning, **collaborative filtering** is more commonly used for **recommender systems**. A recommender system is a technique that's used to filter information by considering user preference. Based on user preference and taking into consideration their past behavior, recommender systems can make predictions on items that the user might like. Collaborative filtering performs information filtering by making use of historical user behavior data and their preferences to build a user-item association matrix. Spark ML uses the **alternating least squares** algorithm to implement the collaborative filtering technique.

The following code example demonstrates Spark MLlib's implementation of the alternating least squares algorithm:

```python
from pyspark.ml.evaluation import RegressionEvaluator
from pyspark.ml.recommendation import ALS
from pyspark.sql import Row
ratings_df = (spark.read.table("retail_features").selectExpr(
    "CAST(invoice_num AS INT) as user_id",
    "CAST(stock_code AS INT) as item_id",
    "CAST(quantity AS INT) as rating")
    .where("user_id is NOT NULL AND item_id is NOT NULL"))
df.display()
(train_df, test_df) = ratings_df.randomSplit([0.7, 0.3])
als = ALS(maxIter=3, regParam=0.03, userCol="user_id",
          itemCol="item_id", ratingCol="rating",
          coldStartStrategy="drop")
als_model = als.fit(train_df)
predictions = model.transform(test_df)
evaluator = RegressionEvaluator(metricName="rmse",
                                labelCol="rating",
                                predictionCol="prediction")
rmse = evaluator.evaluate(predictions)
print("Root-mean-square error = " + str(rmse))
user_recs = als_model.recommendForAllUsers(5)
user_recs.show()
item_recs = als_model.recommendForAllItems(5)
item_recs.show()
```

In the previous code block, we did the following:

1. First, we generated the ratings dataset as a Spark DataFrame using the feature dataset stored in the Delta Lake. A few of the columns that the ALS algorithm required, such as `user_id`, `item_id`, and `ratings` were not in the required integer format. Thus, we used the `CAST` Spark SQL method to convert them into the required data format.

2. Next, we initialized an ALS object with the desired parameters and split our training dataset into two random parts using the `randomSplit()` method.

3. After, we started the learning process by calling the `fit()` method on the training dataset.

4. Then, we evaluated the accuracy metric's `RMSE` using the evaluator provided by Spark MLlib.

5. Finally, we gathered the predictions for the top 5 item recommendations for each user and the top 5 user recommendations per item using the built-in `recommendForAllUsers()` and `recommendForAllItems()` methods, respectively.

This way, you can leverage alternating least squares to build recommender systems for use cases such as movie recommendations for a **video on demand** platform, product recommendations, or **market basket analysis** for an e-tailer application. Spark MLlib helps you implement this scale with only a few lines of code.

In addition to clustering and association rules, Spark MLlib also allows you to implement **dimensionality reduction** algorithms such as **singular value decomposition (SVD)** and **principal component analysis (PCA)**. Dimensionality reduction is the process of reducing the number of random variables under consideration. Though an unsupervised learning method, dimensionality reduction is useful for feature extraction and selection. A detailed discussion of this topic is beyond the scope of this book, and Spark MLlib only has the dimensionality reduction algorithm's implementation available for the RDD API. More details on dimensionality reduction can be found in Apache Spark's public documentation at `https://spark.apache.org/docs/latest/mllib-dimensionality-reduction.html`.

In the next section, we will delve into a few more real-life applications of unsupervised learning algorithms that are in use today by various businesses.

Real-world applications of unsupervised learning

Unsupervised learning algorithms are being used today to solve some real-world business challenges. We will take a look at a few such challenges in this section.

Clustering applications

This section presents some of the real-world business applications of clustering algorithms.

Customer segmentation

Retail marketing teams, as well as business-to-customer organizations, are always trying to optimize their marketing spends. Marketing teams in particular are concerned with one specific metric called **cost per acquisition** (**CPA**). CPA is indicative of the amount that an organization needs to spend to acquire a single customer, and an optimal CPA means a better return on marketing investments. The best way to optimize CPA is via customer segmentation as this improves the effectiveness of marketing campaigns. Traditional customer segmentation takes standard customer features such as demographic, geographic, and social information into consideration, along with historical transactional data, to define standard customer segments. This traditional way of customer segmentation is time-consuming and involves a lot of manual work and is prone to errors. However, machine learning algorithms can be leveraged to find hidden patterns and associations among data sources. Also, in recent years. the number of customer touchpoints has increased, and it is not practical and intuitive to identify patterns among all those customer touchpoints to identify patterns manually. However, machine learning algorithms can easily parse through millions of records and surface insights that can be leveraged promptly by marketing teams to meet their customers where they want, when they want. Thus, by leveraging clustering algorithms, marketers can improve the efficacy of their marketing campaigns via refined customer segmentation.

Retail assortment optimization

Retailers with brick-and-mortar stores have limited store space. Thus, they need to ensure that their store space is utilized optimally by placing only those products that are highly likely to sell. A classic example of assortment optimization is that of a hardware retailer, stocking up on lawnmowers during the deep winter season in the midwestern parts of the United States, when it is highly likely to snow through the season. In this example, the store space is being sub-optimally utilized by having lawnmowers in there, which have a very small chance of selling during the snow season. A better choice would have been space heaters, snow shovels, or other winter season equipment. To overcome this problem, retailers usually employ analysts, who take historical transactional data, seasonality, and current trends into consideration to make recommendations on the optimal assortment of products that are appropriate for the season and location of the store. However, what if we increase the scale of this problem to a much larger retailer, with thousands of warehouses and tens of thousands of retail outlets? At such a scale, manually planning optimal assortments of products becomes impractical and very time-consuming, reducing the time to value drastically. Assortment optimization can be treated as a clustering problem, and clustering algorithms can be applied to help plan how these clusters will be sorted. Here, several more data points must be taken into consideration, including historical consumer buying patterns, seasonality, trends on social media, search patterns on search engines, and more. This not only helps with better assortment optimization but also in increased revenues, a decrease in product waste, and faster time to market for businesses.

Customer churn analysis

It is becoming increasingly difficult for businesses to acquire customers because of ever-changing customer preferences and fierce competition in the marketplace. Thus, businesses need to retain existing customers. **Customer churn rate** is one of the prominent metrics that business executives want to minimize. Machine learning classification algorithms can be used to predict if a particular customer will churn. However, having an understanding of the factors that affect churn would be useful, so that they can change or improve their operations to increase customer satisfaction. Clustering algorithms can be used not only to identify which group of customers are likely to churn, but also to further the analysis by identifying a set of factors that are affecting churn. Businesses can then act on these churn factors to either bring new products into the mix or improve churn to improve customer satisfaction and, in turn, decrease customer churn.

Insurance fraud detection

Insurance companies traditionally use manual inspection, along with rules engines, to flag insurance claims as fraudulent. However, as the size of the data increases, the traditional methods might miss a sizeable portion of the claims since manual inspection is time-consuming and error-prone, and fraudsters are constantly innovating and devising new ways of committing fraud. Machine learning clustering algorithms can be used to group new claims with existing fraud clusters, and classification algorithms can be used to classify whether these claims are fraudulent. This way, by leveraging machine learning and clustering algorithms, insurance companies can constantly detect and prevent insurance fraud.

Association rules and collaborative filtering applications

Association rules and collaborative filtering are techniques that are used for building recommender systems. This section will explore some practical use cases of recommendation systems for practical business applications.

Recommendation systems

Recommendation systems are employed by e-retailers to perform market basket analysis, where the system makes product recommendations to users based on their preferences, as well as items already in their cart. Recommendation systems can also be used for location- or proximity-based recommendations, such as displaying ads or coupons when a customer is near a particular store. Recommendation systems are also used in marketing, where marketers can get recommendations regarding users who are likely to buy an item, which helps with the effectiveness of marketing campaigns.

Recommendation systems are also heavily employed by online music and video service providers for user content personalization. Here, recommendation systems are used to make new music or video recommendations to users based on their preferences and historical usage patterns.

Summary

This chapter introduced you to unsupervised learning algorithms, as well as how to categorize unlabeled data and identify associations between data entities. Two main areas of unsupervised learning algorithms, namely clustering and association rules, were presented. You were introduced to the most popular clustering and collaborative filtering algorithms. You were also presented with working code examples of clustering algorithms such as K-means, bisecting K-means, LDA, and GSM using code in Spark MLlib. You also saw code examples for building a recommendation engine using the alternative least-squares algorithm in Spark MLlib. Finally, a few real-world business applications of unsupervised learning algorithms were presented. We looked at several concepts, techniques, and code examples surrounding unsupervised learning algorithms so that you can train your models at scale using Spark MLlib.

So far, in this and the previous chapter, you have only explored the data wrangling, feature engineering, and model training parts of the machine learning process. In the next chapter, you will be introduced to machine learning life cycle management, where you will explore concepts such as model performance tuning, tracking machine learning experiments, storing machine learning models in a central repository, and operationalizing ML models before putting them in production applications. Finally, an open end-to-end ML life cycle management tool called MLflow will also be introduced and explored.

9
Machine Learning Life Cycle Management

In the previous chapters, we explored the basics of **scalable machine learning** using Apache Spark. Algorithms dealing with **supervised** and **unsupervised** learning were introduced and their implementation details were presented using **Apache Spark MLlib**. In real-world scenarios, it is not sufficient to just train one model. Instead, multiple versions of the same model must be built using the same dataset by varying the model parameters to get the best possible model. Also, the same model might not be suitable for all applications, so multiple models are trained. Thus, it is necessary to track various experiments, their parameters, their metrics, and the version of the data they were trained on. Furthermore, models often drift, meaning that their prediction power decreases due to changes in the environment, so they need to be monitored and retrained when necessary.

This chapter will introduce the concepts of experiment tracking, model tuning, productionizing models, and model inferencing using offline and online techniques. This chapter will present these concepts using an end-to-end open source machine learning life cycle management tool called **MLflow**. Finally, we will look at the concept of continuous deployment for machine learning to automate the entire **machine learning (ML)** life cycle management process.

In this chapter, we're going to cover the following main topics:

- Introduction to the ML life cycle

- Tracking experiments with **MLflow**

- Tracking model versions using **MLflow Model Registry**

- Model serving and inferencing

- Continuous deployment for ML

Technical requirements

In this chapter, we will be using Databricks Community Edition to run our code (`https://community.cloud.databricks.com`).

- Sign-up instructions can be found at `https://databricks.com/try-databricks`.

- The code for this chapter can be downloaded from `https://github.com/PacktPublishing/Essential-PySpark-for-Data-Analytics/tree/main/Chapter09`, while the datasets for this chapter can be found at `https://github.com/PacktPublishing/Essential-PySpark-for-Data-Analytics/tree/main/data`.

We will also be using a managed MLflow that comes with Databricks Community Edition. Instructions for installing a standalone version of MLflow can be found here: `https://mlflow.org/docs/latest/quickstart.html`.

Introduction to the ML life cycle

The **ML life cycle** is a continuous process that a data science project follows. It contains four major stages, starting with data collection and preparation, model training, model evaluation, and finally model inferencing and monitoring. The ML process is a continuous one, where the cycle iterates between improving the data and constantly improving the model's performance; or, rather, keeping it from degrading over time:

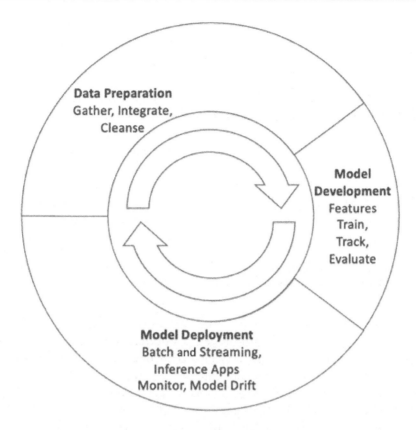

Figure 9.1 – ML life cycle

The previous diagram presents the continuous process of ML life cycle management, from data preparation to model development, and then from training to model deployment and monitoring. When model performance degrades due to either a change in the training data or the model code or changes in model parameters, the cyclic process starts all over again.

Processes for data collection and preparation, cleansing, and consolidation, as well as techniques for training various ML models at scale, were introduced in the previous chapters. This chapter will introduce the remaining stages of the ML life cycle, including model evaluation and model inferencing and monitoring.

This cyclic process of ML life cycle management helps you continuously refine your datasets and models and maintain model performance. The speed at which you can iterate through the ML life cycle determines how fast you can put the model to practical use, which determines the value of your data science project to businesses, as well as the cost associated with the data science project. Thus, it is important to make use of an ML life cycle management tool to streamline the entire ML process, derive the maximum value out of your data science project, and ensure that business users can derive tangible benefits from it. Several ML life cycle management tools exist today that can handle this task. *Pacyderm, Kubeflow, MLflow,* and *Metaflow* are a few of the available open source tools, while *AWS Sagemaker, Google Cloud AutoML,* and *Microsoft Azure ML* are all cloud-native services with full ML life cycle management support. In this chapter, we will explore MLflow as an ML life cycle management tool. The following sections will explore MLflow in greater detail.

Introduction to MLflow

In traditional software development, life cycle code is written to a given functional specification. However, in ML, the goal is to optimize a specific metric until you have achieved a desired level of accuracy. This process of optimizing a certain metric doesn't happen just once; it is a continuous process of experimentation and improvement. Moreover, in ML, the quality of the outcome not just depends on the quality of the code but also on other parameters, such as the data that's used for the ML training process and the parameters that are supplied to the training algorithm. The programming stack that's used by traditional ML also varies widely between different data scientists. Finally, ML models created in one environment are typically deployed in a different environment, so it is also important to ensure model portability and reproducibility. Thus, the entire ML life cycle is very iterative and involves multiple parameters, datasets, and various programming libraries.

MLflow is an easy-to-use, modular, end-to-end ML life cycle management open source software, developed to solve the aforementioned challenges of the ML life cycle:

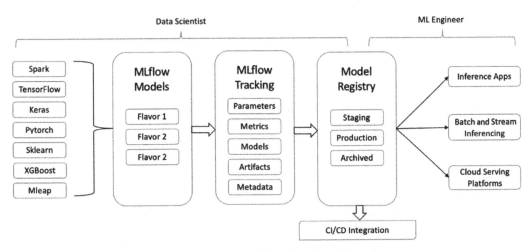

Figure 9.2 – ML life cycle with Mlflow

MLflow consists of the following four components to solve the challenges of the ML life cycle, such as management experiment tracking, experiment reproducibility, model repositories, and model deployment:

- MLflow Tracking
- MLflow Projects
- MLflow Model
- Model Registry

Each of these components will be explored further in the following sections. You will learn how these components help solve your ML life cycle management challenges while looking at some code samples.

Tracking experiments with MLflow

In real life, building a single model is never sufficient. A typical model-building process requires iterating over the process several times, sometimes changing the model parameters and other times tweaking the training dataset, until the desired level of model accuracy is achieved. Sometimes, a model that's suitable for a certain use case might not be useful for another. This means that a typical data science process involves experimenting with several models to solve a single business problem and keeping track of all the datasets, model parameters, and model metrics for future reference. Traditionally, experiment tracking is done using rudimentary tools such as spreadsheets, but this slows down the time to production and is also a tedious process that's prone to mistakes.

The MLflow Tracking component solves this problem with its API and UI for logging ML experiments, including model parameters, model code, metrics, the output of the model training process, as well as any arbitrary artifacts associated with the experiment. Let's learn how to install MLflow and track our experiments using the tracking server:

```
%pip install mlflow
```

The previous command will install MLflow in your Databricks notebook and restart the Python session.

> **Note**
>
> The previous command only installs the MLflow client libraries in your local Python session in your notebook. We will be using the managed MLflow that comes with Databricks Community Edition for the tracking server component. Instructions for configuring and running an MLflow Tracking server outside of Databricks can be found here: https://mlflow.org/docs/latest/tracking.html#how-runs-and-artifacts-are-recorded.

In the following code sample, we are building a simple regression model that we used in the previous chapters and use MLflow Tracking to track the experiment:

```
import mlflow
import mlflow.spark
from pyspark.ml.evaluation import RegressionEvaluator
from pyspark.ml.regression import LinearRegression
from pyspark.ml.tuning import ParamGridBuilder, CrossValidator
```

In the previous code example, we performed the following actions:

- First, we imported the relevant libraries. Here, we imported various MLflow client libraries and also imported the Spark-specific MLflow components via `mlflow.spark`.

- In this code sample, we built multiple regression models using the **cross-validation** technique, so we imported the relevant `pyspark.ml` libraries to perform these actions to measure the accuracy of our models.

Now, we need to initialize MLflow Tracking so that we can start tracking our experiments, as shown in the following code block:

```
mlflow.set_tracking_uri("databricks")
retail_features = spark.read.table("retail_features")
retail_df = retail_features.selectExpr("cust_age as label",
"selected_features as features")
train_df, test_df = retail_df.randomSplit([0.9, 0.1])
```

Now, we must initialize the training dataset, as shown in the following code block:

- First, create a `retail_features` DataFrame out of the features Delta table that we created in the previous chapters. We must select the label and feature columns that are required for our model training from the DataFrame, which contains all the features that we extracted from the enriched retail transactional data.

- Now, we must randomly split the DataFrame containing the label and the feature columns into two separate DataFrames using the `randomSplit()` function. The training DataFrame is used for model training purposes, while the test DataFrame is preserved to check the accuracy of the model once a model has been trained.

At this point, we can get started with the experimentation process, as shown in the following code block:

```
evaluator = RegressionEvaluator(labelCol="label",
                                metricName="rmse")
mlflow.set_tracking_uri("databricks")
mlflow.set_experiment("/Users/snudurupati@outlook.com/
linregexp")
experiment = mlflow.get_experiment_by_name("/Users/snudurupati@
outlook.com/linregexp")
```

In the previous code block, we set our initial algorithm parameters and the MLflow Tracking server parameters:

- We instantiated the `RegressionEvaluator` object, which passes the label column and uses RMSE as the accuracy metric. This is useful in calculating `rmse` on the label column during the cross-validation process.

- Now that we are ready to start our experimentation, we configured our experiment with the MLflow Tracking server by providing the URI for the tracking server using the `mlflow.set_tracking_uri("databricks")` function.

- The MLflow Tracking server can track multiple experiments from multiple users from multiple sessions. Thus, you must provide your experiment with a unique name, which we can achieve using `mlflow.set_experiment("/Users/ user_name/exp_name")`. The path specified for the experiment name needs to be a form of persistent storage, such as a local disk or a data lake location. In this case, we made use of the **Databricks filesystem (DBFS)**.

In the previous code block, we specified the URI as `databricks` because we intend to use the MLflow Tracking server that comes with Databricks Community Edition. You can specify the URI as `./mlruns` if you are running MLflow locally or provide the URI for your remote tracking server if you have set one up yourself. Instructions on how to set up your own tracking server can be found at `https://mlflow.org/docs/latest/ tracking.html#mlflow-tracking-servers`:

```
lr = LinearRegression(maxIter=10)
paramGrid = (ParamGridBuilder()
    .addGrid(lr.regParam, [0.1, 0.01])
    .addGrid(lr.fitIntercept, [False, True])
    .addGrid(lr.elasticNetParam, [0.0, 0.5, 1.0])
    .build())
csv = CrossValidator(estimator=lr,
                        estimatorParamMaps=param_grid,
                        evaluator=RegressionEvaluator(),
                        numFolds=2)
```

Now that we have initialized all the required objects for experimentation and configured experiment tracking with MLflow, we can start the training process:

- First, we must instantiate the `LinearRegression` model object with the `maxIter` parameter set to `10`.

- Then, we must set up a parameter grid for the cross-validation process and specify a range of values for model parameters.

- Finally, we must configure the train-validation split process by initializing the `CrossValidator` object. We can do this by passing in the actual model object, the parameter grid object, and the evaluation objects as parameters.

More details on how the `CrossValidator` objects works will be provided in the following section. Now, we are ready to start the model training experimentation process, as shown in the following code block:

```
with mlflow.start_run() as run_id:
  lr_model = csv.fit(train_df)
  test_metric = evaluator.evaluate(lr_model.transform(test_df))
  mlflow.log_metric(evaluator.getMetricName(),
                    test_metric)
  mlflow.spark.log_model(spark_model=lr_model.bestModel,
                         artifact_path='best-model')
```

In the previous code example, we invoked the MLflow Tracking server to start tracking our experiments:

- Since we are using the cross-validation technique and have defined a parameter grid with a range of values, the `fit()` process builds multiple models instead of a single model and records the best model based on the specified accuracy metric. Since we would like to keep a record of all the models we've built in this process, we must invoke the MLflow Tracking service using the `mlflow.start_run()` method.

- The metrics that were generated during the cross-validation process are logged to the MLflow Tracking server using the `mlflow.log_metric()` function. Within the Databricks managed MLflow environment, the model parameters are automatically logged when `CrossValidator` is used. However, model parameters can also be explicitly logged using the `mlflow.log_parameter()` function and any arbitrary artifacts such as graphs or charts can be logged using the `mlflow.log_artifact()` function.

- `CrossValidator` iterates over multiple models and generates the best model based on the specified accuracy metric. The best model that's generated during this process is available as a `bestModel` object. This can be logged using the `mlflow.spark.log_model(spark_model=lr_model.bestModel, artifact_path='best-model')` command. Here, `artifact_path` denotes the path where the model is stored in the MLflow Tracking server.

The following screenshot shows the MLflow Tracking UI for the ML experiment that we just executed:

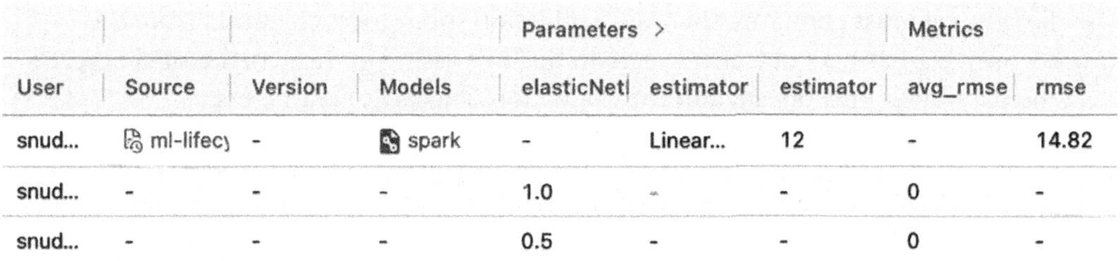

				Parameters >			Metrics	
User	Source	Version	Models	elasticNetl	estimator	estimator	avg_rmse	rmse
snud...	⌕ ml-lifecy	-	⬡ spark	-	Linear...	12	-	14.82
snud...	-	-	-	1.0	–	-	0	-
snud...	-	-	-	0.5	-	-	0	-

Figure 9.3 – MLflow Model tracking UI

In the preceding screenshot, we can see that MLflow recorded the accuracy metrics and model parameters for each of the models we built during the **cross-validation** process as a single experiment. However, only the best model out of all the runs was recorded. Details of an individual run can be accessed by clicking on one of the runs, as shown in the following screenshot:

Date : 2021-06-11 07:33:44   Source : ⌕ ml-lifecycle

Duration : 1.1min   Status : FINISHED

‣ Notes ✎

▾ Parameters

Name	Value
estimator	LinearRegression
estimatorParamMapsLength	12
evaluator	RegressionEvaluator
mlEstimatorUid	CrossValidator_4bcefcebff93
mlModelClass	CrossValidator
numFolds	2

▾ Metrics

Name	Value
rmse ⬈	14.82

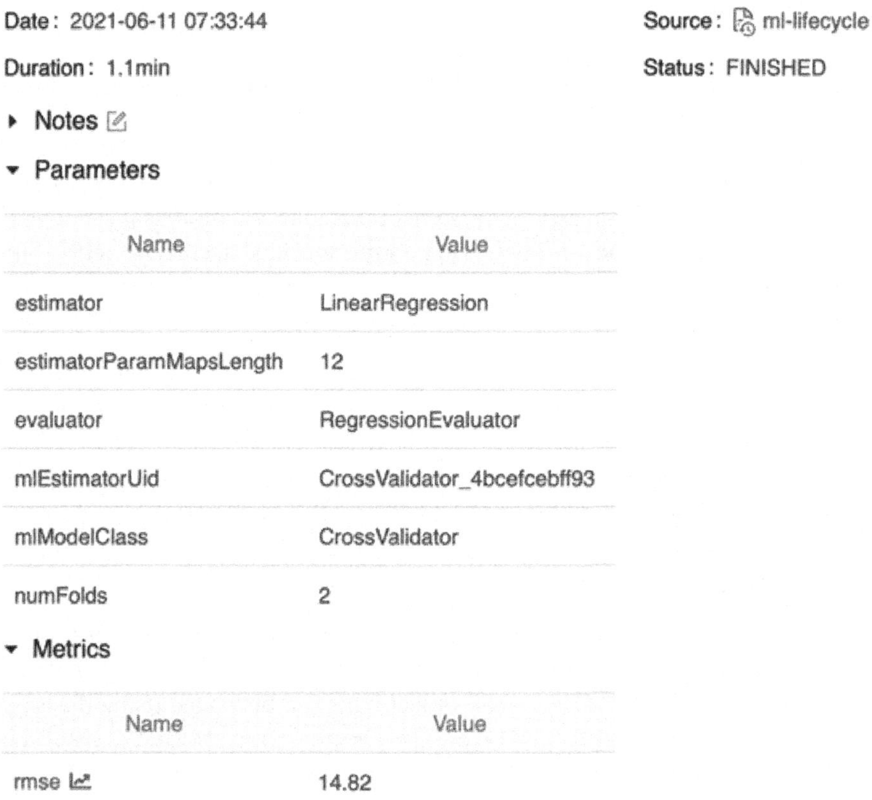

Figure 9.4 – Individual models being run from the MLflow Tracking UI

In the preceding screenshot, all the model parameters and metrics have been recorded in the MLflow Tracking UI, along with other metadata such as the model's run date and time, username, the source code version for this specific model run, the duration of the model's run, and the status of the model. This information is very useful in reproducing the experiment in the future or reproducing the same experiment in a different environment, so long as the same version of the data is available.

> **Tip**
> MLflow Tracking can also be used to track the version of the data that's being used for the experiment if the data is stored in a Delta table, as Delta provides built-in data versioning. This can be done by logging the Delta table's version as an arbitrary artifact to MLflow.

The `mlflow.` command in the previous code snippet specifies that we are using a Spark flavor of the MLflow Model. MLflow supports other flavors of models, as described in the following section.

MLflow Model

MLflow Model is a general-purpose, portable model format that supports a variety of model flavors, ranging from simple Python pickle objects to scikit-learn, TensorFlow, PyTorch, MLeap, and other model formats, including Spark models in Parquet format. MLflow Models present abstractions that can be produced using a variety of common ML tools and then deployed to a variety of ML environments. MLflow Model provides models from popular ML frameworks in MLflow format. An MLflow Model has a standard directory structure that contains configuration files and a serialized model artifact. It also contains all the model evaluation dependencies for model portability and reproducibility in the form of a `conda` environment via the `conda.yaml` file:

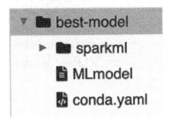

Figure 9.5 – MLflow Model

The preceding screenshot shows the structure of a typical MLflow Model. This standard model format creates a model flavor that can be understood by any downstream tool. Model flavors are used for deployment purposes to help us understand the models from any ML library, without having to integrate each tool with each library. MLflow supports many of the prominent model flavors that all its built-in deployment tools support, such as a simple Python function flavor that describes how to run the model as a Python function. For instance, in the previous code example, we stored our model as a Spark model, which can then be loaded as a **Spark** object or as a simple Python function that can be used in any Python application, even those that may not understand Spark at all.

ML model tuning

Model tuning is an important aspect of the model building process, where the best model parameters are identified programmatically to achieve optimal model performance. This process of model selection by iteratively varying the model parameters is called *hyperparameter tuning*. A typical hyperparameter tuning process involves splitting the available data into multiple training and test datasets. Then, for each training dataset, a test pair iterates through a set of model parameters, called the parameter grid, and selects the model that yields the best performance among all the models that have been trained.

Spark ML provides a `ParamGridbuilder` utility to help build the parameter grid, as well as the `CrossValidator` and `TrainValidationSplit` classes to handle model selection. `CrossValidator` performs model selection by splitting the dataset into a set of folds that are used as separate training and test dataset pairs, and each fold is used as the test set exactly once. The use of model tuning and selection using `ParamGridBuilder` and `CrossValidator` was presented in the code sample presented in the previous section. `TrainValidationSplit` is another popular technique for model selection that uses hyperparameter tuning. Details on its implementation in Apache Spark can be found on Spark's documentation page at `https://spark.apache.org/docs/latest/ml-tuning.html#train-validation-split`.

Now that we have learned how to perform model selection tuning using Apache Spark and how to track experiments using MLflow, the next step in ML life cycle management is storing the models and their versions in a central model repository for use later. We will explore this in the following section using **MLflow Model Registry**.

Tracking model versions using MLflow Model Registry

While the MLflow Tracking server lets you track all the attributes of your ML experiments, MLflow Model Registry provides a central model repository that lets you track all the aspects of your model life cycle. MLflow Model Registry consists of a user interface and APIs to track the model's version, lineage, stage transitions, annotations, and any developer comments. MLflow Model Registry also contains webhooks for CI/CD integrations and a model server for online model serving.

MLflow Model Registry provides us with a way to track and organize the many ML models that are produced and used by businesses during development, testing, and production. Model Registry provides a secure way to share models by leveraging access control lists and provides a way to integrate with model governance and approval workflows. Model Registry also allows us to monitor ML deployments and their performance via its API.

> **Tip**
> Model Registry's access controls and the ability to set permissions on registered models are only available in the full version of Databricks. They are not available in the Community Edition of Databricks or the open source version of MLflow.

Once a model has been logged to the Model Registry, you can add, modify, update, transition, or delete the model through the UI or the API, as shown in the following code sample:

```
import mlflow
from mlflow.tracking.client import MlflowClient
client = MlflowClient()
model_name = "linear-regression-model"
artifact_path = "best_model"
model_uri = "runs:/{run_id}/{artifact_path}".format (run_
id=run_id, artifact_path=artifact_path)
registered_model = mlflow.register_model(model_uri=model_uri,
name=model_name, )
client.update_model_version(
  name=registered_model.name,
  version=registered_model.version,
  description="This predicts the age of a customer using
```

```
transaction history."
)
client.transition_model_version_stage(
  name=registered_model.name,
  version=registered_model.version,
  stage='Staging',
)
model_version = client.get_model_version(
  name=registered_model.name,
  version=registered_model.version,
)
model_uri = "models:/{model_name}/staging".format(model_
name=model_name)
spark_model = mlflow.spark.load_model(model_uri)
```

In the previous code snippet, we did the following:

1. First, we imported the relevant MLflow libraries and `MlflowClient`, an MLflow interface for accessing the MLflow Tracking server and Model Registry artifacts via Python. The client interface is invoked using the `MlflowClient()` method.

2. Then, we constructed `model_uri` by providing the model, name, the model artifact location, and the `run_id` property from a tracked experiment. This information can be accessed via the MLflow Tracking server, either via the API or the UI.

3. Since we had reconstructed the model URI from the tracking server, we registered the model to the Model Registry using the `register_model()` function. If the model doesn't already exist in the Model Registry, a new model with a version of **1** is registered instead.

4. Once the model was registered, we had the opportunity to add or update the model description using the `update_model_version()` method.

5. During the life cycle of a model, it often evolves and needs to transition its stage, say from staging to production or the archival stage. This can be accomplished using the `transition_model_version_stage()` method.

6. A registered model's version and stage can be listed using the `get_model_version()` method.

7. Finally, we loaded a specific version/stage of the model from the Model Registry using the `load_model()` method after constructing the model URI using the `models` keyword, the model's name, and its version or stage name.

Model Registry also provides other handy functions for listing and searching through various versions of an individual registered model, as well as archiving and deleting registered models. References for those methods can be found at `https://www.mlflow.org/docs/latest/model-registry.html#model-registry-workflows`.

> **Important Note**
> Databricks Community Edition, which we will be using throughout this book, does not include Model Registry, so you will have to use the full version of Databricks to execute the preceding code sample. Alternatively, you can deploy your own MLflow Remote Tracking Server, along with a database-backed backend store outside of the Databricks environment, as described here: `https://mlflow.org/docs/latest/tracking.html#mlflow-tracking-servers`.

Now that you have learned how to store, version, and retrieve models using MLflow Model Registry, the next step of the ML life cycle is putting the trained, evaluated, and tuned models to practical use by leveraging them in business applications to draw inferences. We will discuss this in the next section.

Model serving and inferencing

Model serving and inferencing is the most important step of the entire ML life cycle. This is where the models that have been build are deployed to business applications so that we can draw inferences from them. Model serving and inferencing can happen in two ways: using batch processing in offline mode or in real time in online mode.

Offline model inferencing

Offline model inferencing is the process of generating predictions from a ML model using batch processing. The batch processing inference jobs run periodically on a recurring schedule, producing predictions on a new set of fresh data every time. These predictions are then stored in a database or on the data lake and are consumed by business applications in an offline or asynchronous way. An example of batch inferencing would be data-driven customer segmentation being used by the marketing teams at an organization or a retailer predicting customer lifetime value. These use cases do not demand real-time predictions; batch inferencing can serve the purpose here.

In the case of Apache Spark, batch inferencing can take advantage of Spark's scalability to produce predictions at scale on very large datasets, as demonstrated in the following code sample:

```
model_uri = "runs:/{run_id}/{artifact_path}".format(run_
id=active_run.info.run_id, artifact_path="best-model")
spark_udf = mlflow.pyfunc.spark_udf(spark, model_uri)
predictions_df = retail_df.withColumn("predictions", spark_
udf(struct("features")))
predictions_df.write.format("delta").save("/tmp/retail_
predictions")
```

In the previous code block, we recreated the model URI using the model's name and the artifact location from the tracking server. Then, we created a Spark **user-defined function** (**UDF**) using the MLflow Python function model flavor from the Spark model stored on the tracking server. This Spark UDF can be used with a Spark DataFrame to produce inferences in a batch manner at scale. This piece of code can be scheduled as a job that runs periodically, and the predictions can be saved to a location on the data lake.

The Apache Spark framework can help us implement the complete ML life cycle, from model training to model inferencing, using a single, unified data processing framework. Spark can also be used to extend batch inferencing to near-real-time inferencing using Spark Structured Streaming. However, when it comes to ultra-low latency real-time model serving, Apache Spark is not suitable. We will explore this further in the next section.

Online model inferencing

Online inference is the process of generating ML predictions in real time, either by embedding the inference code in the business application itself or by using ultra-low latency APIs. Unlike batch inferences, which are generated in bulk on a large dataset, real-time online inferences are typically generated on one observation at a time. Online inferencing can help with a new and novel application of ML by generating predictions in milliseconds to seconds instead of hours to days.

Consider the example of a mobile gaming application, where you want to show personalized promotions to a gamer based on their level or the type of game they are playing. Online inferencing can quickly collect user behavior data from the mobile app and either generate a predictive recommendation within the app itself or by using a low latency API server. This can, for example, help businesses generate personalized experiences in real time for their customers. While Apache Spark itself is not suitable for online inferencing, MLflow Model Registry includes a model serving component that can be activated using the following command:

```
mlflow models serve -m "models:/ linear-regression-model/
Production"
```

In the previous command, we invoked MLflow's built-in model server to serve the model that we previously registered with Model Registry. This model server makes a RESTful API available for external applications to communicate via HTTP with the model server, sends in a single observation called the payload, and receives a single prediction at a time.

> **Note**
> MLflow's model serving capabilities are not available in Databricks Community Edition, so the previous command will not execute if you are using that version. This feature can be used either in open source MLflow or Databrick's full version.

MLflow's model serving feature is still in preview at the time of writing and has some limitations, such as a target throughput of 20 queries per second and a payload size limitation of 16 MB per request. Thus, this option is only recommended for low throughput, non-production applications. MLflow does offer integrations with other model serving platforms, however, such as **AWS Sagemaker**, **Azure ML**, and **Google Cloud AI**. Details of these integrations can be found in the respective cloud provider's documentation.

Continuous delivery for ML

ML code, unlike traditional software code, is dynamic and is constantly affected by changes to the model code itself, the underlying training data, or the model parameters. Thus, ML model performance needs to be continuously monitored, and models need to be retrained and redeployed periodically to maintain the desired level of model performance. This process can be daunting and time-consuming and prone to mistakes when performed manually. However **Continuous Delivery for ML (CD4ML)** can help streamline and automate this process.

CD4ML is derived from the software engineering principles of **continuous integration** and **continuous delivery (CI/CD)**, which were developed to promote automation, quality, and discipline and help create a reliable and repeatable process that can release software into production. CD4ML builds on and adapts this CI/CD process to ML, where data teams produce artifacts related to the ML process, such as code data and models, in safe and small increments that can be reproduced and released reliably at any time.

The CD4ML process involves a data scientist building a model and its parameters, source code, and the training data required. The next step is model evaluation and tuning. After an acceptable level of model accuracy has been achieved, the model needs to be productionized, and testing must be performed on the model. The final step is deploying and monitoring the model. If the model needs to be adjusted, the CD4ML pipeline should trigger the ML process so that it starts from the beginning. This ensures the continuous delivery occurs and that the latest code changes and models are pushed to the production environment. MLflow provides most of the components that are required to implement this CD4ML process, as follows:

1. Firstly, the MLflow Tracking server can help you track the model training process, including all the training artifacts, along with the data version and the models that have been versioned and marked for testing or production using Model Registry.

2. Then, the registered models can be annotated with custom tags, which helps encode a variety of information. This includes indicating the deployment mode of the model, whether it be batch or online mode, or the region where the model was deployed.

3. Comments can be added to models to specify test failures, model inaccuracies, or production deployment failure notes by data scientists, test engineers, and ML engineers to aid discussion between cross-functional teams.

4. Notifications can be pushed via webhooks within Model Registry to help invoke various actions and automated tests via external CI/CD tools. Actions can be triggered for events such as model creation, version change, adding new comments, and more.

5. Finally, MLflow Projects helps package the entire model development workflow into a reusable, parameterized module.

This way, by leveraging MLflow components such as the MLflow Tracking server, Model Registry, MLflow Projects, and its webhooks functionality, combined with a process automation server such as Jenkins, an entire CD4ML pipeline can be orchestrated.

> **Note**
>
> MLflow Model Registry's webhooks feature is only available in the full version of Databricks; it's not available in the Community Edition or open source MLflow. More information on MLflow Projects and their usage can be found here: `https://www.mlflow.org/docs/latest/projects.html`.

This way, MLflow, with its Model Tracking and Model Registry processes, can help streamline the entire CD4ML process, which would otherwise be a difficult process with a lot of manual steps, lack reproducibility, and cause errors and confusion among cross-functional teams.

Summary

In this chapter, you were introduced to the end-to-end ML life cycle and the various steps involved in it. MLflow is a complete, end-to-end ML life cycle management tool. The MLflow Tracking component was presented, which is useful for streaming the ML experimentation process and helps you track all its attributes, including the data version, ML code, model parameters and metrics, and any other arbitrary artifacts. MLflow Model was introduced as a standards-based model format that provides model portability and reproducibility. MLflow Model Registry was also explored, which is a central model repository that supports the entire life cycle of a newly created model, from staging to production to archival. Model serving mechanisms, such as using batch and online processes, were also introduced. Finally, continuous delivery for ML was introduced. It is used to streamline the entire ML life cycle and automate the model life cycle using Model Registry features, such as the ability to transition model stages, a way to add comments and annotations, and using webhooks to help automate the model life cycle process via external orchestration tools.

So far in this book, you have acquired practical skills to perform data engineering and data science at scale. In the next chapter, we will focus on techniques for scaling out single-machine-based ML libraries based on standard Python.

10
Scaling Out Single-Node Machine Learning Using PySpark

In *Chapter 5, Scalable Machine Learning with PySpark*, you learned how you could use the power of **Apache Spark**'s distributed computing framework to train and score **machine learning (ML)** models at scale. Spark's native ML library provides good coverage of standard tasks that data scientists typically perform; however, there is a wide variety of functionality provided by standard single-node **Python** libraries that were not designed to work in a distributed manner. This chapter deals with techniques for horizontally scaling out standard Python data processing and ML libraries such as **pandas, scikit-learn, XGBoost**, and more. It also covers scaling out of typical data science tasks such as **exploratory data analysis (EDA), model training, model inferencing**, and, finally, also covers a scalable Python library named **Koalas** that lets you effortlessly write **PySpark** code using the very familiar and easy-to-use pandas-like syntax.

In this chapter, we're going to cover the following main topics:

- Scaling out EDA
- Scaling out model inferencing
- Distributed hyperparameter tuning
- Model training using **embarrassingly parallel computing**
- Upgrading pandas to PySpark using Koalas

Some of the skills gained in this chapter will be performing EDA at scale, performing model inferencing and scoring in a scalable fashion, hyperparameter tuning, and best model selection at scale for single-node models. You will also learn to horizontally scale out pretty much any single-node ML model and finally Koalas that lets us use pandas-like API to write scalable PySpark code.

Technical requirements

- In this chapter, we will be using the Databricks Community Edition to run our code:

  `https://community.cloud.databricks.com`

  Sign-up instructions can be found at `https://databricks.com/try-databricks`.

- The code and data used in this chapter can be downloaded from `https://github.com/PacktPublishing/Essential-PySpark-for-Scalable-Data-Analytics/tree/main/Chapter10`.

Scaling out EDA

EDA is a data science process that involves analysis of a given dataset to understand its main characteristics, sometimes graphically using visualizations and other times just by aggregating and slicing data. You have already learned some visual EDA techniques in *Chapter 11, Data Visualization with PySpark*. In this section, we will explore non-graphical EDA using pandas and compare it with the same process using PySpark and Koalas.

EDA using pandas

Typical EDA in standard Python involves using pandas for data manipulation and `matplotlib` for data visualization. Let's take a sample dataset that comes with scikit-learn and perform some basic EDA steps on it, as shown in the following code example:

```
import pandas as pd
from sklearn.datasets import load_boston
boston_data = datasets.load_boston()
boston_pd = pd.DataFrame(boston_data.data,
                         columns=boston_data.feature_names)
boston_pd.info()
boston_pd.head()
boston_pd.shape
boston_pd.isnull().sum()
boston_pd.describe()
```

In the previous code example, we perform the following steps:

1. We import the pandas library and import the sample dataset, `load_boston`, that comes with scikit-learn.

2. Then, we convert the scikit-learn dataset into a pandas DataFrame using the `pd.DataFrame()` method.

3. Now that we have a pandas DataFrame, we can perform analysis on it, starting with the `info()` method, which prints information about the pandas DataFrame such as its column names and their data types.

4. The `head()` function on the pandas DataFrame prints a few rows and columns of the actual DataFrame and helps us visually examine some sample data from the DataFrame.

5. The `shape` attribute on the pandas DataFrame prints the number of rows and columns.

6. The `isnull()` method shows the number of NULL values in each column in the DataFrame.

7. Finally, the `describe()` method prints some statistics on each column sum as the mean, median, and standard deviation.

This code snippet shows some typical EDA steps performed using the Python pandas data processing library. Now, let's see how you can perform similar EDA steps using PySpark.

EDA using PySpark

PySpark also has a DataFrame construct similar to pandas DataFrames, and you can perform EDA using PySpark, as shown in the following code example:

```
boston_df = spark.createDataFrame(boston_pd)
boston_df.show()
print((boston_df.count(), len(boston_df.columns)))
boston_df.where(boston_df.AGE.isNull()).count()
boston_df.describe().display()
```

In the previous code example, we perform the following steps:

1. We first convert the pandas DataFrame created in the previous section to a Spark DataFrame using the `createDataFrame()` function.

2. Then, we use the `show()` function to display a small sample of data from the Spark DataFrame. While the `head()` function is available, `show()` shows the data in a better formatted and more readable way.

3. Spark DataFrames do not have a built-in function to display the shape of the Spark DataFrame. Instead, we use the `count()` function on the rows and the `len()` method on the columns to accomplish the same functionality.

4. Similarly, Spark DataFrames also do not support a pandas-equivalent `isnull()` function to count NULL values in all columns. Instead, a combination of `isNull()` and `where()` is used to filter out NULL values from each column individually and then count them.

5. Spark DataFrames do support a `describe()` function that can calculate basic statistics on each of the DataFrames' columns in a distributed manner by running a Spark job behind the scenes. This may not seem very useful for small datasets but can be very useful when describing very large datasets.

This way, by using the built-in functions and operations available with Spark DataFrames, you can easily scale out your EDA. Since Spark DataFrames inherently support **Spark SQL**, you can also perform your scalable EDA using Spark SQL in addition to using DataFrame APIs.

Scaling out model inferencing

Another important aspect of the whole ML process, apart from data cleansing and model training and tuning, is the productionization of models itself. Despite having access to huge amounts of data, sometimes it is useful to downsample the data and train models on a smaller subset of the larger dataset. This could be due to reasons such as low signal-to-noise ratio, for example. In this, it is not necessary to scale up or scale out the model training process itself. However, since the raw dataset size is very large, it becomes necessary to scale out the actual model inferencing process to keep up with the large amount of raw data that is being generated.

Apache Spark, along with **MLflow**, can be used to score models trained using standard, non-distributed Python libraries like scikit-learn. An example of a model trained using scikit-learn and then productionized at scale using Spark is shown in the following code example:

```
import mlflow
from sklearn.model_selection import train_test_split
from sklearn.linear_model import LinearRegression
X = boston_pd[features]
y = boston_pd['MEDV']
with mlflow.start_run() as run1:
    lr = LinearRegression()
    lr_model = lr.fit(X_train,y_train)
    mlflow.sklearn.log_model(lr_model,  "model")
```

In the previous code example, we perform the following steps:

1. We intend to train a linear regression model using scikit-learn that predicts the median house value (given a set of features) on the sample Boston housing dataset that comes with scikit-learn.

2. First, we import all the required scikit-learn modules, and we also import MLflow, as we intend to log the trained model to the **MLflow Tracking Server**.

3. Then, we define the feature columns as a variable, X, and the label column as y.

4. Then, we invoke an MLflow experiment using the `with mlflow.start_run()` method.

5. Then, we train the actual linear regression model by using the `LinearRegression` class and calling the `fit()` method on the training pandas DataFrame.

6.   Then, we log the resultant model to the MLflow Tracking Server using the `mlflow.sklearn.log_model()` method. The `sklearn` qualifier specifies that the model being logged is of a scikit-learn flavor.

Once we have the trained linear regression model logged to the MLflow Tracking Server, we need to convert it into a PySpark **user-defined function** (**UDF**) to allow it to be used for inferencing in a distributed manner. The code required to achieve this is presented in the following code example:

```
import mlflow.pyfunc
from pyspark.sql.functions import struct
model_uri = "runs:/" + run1.info.run_id + "/model"
pyfunc_udf = mlflow.pyfunc.spark_udf(spark, model_uri=model_
uri)
predicted_df = boston_df.withColumn("prediction", pyfunc_
udf(struct('CRIM','ZN','INDUS','CHAS','NOX','RM','AGE','DIS',
'RAD','TAX','PTRATIO', 'B', 'LSTAT')))
predicted_df.show()
```

In the previous code example, we perform the following steps:

1.   We import the `pyfunc` method used to convert the mlflow model into a PySpark UDF from the mlflow library.

2.   Then, we construct the `model_uri` from MLflow using the `run_id` experiment.

3.   Once we have the `model_uri`, we register the model as a PySpark UDF using the `mlflow.pyfunc()` method. We specify the model flavor as `spark` as we intend to use this with a Spark DataFrame.

4.   Now that the model has been registered as a PySpark UDF, we use it to make predictions on a Spark DataFrame. We do this by using it to create a new column in the Spark DataFrame, then pass in all the feature columns as input. The result is a new DataFrame with a new column that consists of the predictions for each row.

5.   It should be noted that when the `show` action is called it invokes a Spark job and performs the model scoring in a distributed way.

In this way, using the `pyfunc` method of MLflow along with Spark DataFrame operations, a model built using a standard, single-node Python ML library like scikit-learn can also be used to derive inferences at scale in a distributed manner. Furthermore, the inferencing Spark job can be made to write predictions to a persistent storage method like a database, data warehouse, or data lake, and the job itself can be scheduled to run periodically. This can also be easily extended to perform model inferencing in near real-time by using **structured streaming** to perform predictions on a streaming DataFrame.

Model training using embarrassingly parallel computing

As you learned previously, Apache Spark follows the **data parallel processing** paradigm of **distributed computing**. In data parallel processing, the data processing code is moved to where the data resides. However, in traditional computing models, such as those used by standard Python and single-node ML libraries, data is processed on a single machine and the data is expected to be present locally. Algorithms designed for single-node computing can be designed to be multiprocessed, where the process makes use of multiprocessing and multithreading techniques offered by the local CPUs to achieve some level of parallel computing. However, these algorithms are not inherently capable of being distributed and need to be rewritten entirely to be capable of distributed computing. **Spark ML library** is an example where traditional ML algorithms have been completely redesigned to work in a distributed computing environment. However, redesigning every existing algorithm would be very time-consuming and impractical as well. Moreover, a rich set of standard-based Python libraries for ML and data processing already exist and it would be useful if there was a way to leverage them in a distributed computing setting. This is where the embarrassingly parallel computing paradigm comes into play.

In distributed computing, the same compute process executes on different chunks of data residing on different machines, and these compute processes need to communicate with each other to achieve the overall compute task at hand. However, in embarrassingly parallel computing, the algorithm requires no communication between the various processes, and they can run completely independently. There are two ways of exploiting embarrassingly parallel computing for ML training within the Apache Spark framework, and they are presented in the following sections.

Distributed hyperparameter tuning

One of the critical steps of ML processes is model tuning, where data scientists train several models by varying the model hyperparameters. This technique is commonly known as hyperparameter tuning. A common technique for hyperparameter tuning is called **grid search**, which is a method to find the best combination of hyper-parameters that yield the best-performing model. Grid search selects the best model out of all the trained models using **cross-validation**, where data is split into train and test sets, and the trained model's performance is evaluated using the test dataset. In grid search, since multiple models are trained on the same dataset, they can all be trained independently of each other, making it a good candidate for embarrassingly parallel computing.

A typical grid search implementation using standard scikit-learn is illustrated using the following code example:

```
from sklearn.datasets import load_digits
from sklearn.ensemble import RandomForestClassifier
from sklearn.model_selection import GridSearchCV
digits_pd = load_digits()
X = digits_pd.data
y = digits_pd.target
parameter_grid = {"max_depth": [2, None],
                "max_features": [1, 2, 5],
                "min_samples_split": [2, 3, 5],
                "min_samples_leaf": [1, 2, 5],
                "bootstrap": [True, False],
                "criterion": ["gini", "entropy"],
                "n_estimators": [5, 10, 15, 20]}
grid_search = GridSearchCV(RandomForestClassifier(),
                        param_grid=parameter_grid)
grid_search.fit(X, y)
```

In the previous code example, we perform the following steps:

1. First, we import the `GridSearchCV` module and `load_digits` sample dataset, and the `RandomForestClassifier` related modules from scikit-learn.

2. Then, we load the `load_digits` data from the scikit-learn sample datasets, and map the features to the `X` variable and the label column to the `y` variable.

3. Then, we define the parameter grid space to be searched by specifying various values for the hyperparameters used by the RandomForestClassifier algorithm, such as max_depth, max_features, and so on.

4. Then, we invoke the grid search cross validator by invoking the GridSearchCV() method, and perform the actual grid search using the fit() method.

In this way, using the built-in grid search and cross validator methods of scikit-learn, you can perform model hyperparameter tuning and identify the best model among the many models trained. However, this process runs on a single machine, so the models are trained one after another instead of being trained in parallel. Using Apache Spark and a third-party Spark package named spark_sklearn, you can easily implement an embarrassingly parallel implementation of grid search, as shown in the following code example:

```
from sklearn import grid_search
from sklearn.datasets import load_digits
from sklearn.ensemble import RandomForestClassifier
from spark_sklearn import GridSearchCV
digits_pd = load_digits()
X = digits_pd.data
y = digits_pd.target
parameter_grid = {"max_depth": [2, None],
            "max_features": [1, 2, 5],
            "min_samples_split": [2, 3, 5],
            "min_samples_leaf": [1, 2, 5],
            "bootstrap": [True, False],
            "criterion": ["gini", "entropy"],
            "n_estimators": [5, 10, 15, 20]}
grid_search = grid_search.
GridSearchCV(RandomForestClassifier(),
            param_grid=parameter_grid)
grid_search.fit(X, y)
```

The previous code snippet for grid search using `spark_sklearn` is almost the same as the code for grid search using standard scikit-learn. However, instead of using scikit-learn's grid search and cross validators, we make use of the `spark_sklearn` package's grid search and cross validators. This helps run the grid search in a distributed manner, training a different model with a different combination of hyperparameters on the same dataset but on different machines. This helps speed up the model tuning process by orders of magnitude, helping you choose a model from a much larger pool of trained models than was possible using just a single machine. In this way, using the concept of embarrassingly parallel computing on Apache Spark, you can scale out your model tuning task while still using Python's standard single-node machine libraries.

In the following section, we will see how you can scale out the actual model training using Apache Spark's pandas UDFs, and not just the model tuning part.

Scaling out arbitrary Python code using pandas UDF

A UDF, in general, lets you execute arbitrary code on Spark's executors. Thus, UDFs can be used to scale out any arbitrary Python code, including feature engineering and model training, within data science workflows. They can also be used for scaling out data engineering tasks using standard Python. However, UDFs execute code one row at a time, and incur **serialization** and **deserialization** costs between the JVM and the Python processes running on the Spark executors. This limitation makes UDFs less lucrative in scaling out arbitrary Python code onto Spark executors.

With **Spark 2.3**, **pandas UDFs** were introduced. These are executed by Spark using **Apache Arrow** to transfer data, and pandas to perform data manipulation and allow for vectorized operations. This gives pandas UDFs the ability to define high-performance, low-overhead UDFs using standard Python. pandas UDFs are of two types: **scalar** and **grouped** UDFs. Scalar pandas UDFs are used for vectorizing scalar operations, and they take a pandas series as input and return another pandas series of the same size. While grouped pandas UDFs split a Spark DataFrame into groups based on the conditions specified in the `groupby` operator, apply the UDF to each group and finally combine the individual DataFrames produced by each group into a new Spark DataFrame and return it. Examples of scalar, as well as grouped pandas UDFs, can be found on Apache Spark's public documentation:

```
https://spark.apache.org/docs/latest/api/python/reference/api/
pyspark.sql.functions.pandas_udf.html
```

So far, you have seen how to scale the EDA process, or the model tuning process, or to scale out arbitrary Python functions using different techniques supported by Apache Spark. In the following section, we will explore a library built on top of Apache Spark that lets us use pandas-like API for writing PySpark code.

Upgrading pandas to PySpark using Koalas

pandas is the defacto standard for data processing in standard Python, the same as Spark has become the defacto standard for distributed data processing. The pandas API is Python-related and leverages a coding style that makes use of Python's unique features to write code that is readable and beautiful. However, Spark is based on the JVM, and even the PySpark draws heavily on the Java language, including in naming conventions and function names. Thus, it is not very easy or intuitive for a pandas user to switch to PySpark, and a considerable learning curve is involved. Moreover, PySpark executes code in a distributed manner and the user needs to understand the nuances of how distributed code works when intermixing PySpark code with standard single-node Python code. This is a deterrent to an average pandas user to pick up and use PySpark. To overcome this issue, the Apache Spark developer community came up with another open source library on top of PySpark, called Koalas.

The Koalas project is an implementation of the pandas API on top of Apache Spark. Koalas helps data scientists to be immediately productive with Spark, instead of needing to learn a new set of APIs altogether. Moreover, Koalas helps developers maintain a single code base for both pandas and Spark without having to switch between the two frameworks. Koalas comes bundled with the **Databricks Runtime** and is available in the **PyPI** repository. It can be installed using a package manager such as `pip`.

Let's look at a few code examples to see how Koalas presents a pandas-like API for working with Spark:

```
import koalas as ks
boston_data = load_boston()
boston_pd = ks.DataFrame(boston_data.data, columns=boston_data.feature_names)
features = boston_data.feature_names
boston_pd['MEDV'] = boston_data.target
boston_pd.info()
boston_pd.head()
boston_pd.isnull().sum()
boston_pd.describe()
```

In the previous code snippet, we perform the same basic EDA steps that we have performed earlier in this chapter. The only difference here is that instead of creating a pandas DataFrame from the scikit-learn dataset, we create a Koalas DataFrame after importing the Koalas library. You can see that the code is exactly the same as the pandas code written earlier, however, behind the scenes, Koalas converts this code to PySpark code and executes it on the cluster in a distributed manner. Koalas also supports visualization using the `DataFrame.plot()` method, just like pandas. This way you can leverage Koalas to scale out any existing pandas-based ML code, such as feature engineering, or custom ML code, without first having to rewrite the code using PySpark.

Koalas is an active open source project with good community support. However, Koalas is still in a nascent state and comes with its own set of limitations. Currently, only about *70%* of pandas APIs are available in Koalas, which means that some pandas code might not be readily implementable using Koalas. There are a few implementation differences between Koalas and pandas, and it would not make sense to implement certain pandas APIs in Koalas. A common workaround for dealing with missing Koalas functionality is to convert Koalas DataFrames to pandas or PySpark DataFrames, and then apply either pandas or PySpark code to solve the problem. Koalas DataFrames can be easily converted to pandas and PySpark DataFrames using `DataFrame.to_pandas()` and `DataFrame.to_spark()` functions respectively. However, do keep in mind that Koalas does use Spark DataFrames behind the scenes, and a Koalas DataFrame might be too large to fit into a pandas DataFrame on a single machine, causing an out-of-memory error.

Summary

In this chapter, you learned a few techniques to horizontally scale out standard Python-based ML libraries such as scikit-learn, XGBoost, and more. First, techniques for scaling out EDA using a PySpark DataFrame API were introduced and presented along with code examples. Then, techniques for distributing ML model inferencing and scoring were presented using a combination of MLflow pyfunc functionality and Spark DataFrames. Techniques for scaling out ML models using embarrassingly parallel computing techniques using Apache Spark were also presented. Distributed model tuning of models, trained using standard Python ML libraries using a third-party package called `spark_sklearn`, were presented. Then, pandas UDFs were introduced to scale out arbitrary Python code in a vectorized manner for creating high-performance, low-overhead Python user-defined functions right within PySpark. Finally, Koalas was introduced as a way for pandas developers to use a pandas-like API without having to learn the PySpark APIs first, while still leveraging Apache Spark's power and efficiency for data processing at scale.

Section 3: Data Analysis

Once we have clean and integrated data in the data lake and have trained and built machine learning models at scale, the final step is to convey actionable insights to business owners in a meaningful manner to help them make business decisions. This section covers the **business intelligence (BI)** and SQL Analytics part of data analytics. It starts with various data visualization techniques using notebooks. Then, it introduces you to Spark SQL to perform business analytics at scale and shows techniques to connect BI and SQL Analysis tools to Apache Spark clusters. The section ends with an introduction to the Data Lakehouse paradigm to bridge the gap between data warehouses and data lakes to provide a single, unified, scalable storage to cater to all aspects of data analytics, including data engineering, data science, and business analytics.

This section includes the following chapters:

- *Chapter 11, Data Visualization with PySpark*
- *Chapter 12, Spark SQL Primer*
- *Chapter 13, Integrating External Tools with Spark SQL*
- *Chapter 14, The Data Lakehouse*

11
Data Visualization with PySpark

So far, from *Chapter 1, Distributed Computing Primer*, through *Chapter 9, Machine Learning Life Cycle Management*, you have learned how to ingest, integrate, and cleanse data, as well as how to make data conducive for analytics. You have also learned how to make use of clean data for practical business applications using data science and machine learning. This chapter will introduce you to the basics of deriving meaning out of data using data visualizations.

In this chapter, we're going to cover the following main topics:

- Importance of data visualization

- Techniques for visualizing data using PySpark

- Considerations for PySpark to pandas conversion

Data visualization is the process of graphically representing data using visual elements such as charts, graphs, and maps. Data visualization helps you understand patterns within data in a visual manner. In the big data world, with massive amounts of data, it is even more important to make use of data visualizations to derive meaning out of such data and present it in a simple and easy-to-understand way to business users; this helps them make data-driven decisions.

Technical requirements

In this chapter, we will be using Databricks Community Edition to run our code.

- Databricks Community Edition can be accessed at `https://community.cloud.databricks.com`.

- Sign-up instructions can be found at `https://databricks.com/try-databricks`.

- The code and data for this chapter can be downloaded from `https://github.com/PacktPublishing/Essential-PySpark-for-Scalable-Data-Analytics/tree/main/Chapter11`.

Importance of data visualization

Data visualization is the process of translating data into a pictorial representation in the form of graphs, charts, or maps. This makes it easier for the human mind to comprehend complex information. Typically, data visualization is the final stage of business analytics and the first step of any data science process. Though there are professionals who deal solely with data visualizations, any data professional needs to be able to understand and produce data visualizations. They help convey complex patterns that are hidden within data in an easy-to-understand way to business users. Every business needs information for optimal performance, and data visualization helps businesses make easier data-driven decisions by representing relationships between datasets in a visual way and surfacing actionable insights. With the advent of big data, there has been an explosion of both structured and unstructured data, and it is difficult to make sense of it without the help of visual aids. Data visualization helps in accelerating the decision-making process by surfacing key business information and helps business users act on those insights quickly. Data visualization also aids the storytelling process by helping convey the right message to the right audience.

A data visualization can be a simple graph representing a single aspect of the current state of the business, a complex sales report, or a dashboard that gives a holistic view of an organization's performance. Data visualization tools are key to unlocking the power of data visualizations. We will explore the different types of data visualization tools that are available in the following section.

Types of data visualization tools

Data visualization tools provide us with an easier way to create data visualizations. They allow data analysts and data scientists to create data visualizations conveniently by providing a graphical user interface, database connections, and sometimes data manipulation tools in a single, unified interface. There are different types of data visualizations tools, and each serves a slightly different purpose. We will explore them in this section.

Business intelligence tools

Business intelligence (BI) tools are typically enterprise-grade tools that help organizations track and visually represent their **Key Performance Indicators (KPIs)**. BI tools typically include provisions for creating complex logical data models and contain data cleansing and integration mechanisms. BI tools also include connectors to a myriad of data sources and built-in data visualizations with drag-and-drop features to help business users quickly create data visualizations, operational and performance dashboards, and scorecards to track the performance of an individual department or the entire organization. The primary users of BI tools are business analysts and business executives involved in making tactical and strategic decisions.

BI tools traditionally use data warehouses as their data sources, but modern BI tools support RDMS, NoSQL databases, and data lakes as data sources. Some examples of prominent BI tools include **Tableau, Looker, Microsoft Power BI, SAP Business Objects, MicroStrategy, IBM Cognos**, and **Qlikview**, to name a few. BI tools can connect to Apache Spark and consume data stored in Spark SQL tables using an ODBC connection. These concepts will be explored in detail in *Chapter 13, Integrating External Tools with Spark SQL*. A class of data visualization tools with all the necessary data visualization and data connectivity components, minus any data processing capabilities such as Redash, also exist and they can also connect to Apache Spark via an ODBC connection.

Observability tools

Observability is the process of constantly monitoring and understanding what's happening in highly distributed systems. Observability helps us understand what is slow or broken, as well as what needs to be fixed to improve performance. However, since modern cloud environments are dynamic and constantly increasing in scale and complexity, most problems are neither known nor monitored. Observability addresses common issues with modern cloud environments that are dynamic and ever-increasing in scale by enabling you to continuously monitor and surface any issues that might arise. Observability tools help businesses continuously monitor systems and applications and enable a business to receive actionable insights into system behavior, as well as predict outages or problems before they occur. Data visualization is an important component of observability tools; a few popular examples include Grafana and Kibana.

Data teams are typically not responsible for monitoring and maintaining the health of data processing systems – this is usually handled by specialists such as **DevOps** engineers. Apache Spark doesn't have any direct integrations with any observability tools out of the box, but it can be integrated with popular observability platforms such as **Prometheus** and **Grafana**. Apache Spark's integration with observability tools is outside the scope of this book, so we won't discuss this here.

Notebooks

Notebooks are interactive computing tools that are used to execute code, visualize results, and share insights. Notebooks are indispensable tools in the data science process and are becoming prominent in the entire data analytics development life cycle, as you have witnessed throughout this book. Notebooks are also excellent data visualization tools as they help you convert your Python or SQL code into easy-to-understand interactive data visualizations. Some notebooks, such as Databricks, Jupyter, and Zeppelin notebooks can also be used as standalone dashboards. The remainder of this chapter will focus on how notebooks can be used as data visualization tools when using PySpark.

Techniques for visualizing data using PySpark

Apache Spark is a unified data processing engine and doesn't come out of the box with a graphical user interface, per se. As discussed in the previous sections, data that's been processed by Apache Spark can be stored in data warehouses and visualized using BI tools or natively visualized using notebooks. In this section, we will focus on how to leverage notebooks to interactively process and visualize data using PySpark. As we have done throughout this book, we will be making use of notebooks that come with **Databricks Community Edition**, though **Jupyter** and **Zeppelin** notebooks can also be used.

PySpark native data visualizations

There aren't any data visualization libraries that can work with PySpark DataFrames natively. However, the notebook implementations of cloud-based Spark distributions such as Databricks and Qubole support natively visualizing Spark DataFrames using the built-in `display()` function. Let's see how we can use the `display()` function to visualize PySpark DataFrames in Databricks Community Edition.

We will use the cleansed, integrated, and wrangled dataset that we produced toward the end of *Chapter 6, Feature Engineering – Extraction, Transformation, and Selection*, here, as shown in the following code snippet:

```
retail_df = spark.read.table("feature_store.retail_features")
viz_df = retail_df.select("invoice_num", "description",
                          "invoice_date", "invoice_month",
                          "country_code", "quantity",
                          "unit_price", "occupation",
                          "gender")
viz_df.display()
```

In the previous code snippet, we read a table into a Spark DataFrame and selected the columns that we intend to visualize. Then, we called the `display()` method on the Spark DataFrame. The result is a grid display in the notebook, as shown in the following screenshot:

	invoice_num	description	invoice_date	invoice_month	country_code
1	536373	WHITE HANGING HEART T-LIGHT HOLDER	01/12/10 09:02	12	EN
2	536382	ANTIQUE GLASS DRESSING TABLE POT	01/12/10 09:45	12	EN
3	536387	RED TOADSTOOL LED NIGHT LIGHT	01/12/10 09:58	12	EN
4	536388	LOVE BUILDING BLOCK WORD	01/12/10 09:59	12	EN
5	536390	JAM MAKING SET WITH JARS	01/12/10 10:19	12	EN
6	536437	NAMASTE SWAGAT INCENSE	01/12/10 12:12	12	EN

Figure 11.1 – The grid widget

The previous screenshot shows the result of calling the `display()` function on a Spark DataFrame within a Databricks notebook. This way, any Spark DataFrame can be visualized in a tabular format within Databricks notebooks. The tabular grid supports sorting arbitrary columns. Databricks notebooks also support charts and graphs that can be used from within the notebooks.

> **Tip**
> Databricks's `display()` method supports all of Spark's programming APIs, including Python, Scala, R, and SQL. In addition, the `display()` method can also render Python pandas DataFrames.

We can use the same grid display and convert it into a graph by clicking on the graph icon and choosing the desired graph from the list, as shown in the following screenshot:

Figure 11.2 – Graph options

As we can see, the graph menu has multiple chart options, with the bar chart being the first on the list. If you choose the bar chart, plot options can be used to configure the chart's key, value, and series grouping options. Similarly, we can use a line graph or a pie chart, as shown here:

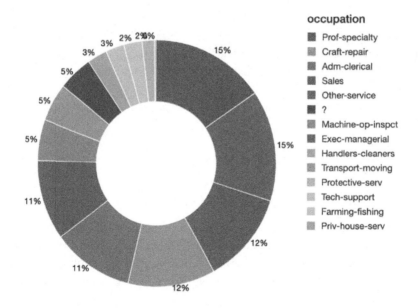

Figure 11.3 – Pie chart

Here, the display() function can be used to display various kinds of charts within the notebook and help configure various graph options. Databricks notebooks also support a rudimentary map widget that can visualize metrics on a world map, as illustrated in the following screenshot:

Figure 11.4 – World map

The previous screenshot shows metrics on a world map. Since our dataset only contains a few European countries, France and the UK have been shaded in on the map widget.

> **Note**
>
> For this widget, the values should be either country codes in ISO 3166-1 alpha-3 format ("GBR") or US state abbreviations ("TX").

In addition to basic bars and charts, Databricks notebooks also support scientific visualizations such as **scatter plots**, **histograms**, **quantile plots**, and **Q-Q** plots, as illustrated in the following figure:

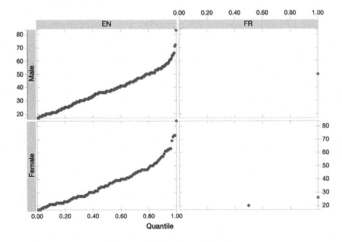

Figure 11.5 – Quantile plot

A quantile plot, as illustrated in the previous figure, helps determine whether two datasets have a common distribution. Quantile plots are available in Databricks notebooks via the graph menu, and plot properties such as keys, values, and series groupings are available via the plot options menu.

We can use the following code to make Databricks notebooks display images:

```
image_df = spark.read.format("image").load("/FileStore/
FileStore/shared_uploads/images")
```

The previous code snippet uses Apache Spark's built-in image data source to load images from a directory on persistent storage such as a data lake:

Figure 11.6 – Image data

This image is rendered in a notebook using Databricks's `display()` function as it is capable of displaying image previews.

Databricks notebooks are also capable of rendering machine learning-specific visualizations such as **residuals**, **ROC curves**, and **decision trees**. In *Chapter 7, Supervised Machine Learning*, we used the `display()` function to visualize a **decision tree** model that we had trained, as illustrated in the following screenshot:

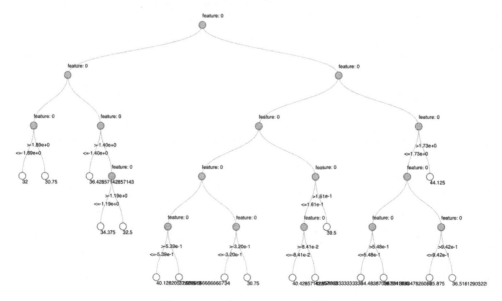

Figure 11.7 – Decision tree model

The previous screenshot shows the decision tree model that we built using Spark ML, rendered in a Databricks notebook.

> **Tip**
> More information on rendering machine learning-specific visualizations using Databricks notebooks can be found in Databricks's public documentation here: `https://docs.databricks.com/notebooks/visualizations/index.html#machine-learning-visualizations`.

Interactive visuals using JavaScript and HTML

Databricks notebooks also support **HTML**, **JavaScript**, and **CSS** for interactive visualizations via **D3.js** and **SVG** and the `displayHTML()` function. You can pass any arbitrary HTML code to `displayHTML()` and have it rendered in a notebook, as shown in the following code snippet:

```
displayHTML("<a href ='/files/image.jpg'>Arbitrary Hyperlink</a>")
```

The preceding code snippet displays an arbitrary HTML hyperlink in a notebook. Other HTML elements such as paragraphs, headings, images, and more can also be used with the `displayHTML()` function.

> **Tip**
> HTML blocks such as hyperlinks, images, and tables can be used to make your notebooks more descriptive and interactive for end users and can aid in the storytelling process.

Similarly, SVG graphics can also be rendered using the `displayHTML()` function, as shown in the following code block:

```
displayHTML("""<svg width="400" height="400">
  <ellipse cx="300" cy="300" rx="100" ry="60"
style="fill:orange">
    <animate attributeType="CSS" attributeName="opacity"
from="1" to="0" dur="5s" repeatCount="indefinite" />
  </ellipse>
</svg>""")
```

The preceding code renders an orange-colored, animated ellipse that fades in and out. Far more complex SVG graphics can also be rendered and data from a Spark DataFrame can be passed along. Similarly, the popular HTML and JavaScript-based visualization library can also be leveraged with Databricks notebooks, as shown here:

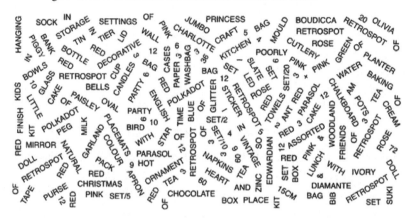

Figure 11.8 – Word cloud using D3.js

Here, we have taken the `description` column from the `retail_sales` Delta table that we created during our data processing steps in the previous chapters, and then we extracted individual words from the item description column. Then, we rendered the words using a word cloud visualization by using HTML, CSS, and JavaScript. After, we used the popular D3.js JavaScript library to manipulate the HTML documents based on data. The code for this visualization can be found at `https://github.com/PacktPublishing/Essential-PySpark-for-Scalable-Data-Analytics/blob/main/Chapter11/databricks-charts-graphs.py`.

So far, you have seen some of the basic and statistical graphs that are available via the Databricks notebook interface, which can work natively with Spark DataFrames. However, sometimes, you may need some additional graphs and charts that aren't available within the notebook, or you may need more control over your graph. In these instances, popular visualization libraries for Python such as `matplotlib`, `plotly`, `seaborn`, `altair`, `bokeh`, and so on can be used with PySpark. We will explore some of these visualization libraries in the next section.

Using Python data visualizations with PySpark

As you learned in the previous section, PySpark doesn't inherently have any visualization capabilities, but you can choose to use Databricks notebook capabilities to visualize data in Spark DataFrames. In situations where using Databricks notebooks is not possible, you can use popular Python-based visualizations libraries to visualize your data using any notebook interface that you are comfortable with. In this section, we will explore some prominent Python visualization libraries and how to use them for data visualization in Databricks notebooks.

Creating two-dimensional plots using Matplotlib

Matplotlib is one of the oldest and most popular Python-based visualization libraries for creating two-dimensional plots from data stored in arrays. Matplotlib comes pre-installed in Databricks Runtime, though it can also be easily installed from the PyPI repository using a package manager such as pip. The following code example shows how Matplotlib can be used with PySpark:

```
import pandas as pd
import matplotlib.pyplot as plt
retail_df = spark.read.table("feature_store.retail_features")
viz_df = retail_df.select("invoice_num", "description",
                          "invoice_date", "invoice_month",
                          "country_code", "quantity",
                          "unit_price", "occupation",
                          "gender")
pdf = viz_df.toPandas()
pdf['quantity'] = pd.to_numeric(pdf['quantity'],
                          errors='coerce')
pdf.plot(kind='bar', x='invoice_month', y='quantity',
         color='orange')
```

In the previous code snippet, we did the following:

1. First, we imported the pandas and matplotlib libraries, assuming they are already installed in the notebook.

2. Then, we generated a Spark DataFrame with the required columns using the online retail dataset that we have created during the data processing steps in the previous chapters.

3. Since Python-based visualization libraries cannot directly use Spark DataFrames, we converted the Spark DataFrame into a pandas DataFrame.

4. Then, we converted the quantity column into a numeric data type so that we could plot it.

5. After that, we defined a plot on the pandas DataFrame using the `plot()` method of the Matplotlib library, specified the type of plot to be generated as a bar graph, and passed the x-axis and y-axis column names.

6. Some notebook environments may require you to explicitly call the `display()` function for the plot to be displayed.

This way, Matplotlib can be used with any Spark DataFrame if we convert it into a pandas DataFrame. The plot that was generated looks as follows:

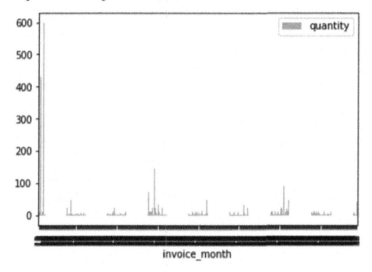

Figure 11.9 – Matplotlib visualization

The previous graph depicts the number of items that have been sold over a certain period.

Scientific visualizations using Seaborn

Seaborn is a visualization library based on Matplotlib and has close integration with pandas. It has a high-level interface for easily plotting statistical data. Seaborn comes pre-installed with Databricks, though it can easily be installed from PyPI using `pip`. The following code sample shows how Seaborn can be used with PySpark DataFrames:

```
import matplotlib.pyplot as plt
import seaborn as sns
```

```
data = retail_df.select("unit_price").toPandas()["unit_price"]
plt.figure(figsize=(10, 3))
sns.boxplot(data)
```

In the previous code snippet, we did the following:

1. First, we imported the `matplotlib` and `seaborn` libraries.

2. Next, we converted the Spark DataFrame, which contains a single column called `unit_price`, into a pandas DataFrame using the `toPandas()` PySpark function.

3. Then, we defined our plot dimensions using the `plot.figure()` Matplotlib method.

4. Finally, we plotted a boxplot by invoking the `seaborn.boxplot()` method and passing the pandas DataFrame with a single column. The resultant plot is shown in the following screenshot:

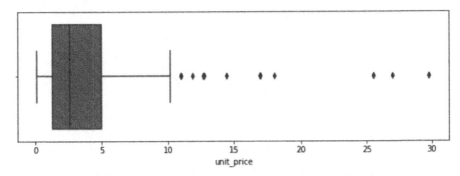

Figure 11.10 – Seaborn boxplot visualization

The previous screenshot depicts how the **unit_price** column can be distributed as a box plot using its minimum, first quartile, median, third quartile, and maximum values.

Interactive visualizations using Plotly

Plotly is a JavaScript-based visualization library that enables Python users to create interactive web-based visualizations that can be displayed in notebooks or saved to standalone HTML files. Plotly comes pre-installed with Databricks and can be used like so:

```
import plotly.express as plot
df = viz_df.toPandas()
fig = plot.scatter(df, x="fin_wt", y="quantity",
                   size="unit_price", color="occupation",
                   hover_name="country_code", log_x=True,
```

```
                              size_max=60)
fig.show()
```

In the previous code snippet, we did the following actions:

1. First, we imported the `matplotlib` and `seaborn` libraries.

2. Next, we converted the Spark DataFrame, along with the required columns, into a pandas DataFrame.

3. Then, we defined the Plotly plot parameters using the `plot.scatter()` method. This method configures a scatter plot with three dimensions.

4. Finally, we rendered the plot using the `fig.show()` method. The resultant plot is shown in the following screenshot:

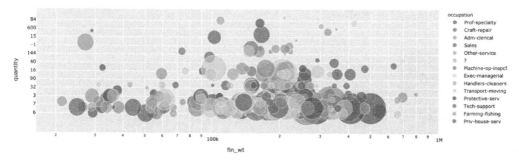

Figure 11.11 – Plotly bubble chart visualization

The preceding screenshot shows a bubble graph that depicts three metrics along three dimensions. The plot is interactive, and information is provided when you hover your mouse over various parts of the graph.

Declarative visualizations using Altair

Altair is a declarative statistical visualization library for Python. Altair is based on an open source, declarative grammar engine called **Vega**. Altair also offers a concise visualization grammar that enables users to build a wide range of visualizations quickly. It can be installed using the following command:

```
%pip install altair
```

The previous command installs Altair in the notebook's local Python kernel and restarts it. Once Altair has been successfully installed, it can be invoked using the usual Python `import` statements, as shown in the following code sample:

```
import altair as alt
import pandas as pd
source = (viz_df.selectExpr("gender as Gender",
"trim(occupation) as Occupation").where("trim(occupation) in
('Farming-fishing', 'Handlers-cleaners', 'Prof-specialty',
'Sales', 'Tech-support') and cust_age > 49").toPandas())
```

In the previous code snippet, we imported the Altair and pandas libraries. Then, we selected the required columns from the Spark table and convert them into a pandas DataFrame. Once we have data in Python in a pandas DataFrame, Altair can be used to create a plot, as shown here:

Figure 11.12 – Altair isotype visualization

The preceding figure depicts an isotype visualization that shows the distribution of occupations by gender, across countries. Other open source libraries such as `bokeh`, `pygal`, and `leather` can also be used to visualize PySpark DataFrames. Bokeh is another popular data visualization library in Python that provides high-performance interactive charts and plots. Bokeh is based on JavaScript and HTML and unlike Matplotlib, it lets users create custom visualizations. Information on using Bokeh in Databricks notebooks can be found in Databricks's public documentation at `https://docs.databricks.com/notebooks/visualizations/bokeh.html#bokeh`.

So far, you have learned how to use some of the popular visualizations that are available for Python with Spark DataFrames by converting PySpark DataFrames into pandas DataFrames. However, there are some performance considerations and limitations you must consider when converting PySpark DataFrames into pandas DataFrames. We will look at these in the next section.

Considerations for PySpark to pandas conversion

This section will introduce **pandas**, demonstrate the differences between pandas and PySpark, and the considerations that need to be kept in mind while converting datasets between PySpark and pandas.

Introduction to pandas

pandas is one of the most widely used open source data analysis libraries for Python. It contains a diverse set of utilities for processing, manipulating, cleaning, munging, and wrangling data. pandas is much easier to work with than Pythons lists, dictionaries, and loops. In some ways, pandas is like other statistical data analysis tools such as R or SPSS, which makes it very popular with data science and machine learning enthusiasts.

The primary abstractions of pandas are **Series** and **DataFrames**, with the former essentially being a one-dimensional array and the latter a two-dimensional array. One of the fundamental differences between pandas and PySpark is that pandas represents its datasets as one- and two-dimensional **NumPy** arrays, while PySpark DataFrames are collections of **Row** and **Column** objects, based on Spark SQL. While pandas DataFrames can only be manipulated using pandas DSL, PySpark DataFrames can be manipulated using Spark's DataFrame DSL, as well as SQL. Owing to this difference, developers familiar with manipulating pandas might find PySpark to be different and may face a learning curve when working with the platform. The Apache Spark community realized this difficulty and launched a new open source project called Koalas. Koalas implements a pandas-like API on top of Spark DataFrames to try and overcome the previously mentioned difference between pandas and PySpark. More information on using Koalas will be presented in *Chapter 10, Scaling Out Single-Node Machine Learning Using PySpark*.

> **Note**
>
> NumPy is a Python package for scientific computing that provides a multi-dimensional array and a set of routines for fast operations on arrays. More information about NumPy can be found here: `https://numpy.org/doc/stable/user/whatisnumpy.html`.

The other fundamental difference, in the context of big data and processing massive amounts of data at big data scale, is that pandas was designed to process data on a single machine and PySpark, by design, is distributed and can process data on multiple machines in a massively parallel manner. This brings up an important limitation of pandas compared to PySpark, as well as some important considerations that the developer needs to keep in mind while converting from pandas into PySpark. We will look at these in the following section.

Converting from PySpark into pandas

The PySpark API comes with a handy utility function called `DataFrame.toPandas()` that converts PySpark DataFrames into pandas DataFrames. This function has been demonstrated throughout this chapter. If you recall our discussions from *Chapter 1, Distributed Computing Primer*, especially the *Spark's cluster architecture* section, a Spark cluster consists of a **Driver** process and a set of executor processes on worker machines, with the Driver being responsible for compiling user code, passing it on to the workers, managing and communicating with the workers, and if required, aggregating and collecting data from the workers. The Spark workers are responsible for all the data processing tasks. However, pandas is not based on the distributed computing paradigm and works solely on a single computing machine. Thus, when you execute pandas code on a Spark cluster, it executes on the Driver or the Master node, as depicted in the following diagram:

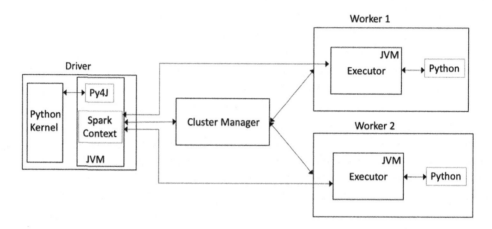

Figure 11.13 – PySpark architecture

As we can see, Python and **JVM** are two separate processes running inside the **Driver**. The communication between the **Python kernel** and the **JVM** happens through another process called Py4J, which is the link between the Spark context and the Python kernel inside the Driver. In the case of pandas, it runs inside the Python kernel, completely independent and oblivious of any knowledge of Spark and its DataFrames. Whenever the `toPandas()` function is called on a Spark DataFrame, it collects rows from all the Spark workers and then creates a pandas DataFrame locally on the Driver inside the Python kernel.

The first issue with this is that `toPandas()` practically collects all the data from the workers and brings it back to the Driver. This may cause the Driver to run out of memory if the dataset being collected is too large. Another issue with this process is that by default, the **Row** objects of the Spark DataFrame are collected on the Driver as a **list** of **tuples**, and then converted to a pandas DataFrame. This ends up using a large amount of memory and sometimes even data that's twice the size of the Spark DataFrame being collected.

To mitigate some of the memory issues during PySpark to pandas conversion, Apache Arrow can be used. Apache Arrow is an in-memory, columnar data format that is similar to Spark's internal representation of datasets and is efficient at transferring data between the JVM and Python processes. Apache Arrow is not enabled by default in Spark and needs to be enabled by setting the `spark.sql.execution.arrow.enabled` Spark configuration to `true`.

> **Note**
>
> PyArrow, the Python binding of Apache Arrow, is pre-installed on Databricks Runtime. However, you might need to install a version of PyArrow that's appropriate for the Spark and Python versions of your Spark cluster.

Apache Arrow helps mitigate some of the memory issues that might arise from using `toPandas()`. Despite this optimization, the conversion operation still results in all records in the Spark DataFrame being collected by the Driver, so you should only perform the conversion on a small subset of the original data. Thus, by making use of the PyArrow format and taking care to sample down datasets, you can still use all the open source visualizations that are compatible with standard Python to visualize your PySpark DataFrames in a notebook environment.

Summary

In this chapter, you learned about the importance of using data visualization to convey meaning from complex datasets in a simple way, as well as to easily surface patterns among data to business users. Various strategies for visualizing data with Spark were introduced. You also learned how to use data visualizations with PySpark natively using Databricks notebooks. We also looked at techniques for using plain Python visualization libraries to visualize data with Spark DataFrames. A few of the prominent open source visualization libraries, such as Matplotlib, Seaborn, Plotly, and Altair, were introduced, along with practical examples of their usage and code samples. Finally, you learned about the pitfalls of using plain Python visualizations with PySpark, the need for PySpark conversion, and some strategies to overcome these issues.

The next chapter will cover the topic of connecting various BI and SQL analysis tools to Spark, which will help you perform ad hoc data analysis and build complex operational and performance dashboards.

12

Spark SQL Primer

In the previous chapter, you learned about data visualizations as a powerful and key tool of data analytics. You also learned about various Python visualization libraries that can be used to visualize data in pandas DataFrames. An equally important and ubiquitous and essential skill in any data analytics professional's repertoire is **Structured Query Language** or **SQL**. **SQL** has existed as long as the field of data analytics has existed, and even with the advent of big data, data science, and **machine learning** (**ML**), SQL is still proving to be indispensable.

This chapter introduces you to the basics of SQL and looks at how SQL can be applied in a distributed computing setting via Spark SQL. You will learn about the various components that make up Spark SQL, including the storage, metastore, and the actual query execution engine. We will look at the differences between **Hadoop Hive** and Spark SQL, and finally, end with some techniques for improving the performance of Spark SQL queries.

In this chapter, we're going to cover the following main topics:

- Introduction to SQL
- Introduction to Spark SQL
- Spark SQL language reference
- Optimizing Spark SQL performance

Some of the areas covered in this chapter include the usefulness of SQL as a language for slicing and dicing of data, the individual components of Spark SQL, and how they come together to create a powerful distributed SQL engine on Apache Spark. You will look at a Spark SQL language reference to help with your data analytics needs and some techniques to optimize the performance of your Spark SQL queries.

Technical requirements

Here is what you'll need for this chapter:

- In this chapter, we will be using Databricks Community Edition to run our code (https://community.cloud.databricks.com). Sign-up instructions can be found at https://databricks.com/try-databricks.

- The code and data used in this chapter can be downloaded from https://github.com/PacktPublishing/Essential-PySpark-for-Scalable-Data-Analytics/tree/main/Chapter12.

Introduction to SQL

SQL is a declarative language for storing, manipulating, and querying data stored in relational databases, also called **relational database management systems (RDBMSes)**. A relational database contains data in tables, which in turn contain rows and columns. In the real world, entities have relationships among themselves, and a relational database tries to mimic these real-world relationships as relationships between tables. Thus, in relational databases, individual tables contain data related to individual entities, and these tables might be related.

SQL is a declarative programming language that helps you specify which rows and columns you want to retrieve from a given table and specify constraints to filter out any data. An RDBMS contains a query optimizer that turns a SQL declaration into a query plan and executes it on the database engine. The query plan is finally translated into an execution plan for the database engine to read table rows and columns into memory and filter them based on the provided constraints.

The SQL language includes subsets for defining schemas—called **Data Definition Language (DDL)**—and modifying and querying data—called **Data Manipulation Language (DML)**, as discussed in the following sections.

DDL

DDL is used to define data structures such as databases, schemas, tables, and columns within a relational database. Basic DDL statements include CREATE, ALTER, DROP, TRUNCATE, and so on. The following SQL query represents a DDL SQL statement:

```
CREATE TABLE db_name.schema_name.table_name (
    column1 datatype,
    column2 datatype,
    column3 datatype,
    ....
);
```

The previous SQL statement represents a typical command to create a new table within a specific database and a schema with a few columns and its data types defined. A database is a collection of data and log files, while a schema is a logical grouping within a database.

DML

DML is used to query, retrieve, and manipulate data stored within a database. Basic DML statements include SELECT, UPDATE, INSERT, DELETE, MERGE, and so on. An example DML query is shown here:

```
SELECT column1, SUM(column2) AS agg_value
FROM db_name.schema_name.table_name
WHERE column3 between value1 AND value2
GROUP BY column1
ORDER BY SUM(column2)
);
```

The previous query results in column2 being aggregated by each distinct value of column1 after filtering rows based on the constraint specified on column3, and finally, the results being sorted by the aggregated value.

> **Note**
>
> Although SQL generally adheres to certain standards set by the **American National Standards Institute** (**ANSI**), each RDBMS vendor has a slightly different implementation of the SQL standards, and you should refer to the specific RDBMS's documentation for the correct syntax.

The previous SQL statement represents standard DDL and DML queries; however, there might be subtle implementation details between each RDBMS's implementation of the SQL standard. Similarly, Apache Spark also has its own implementation of the ANSI SQL 2000 standard.

Joins and sub-queries

Tables within relational databases contain data that is related, and it is often required to join the data between various tables to produce meaningful analytics. Thus, SQL supports operations such as joins and sub-queries for users to be able to combine data across tables, as shown in the following SQL statement:

```
SELECT a.column1, b.cloumn2, b.column3
FROM table1 AS a JOIN  table2 AS b
ON a.column1 = b.column2
```

In the previous SQL query, we join two tables using a common key column and produce columns from both the tables after the JOIN operation. Similarly, sub-queries are queries within queries that can occur in a SELECT, WHERE, or FROM clause that lets you combine data from multiple tables. A specific implementation of these SQL queries within Spark SQL will be explored in the following sections.

Row-based versus columnar storage

Databases physically store data in one of two ways, either in a row-based manner or in a columnar fashion. Each has its own advantages and disadvantages, depending on its use case. In row-based storage, all the values are stored together, and in columnar storage, all the values of a column are stored contiguously on a physical storage medium, as shown in the following screenshot:

Row-based Storage

uid	last_name	first_name	birth_month
1	Asimov	Isaac	January
2	Brown	Dan	June
3	Burroughs	Edgar Rice	September

Columnar Storage

uid	1	2	3
last_name	Asimov	Isaac	January
first_name	Brown	Dan	June
birth_month	Burroughs	Edgar Rice	September

Figure 12.1 – Row-based versus columnar storage

As depicted in the previous screenshot, in row-based storage, an entire row with all its column values is stored together on physical storage. This makes it easier to find an individual row and retrieve all its columns from storage in a fast and efficient manner. Columnar storage, on the other hand, stores all the values of an individual column contiguously on physical storage, which makes retrieving an individual column fast and efficient.

Row-based storage is more popular with transactional systems, where quickly retrieving an individual transactional record or a row is more important. On the other hand, analytical systems typically deal with aggregates of rows and only need to retrieve a few columns per query. Thus, it is more efficient to choose columnar storage while designing analytical systems. Columnar storage also offers a better data compression ratio, thus making optimal use of available storage space when storing huge amounts of historical data. Analytical storage systems including **data warehouses** and **data lakes** prefer columnar storage over row-based storage. Popular big data file formats such as **Parquet** and **Optimized Row Columnar** (**ORC**) are also columnar.

The ease of use and ubiquity of SQL has led the creators of many non-relational data processing frameworks such as Hadoop and Apache Spark to adopt subsets or variations of SQL in creating Hadoop Hive and Spark SQL. We will explore Spark SQL in detail in the following section.

Introduction to Spark SQL

Spark SQL brings native support for SQL to Apache Spark and unifies the process of querying data stored both in Spark DataFrames and in external data sources. Spark SQL unifies DataFrames and relational tables and makes it easy for developers to intermix SQL commands with querying external data for complex analytics. With the release of **Apache Spark 1.3**, Spark DataFrames powered by Spark SQL became the de facto abstraction of Spark for expressing data processing code, while **resilient distributed datasets** (**RDDs**) still remain Spark's core abstraction method, as shown in the following diagram:

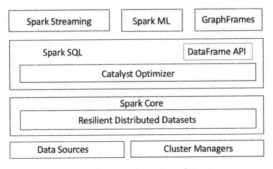

Figure 12.2 – Spark SQL architecture

As shown in the previous diagram, you can see that most of Spark's components now leverage Spark SQL and DataFrames. Spark SQL provides more information about the structure of the data and the computation being performed, and the **Spark SQL engine** uses this extra information to perform additional optimizations to the query. With Spark SQL, all of Spark's components—including **Structured Streaming, DataFrames, Spark ML**, and **GraphFrames**—and all its programming **application programming interfaces (APIs)**—including **Scala, Java, Python, R**, and **SQL**—use the same execution engine to express computations. This unification makes it easy for you to switch back and forth between different APIs and lets you choose the right API for the task at hand. Certain data processing operations, such as joining multiple tables, are expressed much more easily in SQL, and developers can easily mix **SQL** with **Scala, Java**, or **Python** code.

Spark SQL also brings a powerful new optimization framework called **Catalyst**, which can automatically transform any data processing code, whether expressed using Spark DataFrames or using Spark SQL, to execute more efficiently. We will explore the **Catalyst** optimizer in the following section.

Catalyst optimizer

A **SQL query optimizer** in an RDBMS is a process that determines the most efficient way for a given SQL query to process data stored in a database. The SQL optimizer tries to generate the most optimal execution for a given SQL query. The optimizer typically generates multiple query execution plans and chooses the optimal one among them. It typically takes into consideration factors such as the **central processing unit (CPU)**, **input/output (I/O)**, and any available statistics on the tables being queried to choose the most optimal query execution plan. The optimizer based on the chosen query execution plan chooses to re-order, merge, and process a query in any order that yields the optimal results.

The Spark SQL engine also comes equipped with a query optimizer named **Catalyst**. **Catalyst** is based on **functional programming** concepts, like the rest of Spark's code base, and uses Scala's programming language features to build a robust and extensible query optimizer. Spark's Catalyst optimizer generates an optimal execution plan for a given Spark SQL query by following a series of steps, as depicted in the following diagram:

Figure 12.3 – Spark's Catalyst optimizer

As shown in the previous diagram, the Catalyst optimizer first generates a logical plan after resolving references, then optimizes the logical plan based on standard rule-based optimization techniques. It then generates a set of physical execution plans using the optimized logical plan and chooses the best physical plan, and finally, generates **Java virtual machine** (**JVM**) bytecode using the best possible physical plan. This process allows Spark SQL to translate user queries into the best possible data processing code without the developer having any nuanced understanding of the microscopic inner workings of Spark's distributed data processing paradigm. Moreover, Spark SQL DataFrame APIs in the Java, Scala, Python, and R programming languages all go through the same Catalyst optimizer. Thus, Spark SQL or any data processing written using DataFrame APIs irrespective of the programming language yields comparable performance.

> **Tip**
>
> There are a few exceptions where PySpark DataFrame code might not be comparable to Scala or Java code in performance. One such example is when using non-vectorized **user-defined functions** (**UDFs**) in PySpark DataFrame operations. Catalyst doesn't have any visibility into UDFs in Python and will not be able to optimize the code. Thus, these should be replaced with either Spark SQL's built-in function or the UDFs defined in Scala or Java.

A seasoned data engineer with a thorough understanding of the RDD API can possibly write a little more optimized code than the Catalyst optimizer; however, by letting Catalyst handle the code-generation complexity, developers can focus their valuable time on actual data processing tasks, thus making them even more efficient. After gaining an understanding of the inner workings of the Spark SQL engine, it would be useful to understand the kinds of data sources that Spark SQL can work with.

Spark SQL data sources

Since Spark DataFrame API and SQL API are both based on the same Spark SQL engine powered by the Catalyst optimizer, they also support the same set of data sources. A few prominent Spark SQL data sources are presented here.

File data source

File-based data sources such as Parquet, ORC, Delta, and so on are supported by Spark SQL out of the box, as shown in the following SQL query example:

```
SELECT * FROM delta.'/FileStore/shared_uploads/delta/retail_
features.delta' LIMIT 10;
```

In the previous SQL statement, data is directly queried from a **Delta Lake** location by simply using the delta. prefix. The same SQL construct can also be used with a Parquet file location on the data lake.

Other file types such as **JavaScript Object Notation (JSON)** and **comma-separated values (CSV)** would require first registering a table or a view with the metastore, as these files are not self-describing and lack any inherent schema information. An example of using a CSV file with Spark SQL is presented in the following SQL query:

```
CREATE OR REPLACE TEMPORARY VIEW csv_able
USING csv
OPTIONS (
  header "true",
  inferSchema "true",
  path "/FileStore/ConsolidatedCities.csv"
);
SELECT * FROM csv_able LIMIT 5;
```

In the previous SQL statement, we first create a temporary view by using a CSV file on the data lake using a CSV data source. We also use OPTIONS to specify the CSV file has a header row and to infer a schema from the file itself.

> **Note**
> A metastore is an RDBMS database where Spark SQL persists metadata information such as databases, tables, columns, and partitions.

You could also create a permanent table instead of a temporary view if the table needs to persist across cluster restarts and will be reused later.

JDBC data source

Existing RDBMS databases can also be registered with the metastore via **Java Database Connectivity (JDBC)** and used as a data source in Spark SQL. An example is presented in the following code block:

```
CREATE TEMPORARY VIEW jdbcTable
USING org.apache.spark.sql.jdbc
OPTIONS (
  url "jdbc:mysql://localhost:3306/pysparkdb",
  dbtable "authors",
```

```
  user 'username',
  password 'password'
);
SELECT * FROM resultTable;
```

In the previous code block, we create a temporary view using the `jdbc` data source and specify database connectivity options such as the database **Uniform Resource Locator (URL)**, table name, username, password, and so on.

Hive data source

Apache Hive is a data warehouse in the Hadoop ecosystem that can be used to read, write, and manage datasets on a Hadoop filesystem or a data lake using SQL. Spark SQL can be used with Apache Hive, including a Hive metastore, Hive **Serializer/Deserializer (SerDes)**, and Hive UDFs. Spark SQL supports most Hive features such as the Hive query language, Hive expressions, user-defined aggregate functions, window functions, joins, unions, sub-queries, and so on. However, features such as Hive **atomicity, consistency, isolation, durability (ACID)** table updates, Hive I/O formats, and certain Hive-specific optimizations are not supported. A full list of the supported and unsupported features can be found in Databricks' public documentation here: `https://docs.databricks.com/spark/latest/spark-sql/compatibility/hive.html`.

Now that you have gained an understanding of Spark SQL components such as the Catalyst optimizer and its data sources, we can delve into Spark SQL-specific syntax and functions.

Spark SQL language reference

Being a part of the overarching Hadoop ecosystem, Spark has traditionally been Hive-compliant. While the Hive query language diverges greatly from ANSI SQL standards, Spark 3.0 Spark SQL can be made ANSI SQL-compliant using a `spark.sql.ansi.enabled` configuration. With this configuration enabled, Spark SQL uses an ANSI SQL-compliant dialect instead of a Hive dialect.

Even with ANSI SQL compliance enabled, Spark SQL may not entirely conform to ANSI SQL dialect, and in this section, we will explore some of the prominent DDL and DML syntax of Spark SQL.

Spark SQL DDL

The syntax for creating a database and a table using Spark SQL is presented as follows:

```
CREATE DATABASE IF NOT EXISTS feature_store;
CREATE TABLE IF NOT EXISTS feature_store.retail_features
USING DELTA
LOCATION '/FileStore/shared_uploads/delta/retail_features.
delta';
```

In the previous code block, we do the following:

- First, we create a database if it doesn't already exist, using the CREATE DATABASE command. With this command, options such as the physical warehouse location on persistent storage and other database properties can also be specified as options.

- Then, we create a table using delta as the data source and specify the location of the data. Here, data at the specified location already exists, so there is no need to specify any schema information such as column names and their data types. However, to create an empty table structure, columns and their data types need to be specified.

To change certain properties of an existing table such as renaming the table, altering or dropping columns, or ammending table partition information, the ALTER command can be used, as shown in the following code sample:

```
ALTER TABLE feature_store.retail_features RENAME TO feature_
store.etailer_features;
ALTER TABLE feature_store.etailer_features ADD COLUMN (new_col
String);
```

In the previous code sample, we rename the table in the first SQL statement. The second SQL statement alters the table and adds a new column of the String type. Only changing column comments and adding new columns are supported in Spark SQL. The following code sample presents Spark SQL syntax for dropping or deleting artifacts altogether:

```
TRUNCATE TABLE feature_store.etailer_features;
DROP TABLE feature_store.etailer_features;
DROP DATABASE feature_store;
```

In the previous code sample, the TRUNCATE command deletes all the rows of the table and leaves the table structure and schema intact. The DROP TABLE command deletes the table along with its schema, and the DROP DATABASE command deletes the entire database itself.

Spark DML

Data manipulation involves adding, changing, and deleting data from tables. Some examples of this are presented in the following code statements:

```
INSERT INTO feature_store.retail_features
SELECT * FROM delta.'/FileStore/shared_uploads/delta/retail_
features.delta';
```

The previous SQL statement inserts data into an existing table using results from another SQL query. Similarly, the INSERT OVERWRITE command can be used to overwrite existing data and then load new data into a table. The following SQL statement can be used to selectively delete data from a table:

```
DELETE FROM feature_store.retail_features WHERE country_code =
'FR';
```

The previous SQL statement deletes selective data from the table based on a filter condition. Though SELECT statements are not necessary, they are quintessential in data analysis. The following SQL statement depicts the use of SELECT statements for data analysis using Spark SQL:

```
SELECT
    year AS emp_year
    max(m.last_name),
    max(m.first_name),
    avg(s.salary) AS avg_salary
FROM
    author_salary s
    JOIN mysql_authors m ON m.uid = s.id
GROUP BY year
ORDER BY s.salary DESC
```

The previous SQL statement performs an **inner join** of two tables based on a common key and calculates the average salary of each employee by year. The results of this query give insights into employee salary changes over the years and can be easily scheduled to be refreshed periodically.

This way, using the powerful distributed SQL engine of Apache Spark and its expressive Spark SQL language, you can perform complex data analysis in a fast and efficient manner without having to learn any new programming languages. A complete Spark SQL reference guide for an exhaustive list of supported data types, function libraries, and SQL syntax can be found in Apache Spark's public documentation here: `https://spark.apache.org/docs/latest/sql-ref-syntax.html`.

Though Spark SQL's **Catalyst** optimizer does most of the heavy lifting, it's useful to know a few techniques to further tune Spark SQL's performance, and a few prominent ones are presented in the following section.

Optimizing Spark SQL performance

In the previous section, you learned how the Catalyst optimizer optimizes user code by running the code through a set of optimization steps until an optimal execution plan is derived. To take advantage of the Catalyst optimizer, it is recommended to use Spark code that leverages the Spark SQL engine—that is, Spark SQL and DataFrame APIs—and avoid using RDD-based Spark code as much as possible. The Catalyst optimizer has no visibility into UDFs, thus users could end up writing sub-optimal code that might degrade performance. Thus, it is recommended to use built-in functions instead of UDFs or to define functions in Scala and Java and then use them in SQL and Python APIs.

Though Spark SQL supports file-based formats such as CSV and JSON, it is recommended to use serialized data formats such as Parquet, AVRO, and ORC. Semi-structured formats such as CSV or JSON incur performance costs, firstly during the schema inference phase, as they cannot present their schema readily to the Spark SQL engine. Secondly, they do not support any data filtering features such as **Predicate Pushdown**, thus entire files must be loaded into memory before any data can be filtered out at the source. Being inherently uncompressed file formats, CSV and JSON also consume more memory compared to binary compressed formats such as Parquet. Even traditional relational databases are preferred over using semi-structured data formats as they support Predicate Pushdown, and some data processing responsibility can be delegated down to the databases.

For iterative workloads such as ML, where the same dataset is accessed multiple times, it is useful to cache the dataset in memory so that subsequent scans of the table or DataFrame happen in memory, improving query performance greatly.

Spark comes with various **join** strategies to improve performance while joining tables, such as BROADCAST, MERGE, SHUFFLE_HASH, and so on. However, the Spark SQL engine might sometimes not be able to predict the strategy for a given query. This can be mitigated by passing in **hints** to the Spark SQL query, as shown in the following code block:

```
SELECT /*+ BROADCAST(m) */
   year AS emp_year
   max(m.last_name),
   max(m.first_name),
   avg(s.salary) AS avg_salary
FROM
   author_salary s
   JOIN mysql_authors m ON m.uid = s.id
GROUP BY year
ORDER BY s.salary DESC;
```

In the previous code block, we are passing in a **join hint** via a comment in the SELECT clause. This specifies that the smaller table is broadcasted to all the worker nodes, which should improve join performance and thus the overall query performance. Similarly, COALESCE and REPARTITION hints can also be passed to Spark SQL queries; these hints reduce the number of output files, thus improving performance.

> **Note**
> SQL hints, query hints, or optimizer hints are additions to standard SQL statements used to nudge the SQL execution engine to choose a particular physical execution plan that the developer thinks is optimal. SQL hints have traditionally been supported by all RDBMS engines and are now supported by Spark SQL as well as for certain kinds of queries, as discussed previously.

While the Catalyst optimizer does an excellent job of producing the best possible physical query execution plan, it can still be thrown off by stale statistics on the table. Starting with Spark 3.0, **Adaptive Query Execution** can be deployed to make use of runtime statistics to choose the most efficient query execution plan. Adaptive Query Execution can be enabled using a spark.sql.adaptive.enabled configuration. These are just a few of the Spark SQL performance-tuning techniques available, and detailed descriptions of each can be found in the Apache Spark public documentation here: https://spark.apache.org/docs/latest/sql-performance-tuning.html.

Summary

In this chapter, you learned about SQL as a declarative language that has been universally accepted as the language for structured data analysis because of its ease of use and expressiveness. You learned about the basic constructions of SQL, including the DDL and DML dialects of SQL. You were introduced to the Spark SQL engine as the unified distributed query engine that powers both Spark SQL and DataFrame APIs. SQL optimizers, in general, were introduced, and Spark's very own query optimizer Catalyst was also presented, along with its inner workings as to how it takes a Spark SQL query and converts it into Java JVM bytecode. A reference to the Spark SQL language was also presented, along with the most important DDL and DML statements, with examples. Finally, a few performance optimizations techniques were also discussed to help you get the best out of Spark SQL for all your data analysis needs. In the next chapter, we will extend our Spark SQL knowledge and see how external data analysis tools such as **business intelligence** (**BI**) tools and SQL analysis tools can also leverage Apache Spark's distributed SQL engine to process and visualize massive amounts of data in a fast and efficient manner.

13
Integrating External Tools with Spark SQL

Business intelligence (BI) refers to the capabilities that enable organizations to make informed, data-driven decisions. BI is a combination of data processing capabilities, data visualizations, business analytics, and a set of best practices that enable, refine, and streamline organizations' business processes by helping them in both strategic and tactical decision making. Organizations typically rely on specialist software called BI tools for their BI needs. BI tools combine strategy and technology to gather, analyze, and interpret data from various sources and provide business analytics about the past and present state of a business.

BI tools have traditionally relied on data warehouses as data sources and data processing engines. However, with the advent of big data and real-time data, BI tools have branched out to using data lakes and other new data storage and processing technologies as data sources. In this chapter, you will explore how Spark SQL can be used as a distributed **Structured Query Language (SQL)** engine for BI and SQL analysis tools via Spark Thrift **Java Database Connectivity/Open Database Connectivity (JDBC/ODBC)** Server. Spark SQL connectivity requirements with SQL analysis and BI tools will be presented, along with detailed configuration and setup steps. Finally, the chapter will also present options to connect to Spark SQL from arbitrary Python applications.

In this chapter, we're going to cover the following main topics:

- Apache Spark as a **distributed SQL engine**

- Spark connectivity to SQL analysis tools

- Spark connectivity to BI tools

- Connecting Python applications to Spark SQL using `pyodbc`

Some of the skills gained in this chapter are an understanding of Spark Thrift JDBC/ODBC Server, how to connect SQL editors and BI tools to Spark SQL via JDBC and Spark Thrift Server, and connecting business applications built using Python with a Spark SQL engine using Pyodbc.

Technical requirements

Here is what you'll need for this chapter:

- In this chapter, we will be using Databricks Community Edition to run our code (`https://community.cloud.databricks.com`). Sign-up instructions can be found at `https://databricks.com/try-databricks`.

- We will be using a free and open source SQL editor tool called **SQL Workbench/J**, which can be downloaded from `https://www.sql-workbench.eu/downloads.html`.

- You will need to download a JDBC driver for SQL Workbench/J to be able to connect with Databricks Community Edition. This can be downloaded from `https://databricks.com/spark/jdbc-drivers-download`.

- We will also be using **Tableau Online** to demonstrate BI tool integration. You can request a free 14-day Tableau Online trial at `https://www.tableau.com/products/online/request-trial`.

Apache Spark as a distributed SQL engine

One common application of SQL has been its use with BI and SQL analysis tools. These SQL-based tools connect to a **relational database management system (RDBMS)** using a JDBC or ODBC connection and traditional RDBMS JDBC/ODBC connectivity built in. In the previous chapters, you have seen that Spark SQL can be used using notebooks and intermixed with PySpark, Scala, Java, or R applications. However, Apache Spark can also double up as a powerful and fast distributed SQL engine using a JDBC/OCBC connection or via the command line.

> **Note**
>
> JDBC is a SQL-based **application programming interface (API)** used by Java applications to connect to an RDBMS. Similarly, ODBC is a SQL-based API created by Microsoft to provide RDBMS access to Windows-based applications. A JDBC/ODBC driver is a client-side software component either developed by the RDBMS vendor themselves or by a third party that can be used with external tools to connect to an RDBMS via the JDBC/ODBC standard.

In the following section, we will explore how to make use of **JDBC/ODBC** serving capabilities with Apache Spark.

Introduction to Hive Thrift JDBC/ODBC Server

While the JDBC/ODBC driver gives client-side software such as BI or SQL analytics tools the ability to connect to database servers, some server-side components are also required for the database server to utilize JDBC/ODBC standards. Most RDBMSes come built with these JDBC/ODBC serving capabilities, and Apache Spark can also be enabled with this server-side functionality using a Thrift JDBC/ODBC server.

HiveServer2 is a server-side interface developed to enable Hadoop Hive clients to execute Hive queries against Apache Hive. HiveServer2 has been developed to provide multi-client concurrency with open APIs such as JDBC and ODBC. HiveServer2 itself is based on Apache Thrift, which is a binary communication protocol used for creating services in multiple programming languages. Spark Thrift Server is Apache Spark's implementation of HiveServer2 that allows JDBC/ODBC clients to execute Spark SQL queries on Apache Spark.

Spark Thrift Server comes bundled with the Apache Spark distribution, and most Apache Spark vendors enable this service by default on their Spark clusters. In the case of Databricks, this service can be accessed from the **Clusters** page, as shown in the following screenshot:

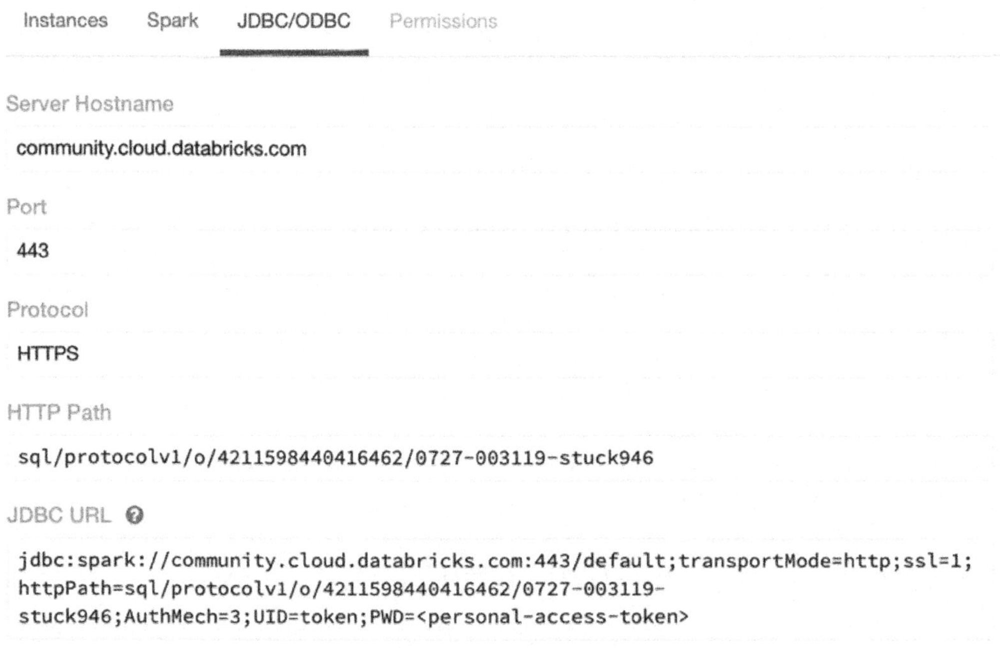

Instances   Spark   JDBC/ODBC   Permissions

Server Hostname

community.cloud.databricks.com

Port

443

Protocol

HTTPS

HTTP Path

```
sql/protocolv1/o/4211598440416462/0727-003119-stuck946
```

JDBC URL ❓

```
jdbc:spark://community.cloud.databricks.com:443/default;transportMode=http;ssl=1;
httpPath=sql/protocolv1/o/4211598440416462/0727-003119-
stuck946;AuthMech=3;UID=token;PWD=<personal-access-token>
```

Figure 13.1 – Databricks JDBC/ODBC interface

You can get to the Databricks JDBC/ODBC interface shown in the previous screenshot by navigating to the **Clusters** page within the Databricks web interface. Then, click on **Advanced Options** and then on the **JDBC/ODBC** tab. The Databricks JDBC/ODBC interface provides you with the hostname, port, protocol, the HTTP path, and the actual JDBC URL required by external tools for connectivity to the Databricks Spark cluster. In the following sections, we will explore how this Spark Thrift Server functionality can be used by external SQL-based clients to utilize Apache Spark as a distributed SQL engine.

Spark connectivity to SQL analysis tools

SQL analysis tools, as the same suggests, are tools with interfaces suited for quick and easy SQL analysis. They let you connect to an RDBMS, sometimes even multiple RDBMSes, at the same time, and browse through various databases, schemas, tables, and columns. They even help you visually analyze tables and their structure. They also have interfaces designed to perform SQL analysis quickly with multiple windows that let you browse tables and columns on one side, compose a SQL query in another window, and look at the results in another window. Once such SQL analysis tool, called **SQL Workbench/J**, is shown in the following screenshot:

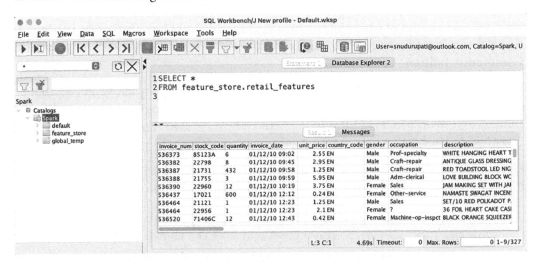

Figure 13.2 – SQL Workbench/J interface

The previous screenshot depicts the interface of **SQL Workbench/J**, which represents a typical SQL editor interface with a database, schema, table, and column browser on the left-hand side pane. The top pane has a text interface for composing actual SQL queries, and the bottom pane shows the results of executed SQL queries and has other tabs to show any error messages, and so on. There is also a menu and a toolbar on the top to establish connections to databases, toggle between various databases, execute SQL queries, browse databases, save SQL queries, browse through query history, and so on. This type of SQL analysis interface is very intuitive and comes in very handy for quick SQL analysis, as well as for building SQL-based data processing jobs, as databases, tables, and columns can easily be browsed. Tables and column names can be easily dragged and dropped into the **Query Composer** window, and results can be quickly viewed and analyzed.

There are, additionally, rather more sophisticated SQL analysis tools that also let you visualize the results of a query right within the same interface. Some open source tools to name are **Redash**, **Metabase**, and **Apache Superset**, and some cloud-native tools are **Google Data Studio**, **Amazon QuickSight**, and so on.

> **Tip**
> Redash was recently acquired by Databricks and is available to use with the Databricks paid versions; it is not available in Databricks Community Edition as of this writing.

Now you have an idea of what SQL analysis tools look like and how they work, let's look at the steps required to connect a SQL analysis tool such as **SQL Workbench/J** to **Databricks Community Edition**.

SQL Workbench/J is a free, RDBMS-independent SQL analysis tool based on Java and can be used with any operating system of your choice. Instructions on downloading and running **SQL Workbench/J** can be found here: `https://www.sql-workbench.eu/downloads.html`.

Once you have **SQL Workbench/J** set up and running on your local machine, the following steps will help you get it connected with **Databricks Community Edition**:

1. Download the Databricks JDBC driver from `https://databricks.com/spark/jdbc-drivers-download`, and store at a known location.

2. Launch **SQL Workbench/J** and open the **File** menu. Then, click on **Connect window**, to take you to the following screen:

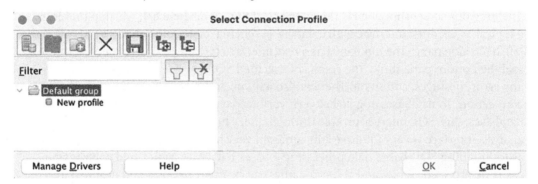

Figure 13.3 – SQL Workbench/J connect window

3. In the previous window, click on **Manage Drivers** to take you to the following screen:

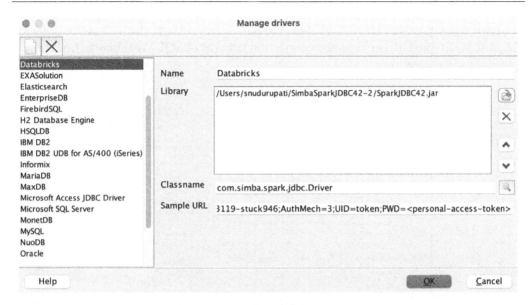

Figure 13.4 – Manage drivers screen

4. As shown in the preceding **Manage drivers** window screenshot, click on the folder icon and navigate to the folder where you stored your previously downloaded Databricks drivers and open it, then click the **OK** button.

5. Now, navigate to your Databricks **Clusters** page, click on a cluster, and navigate to **Advanced Options** and the **JDBC/ODBC** tab, as shown in the following screenshot:

Instances   Spark   JDBC/ODBC   Permissions

Server Hostname

community.cloud.databricks.com

Port

443

Protocol

HTTPS

HTTP Path

sql/protocolv1/o/4211598440416462/0727-003119-stuck946

JDBC URL ❓

jdbc:spark://community.cloud.databricks.com:443/default;transportMode=http;ssl=1;
httpPath=sql/protocolv1/o/4211598440416462/0727-003119-
stuck946;AuthMech=3;UID=token;PWD=<personal-access-token>

Figure 13.5 – Databricks cluster JDBC URL

As shown in the previous screenshot, copy the JDBC URL without the UID and PWD parts and paste it into the **URL** field on the connection window of **SQL Workbench/J**, as shown in the following screenshot:

Figure 13.6 – SQL Workbench/J connection parameters

6. After entering the required JDBC parameters from the Databricks **Clusters** page, enter your Databricks username and password in the **Username** and **Password** fields on the **SQL Workbench/J** connection window. Then, click on the **Test** button to test connectivity to the Databricks clusters. If all the connection parameters have been correctly provided, you should see a **Connection Successful** message pop up.

> **Tip**
>
> Make sure the Databricks cluster is up and running if you see any connection failures or **Host Not Found** types of errors.

This way, by following the previous steps, you can successfully connect a SQL analysis tool such as **SQL Workbench/J** to Databricks clusters and run Spark SQL queries remotely. It is also possible to connect to other Spark clusters running on other vendors' clusters—just make sure to procure the appropriate **HiveServer2** drivers directly from the vendor. Modern BI tools also recognize the importance of connecting to big data technologies and data lakes, and in the following section, we will explore how to connect BI tools with Apache Spark via a JDBC connection.

Spark connectivity to BI tools

In the era of big data and **artificial intelligence** (**AI**), Hadoop and Spark have modernized data warehouses into distributed warehouses that can process up to **petabytes** (**PB**) of data. Thus, BI tools have also evolved to utilize Hadoop- and Spark-based analytical stores as their data sources, connecting to them using JDBC/ODBC. BI tools ranging from Tableau, Looker, Sisense, MicroStrategy, Domo, and so on all feature connectivity support and built-in drivers to Apache Hive and Spark SQL. In this section, we will explore how you can connect a BI tool such as Tableau Online with Databricks Community Edition, via a JDBC connection.

Tableau Online is a BI platform fully hosted in the cloud that lets you perform data analytics, publish reports and dashboards, and create interactive visualizations, all from a web browser. The following steps describe the process of connecting Tableau Online with Databricks Community Edition:

1. If you already have an existing Tableau Online account, sign in. If not, you can request a free trial here: `https://www.tableau.com/products/online/request-trial`.

2. Once you have logged in, click on the **New** button near the top right-hand corner, as shown in the following screenshot:

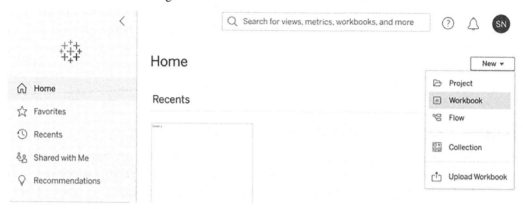

Figure 13.7 – Tableau Online new workbook

3. The newly created workbook will prompt you to **Connect to Data**. Click on the **Connectors** tab and choose **Databricks** from the list of available data sources, as shown in the following screenshot:

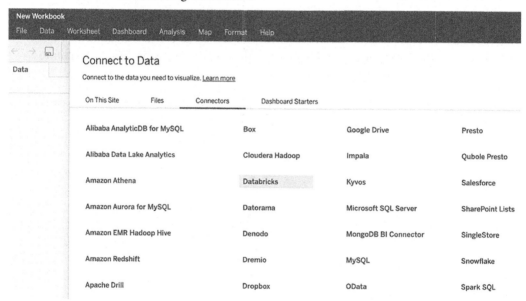

Figure 13.8 – Tableau Online data sources

4. Then, provide Databricks cluster details such as **Server Hostname**, **HTTP Path**, **Authentication**, **Username**, and **Password**, as shown in the following screenshot, and click the **Sign In** button. These details are found on the Databricks **Clusters** page:

Figure 13.9 – Tableau Online Databricks connection

5.   Once your connection is successful, your new workbook will open in the **Data Source** tab, where you can browse through your existing databases and tables, as shown in the following screenshot:

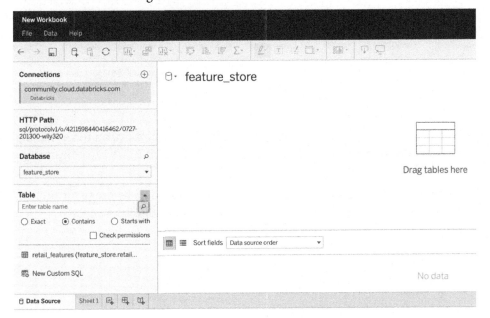

Figure 13.10 – Tableau Online data sources

6. The **Data Source** tab also lets you drag and drop tables and define relationships and joins among tables as well, as shown in the following screenshot:

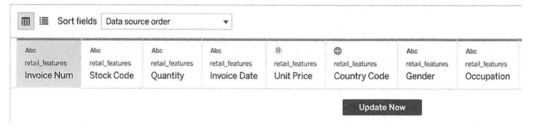

Figure 13.11 – Tableau Online: defining table joins

7. Tableau Online data sources also let you create two types of connections with the underlying data sources—a live connection that queries the underlying data sources with every request and an option to create an **Extract**, which extracts data from the data sources and stores it within Tableau. With big data sources such as Apache Spark, it is recommended to create a live connection because the amount of data being queried could be substantially larger than usual.

8. Sample data can also be browsed in the **Data Source** tab by clicking on the **Update Now** button, as shown in the following screenshot:

Abc	Abc	Abc	Abc	#	⊕	Abc	Abc
retail_features	retail_features	retail_features	retail_features	retail_features	retail_features	retail_features	retail_features
Invoice Num	Stock Code	Quantity	Invoice Date	Unit Price	Country Code	Gender	Occupation

Sort fields: Data source order

Update Now

Figure 13.12 – Tableau Online data source preview

9. Once the data source connection is established, you can move on to visualizing the data and creating reports and dashboards by clicking on `Sheet1` or by creating new additional sheets.

10. Once you are within a sheet, you can start visualizing data by dragging and dropping columns from the **Data** pane onto the blank sheet.

11. Tableau automatically chooses the appropriate visualization based on the fields selected. The visualization can also be changed using the **Visualization** drop-down selector, and data filters can be defined using the **Filters** box. Aggregations can be defined on metrics in the **Columns** field, and columns can also be defined as **Dimension**, **Attribute**, or **Metric** as required. The top menu has additional settings to sort and pivot data and has other formatting options. There are also advanced analytics options such as defining quartiles, medians, and so on available within Tableau Online. This way, using Tableau Online with its built-in Databricks connector data can be analyzed at scale using the power and efficiency of Apache Spark, along with the ease of use and **graphical user interface (GUI)** of a prominent BI tool such as Tableau Online, as shown in the following screenshot:

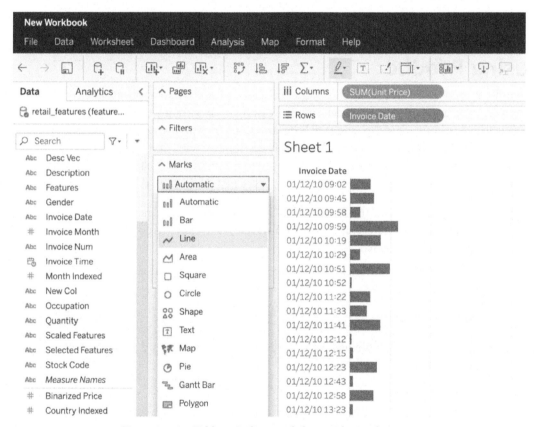

Figure 13.13 – Tableau Online worksheet with visualizations

Tableau Online is one of the many popular BI tools that support native Databricks connectivity out of the box. Modern BI tools also offer Spark SQL connectivity options for connecting to Apache Spark distributions outside of Databricks.

Connectivity to Apache Spark is not just limited to SQL analysis and BI tools. Since the JDBC protocol is based on Java and was meant to be used by Java-based applications, any applications built using **Java Virtual Machine** (**JVM**)-based programming languages such as **Java** or **Scala** can also make use of the JDBC connectivity options to Apache Spark.

But what about applications based on popular programming languages such as Python that are not based on Java? There is a way to connect these types of Python applications to Apache Spark via **Pyodbc**, and we will explore this in the following section.

Connecting Python applications to Spark SQL using Pyodbc

Pyodbc is an open source Python module for connecting Python applications to data sources using an ODBC connection. Pyodbc can be used with any of your local Python applications to connect to Apache Spark via an ODBC driver and access databases and tables defined with Apache Spark SQL. In this section, we will explore how you can connect Python running on your local machine to a Databricks cluster using **Pyodbc** with the following steps:

1. Download and install the Simba ODBC driver provided by Databricks on your local machine from here: `https://databricks.com/spark/odbc-drivers-download`.

2. Install Pyodbc on your local machine's Python using `pip`, as shown in the following command:

    ```
    sudo pip install pyodbc
    ```

3. Create a new Python file using a text editor of your choice and paste the following code into it:

    ```
    import pyodbc
    odbc_conn = pyodbc.connect("Driver /Library/simba/spark/
    lib/libsparkodbc_sbu.dylib;" +
                    "HOST=community.cloud.databricks.
    com;" +
                    "PORT=443;" +
                    "Schema=default;" +
    ```

```
                       "SparkServerType=3;" +
                       "AuthMech=3;" +
                       "UID=username;" +
                       "PWD=password;" +
                       "ThriftTransport=2;" +
                       "SSL=1;" +
                       "HTTPPath= sql/protocolv1/
   o/4211598440416462/0727-201300-wily320",
                       autocommit=True)
cursor = odbc_conn.cursor()
cursor.execute(f"SELECT * FROM retail_features LIMIT 5")
for row in cursor.fetchall():
   print(row)
```

4. The driver paths for the previous code configuration may vary based on your operating systems and are given as follows:

```
macOS: /Library/simba/spark/lib/libsparkodbc_sbu.dylib
Linux 64-bit: /opt/simba/spark/lib/64/libsparkodbc_sb64.
so
Linux 32-bit: /opt/simba/spark/lib/32/libsparkodbc_sb32.
so
```

5. The values for hostname, port, and the HTTP path can be obtained from your Databricks cluster **JDBC/ODBC** tab.

6. Once you have added all the code and put in the appropriate configuration values, save the Python code file and name it pyodbc-databricks.py.

7. You can now execute the code from your Python interpreter using the following command:

```
python pyodbd-databricks.py
```

8. Once the code runs successfully, the first five rows of the table you specified in your SQL query will be displayed on the console.

> **Note**
> Instructions on configuring the ODBC driver on a Microsoft Windows machine to be used with Pyodbc can be found on the Databricks public documentation page here: `https://docs.databricks.com/dev-tools/pyodbc.html#windows`.

This way, using **Pyodbc**, you can integrate Apache Spark SQL into any of your Python applications that may be running locally on your machine or some remote machine in the cloud or a data center somewhere, but still take advantage of the fast and powerful distributed SQL engine that comes with Apache Spark.

Summary

In this chapter, you have explored how you can take advantage of Apache Spark's Thrift server to enable JDBC/ODBC connectivity and use Apache Spark as a distributed SQL engine. You learned how the HiveServer2 service allows external tools to connect to Apache Hive using JDBC/ODBC standards and how Spark Thrift Server extends HiveServer2 to enable similar functionality on Apache Spark clusters. Steps required for connecting SQL analysis tools such as SQL Workbench/J were presented in this chapter, along with detailed instructions required for connecting BI tools such as Tableau Online with Spark clusters. Finally, steps required for connecting arbitrary Python applications, either locally on your machine or on remote servers in the cloud or a data center, to Spark clusters using Pyodbc were also presented. In the following and final chapter of this book, we will explore the Lakehouse paradigm that can help organizations seamlessly cater to all three workloads of data analytics—data engineering, data science, and SQL analysis—using a single unified distributed and persistent storage layer that combines the best features of both data warehouses and data lakes.

14
The Data Lakehouse

Throughout this book, you have encountered two primary data analytics use cases: descriptive analytics, which includes BI and SQL analytics, and advanced analytics, which includes data science and machine learning. You learned how Apache Spark, as a unified data analytics platform, can cater to all these use cases. Apache Spark, being a computational platform, is data storage-agnostic and can work with any traditional storage mechanisms, such as databases and data warehouses, and modern distributed data storage systems, such as data lakes. However, traditional descriptive analytics tools, such as BI tools, are designed around data warehouses and expect data to be presented in a certain way. Modern advanced analytics and data science tools are geared toward working with large amounts of data that can easily be accessed on data lakes. It is also not practical or cost-effective to store redundant data in separate storage to be able to cater to these individual use cases.

This chapter will present a new paradigm called the **data lakehouse**, which tries to overcome the limitations of data warehouses and data lakes and bridge the gap by combining the best elements of both.

The following topics will be covered in this chapter:

- Moving from BI to AI
- The data lakehouse paradigm
- Advantages of data lakehouses

By the end of this chapter, you will have learned about the key challenges of existing data storage architectures, such as data warehouses and data lakes, and how a data lakehouse helps bridge this gap. You will gain an understanding of the core requirements of a data lakehouse and its reference architecture, as well as explore a few existing and commercially available data lakehouses and their limitations. Finally, you will learn about the reference architecture for the data lakehouse, which makes use of Apache Spark and Delta Lake, as well as some of their advantages.

Moving from BI to AI

Business intelligence (**BI**) remains the staple of data analytics. In BI, organizations collect raw transactional from a myriad of data sources and ETL it into a format that is conducive for building operational reports and enterprise dashboards, which depict the overall enterprise over a past period. This also helps business executives make informed decisions on the future strategy of an organization. However, if the amount of transactional data that's been generated has increased by several orders of magnitude, it is difficult (if not impossible) to surface relevant and timely insights that can help businesses make decisions. Moreover, it is also not sufficient to just rely on structured transactional data for business decision-making. Instead, new types of unstructured data, such as customer feedback in the form of natural language, voice transcripts from a customer service center, and videos and images of products and customer reviews need to be considered if you wish to understand the current state of a business, the state of the market, and customer and social trends for businesses to stay relevant and profitable. Thus, you must move on from traditional BI and decision support systems and supplement the operational reports and executive dashboards with predictive analytics, if not completely replace **BI** with **artificial intelligence** (**AI**). Traditional BI and data warehouse tools completely fall apart when catering to AI use cases. This will be explored in more detail in the next few sections.

Challenges with data warehouses

Traditionally, data warehouses have been the primary data sources of BI tools. Data warehouses expect data to be transformed and stored in a predefined schema that makes it easy for BI tools to query it. BI tools have evolved to take advantage of data warehouses, which makes the process very efficient and performant. The following diagram represents the typical reference architecture of a **BI and DW** system:

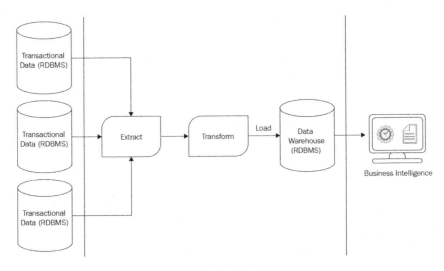

Figure 14.1 – BI and DW architecture

As shown in the preceding diagram, a **BI and DW** system extracts raw transactional data from transactional systems, transforms the data according to a schema that has been defined by the data warehouse, and then loads the data into the data warehouse. This entire process is scheduled to be run periodically, typically nightly. Modern ETL and data warehouse systems have also evolved to support data loads more frequently, such as hourly. However, there are a few key drawbacks to this approach that limit these systems from truly supporting modern AI use cases. They are as follows:

- The compute and storage of traditional data warehouses are typically located on-premises on a single server machine. Their capacity is generally planned for peak workloads as the storage and compute capacity of such databases is tied to the machine or server they are running on. They cannot be scaled easily, if at all. This means that traditional on-premises data warehouses have their data capacity set and cannot handle the rapid influx of data that big data typically brings on. This makes their architecture rigid and not future-proof.

- Data warehouses were designed to only be loaded periodically, and almost all traditional data warehouses were not designed to handle real-time data ingestion. This means data analysts and business executives working off such data warehouses usually only get to work on stale data, delaying their decision-making process.

- Finally, data warehouses are based on relational databases, which, in turn, cannot handle unstructured data such as video, audio, or natural language. This makes them incapable of expanding to cater to advanced analytics use cases such as data science, machine learning, or AI.

To overcome the aforementioned shortcomings of data warehouses, especially the inability to separate compute and storage, and thus the inability to scale on-demand and their shortcomings with dealing with real-time and unstructured data, enterprises have moved toward data lake architectures. These were first introduced by the **Hadoop** ecosystem. We will look at this in more detail in the following sections.

Challenges with data lakes

Data lakes are low-cost storage systems with filesystem-like APIs that can hold any form of data, whether it's structured or unstructured, such as the **Hadoop Distributed File System (HDFS)**. Enterprises adopted the data lake paradigm to solve the scalability and segregation of compute and storage. With the advent of big data and Hadoop, the first HDFS was adopted as data lakes were being stored in generic and open file formats such as Apache Parquet and ORC. With the advent of the cloud, object stores such as Amazon S3, Microsoft Azure ADLS, and Google Cloud Storage were adopted as data lakes. These are very inexpensive and allow us to automatically archive data.

While data lakes are highly scalable, relatively inexpensive, and can support a myriad of data and file types, they do not conform to the strict schema-on-write requirements of BI tools. Thus, the cloud-based data lake architecture was supplemented with an additional layer of cloud-based data warehouses to specifically cater to BI use cases. The architecture of a typical decision support system in the cloud is shown in the following diagram:

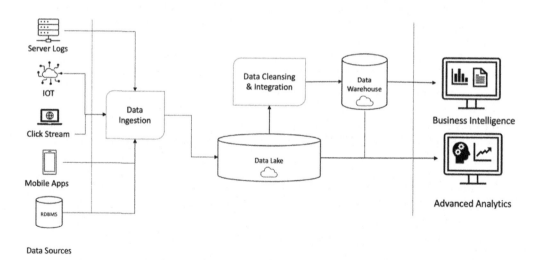

Figure 14.2 – Data lake architecture in the cloud

In the previous diagram, we can see a typical data lake architecture in the cloud. First, raw data is ingested into the data lake as is, without any transformations applied, in a streaming or fashionable manner. The raw data is then ELTed and put back into the data lake for consumption by downstream use cases such as data science, machine learning, and AI. Part of the data that's required for BI and operational reporting is cleaned, integrated, and loaded into a cloud-based data warehouse to be consumed by BI tools. This architecture solves all the issues of a traditional data warehouse. Data lakes are infinitely scalable and completely independent of any compute. This is because compute is only required while either ingesting, transforming, or consuming data. Data lakes can also handle different data types, ranging from structured and semi-structured data to unstructured data.

However, the data lake architecture does present a few key challenges:

- Data lakes do not possess any built-in transactional controls or data quality checks, so data engineers need to build additional code into their data processing pipelines to perform transactional control. This helps ensure the data is consistent and of the right quality for downstream consumption.

- Data lakes can store data in structured files such as Parquet and ORC; however, traditional BI tools may not be capable of reading data in such files, so another layer of a data warehouse must be introduced to cater to these use cases. This introduces an additional layer of complexity as two separate data processing pipelines need to exist – one for ELTing the data to be used by advanced analytics use cases, and another for ETLing the data into the data warehouse. This also increases the operational costs as data storage almost doubles and two separate data storage systems need to be managed.

- While raw data could be streamed into the warehouse, it may not be readily available for downstream business analytics systems until the raw data has been ETLed into the data warehouse, presenting stale data to business users and data analysts, thereby delaying their decision-making process.

The data lakehouse promises to overcome such challenges that are faced by traditional data warehouses, as well as modern data lakes, and help bring the best elements of both to end users. We will explore the data lakehouse paradigm in detail in the following section.

The data lakehouse paradigm

The data lakehouse paradigm combines the best aspects of the data warehouse with those of the data lake. A data lakehouse is based on open standards and implements data structures and data management features such as data warehouses. This paradigm also uses data lakes for its cost-effective and scalable data storage. By combining the best of both data warehousing and data lakes, data lakehouses cater to data analysts and data scientists simultaneously, without having to maintain multiple systems or having to maintain redundant copies of data. Data lakehouses help accelerate data projects as teams access data in a single place, without needing to access multiple systems. Data lakehouses also provide access to the freshest data, which is complete and up to date so that it can be used in BI, data science, machine learning, and AI projects. Though data lakehouses are based on data lakes such as cloud-based object stores, they need to adhere to certain requirements, as described in the following section.

Key requirements of a data lakehouse

A data lakehouse needs to satisfy a few key requirements for it to be able to provide the structure and data management capabilities of a data warehouse, as well as the scalability and ability to work with the unstructured data of a data lake. The following are some key requirements that must be taken into consideration:

- A data lakehouse needs to be able to support **ACID** transactions to ensure data reads for SQL queries. In a data lakehouse, multiple data pipelines could be writing and reading data from the same dataset, and support for transactions guarantees that data readers and writers never have an inconsistent view of data.

- A data lakehouse should be able to decouple compute from storage to make sure that one can scale independently of the other. Not only does it make the data lakehouse more economical but it also helps support concurrent users using multiple clusters and very large datasets.

- A data lakehouse needs to be based on open standards. This allows a variety of tools, APIs, and libraries to be able to access the data lakehouse directly and prevents any sort of expensive vendor or data lock-ins.

- To be able to support structured data and data models such as **Star/Snowflake** schemas from the data warehousing world, a data lakehouse must be able to support schema enforcement and evolution. The data lakehouse should support mechanisms for managing data integrity, governance, and auditing.

- Support for a variety of data types, including structured and unstructured data types, is required as a data lakehouse can be used to store, analyze, and process data, ranging from text, transactions, IoT data, and natural language to audio transcripts and video files.

- Support for traditional structured data analysis such as BI and SQL analytics, as well as advanced analytics workloads including data science, machine learning, and AI, is required. A data lakehouse should be able to directly support BI and data discovery by supporting SQL standard connectivity over **JDBC/ODBC**.

- A data lakehouse should be able to support end-to-end stream processing, starting from the ability to ingest real-time data directly into the data lakehouse, to real-time ELT of data and real-time business analytics. The data lakehouse should also support real-time machine learning and low-latency machine learning inference in real time.

Now that you understand the key requirements of a data lakehouse, let's try to understand its core components and reference architecture.

Data lakehouse architecture

Data lakehouse features such as scalability, the ability to handle unstructured data, and being able to segregate storage and compute are afforded by the underlying data lakes that are used for persistent storage. However, a few core components are required to provide data warehouse-like functionality, such as **ACID** transactions, indexes, data governance and audits, and other data-level optimizations. A scalable metadata layer is one of the core components. A metadata layer sits on top of open file formats such as Apache Parquet and helps keep track of file and table versions and features such as ACID transactions. The metadata layer also enables features such as streaming data ingestion, schema enforcement, and evolution, and enforcing data validation.

Based on these core components, a reference data lakehouse architecture has been produced, as shown in the following diagram:

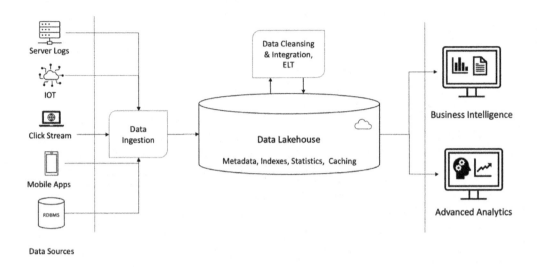

Figure 14.3 – Data lakehouse architecture

Data lakehouses are built on top of inexpensive cloud-based storage, which does not offer very high throughput data access. To be able to cater to low latency and highly concurrent use cases, a data lakehouse needs to be able to provide speedy data access via features such as data skipping indexes, folder- and file-level pruning, and the ability to collect and store table and file statistics to help the query execution engine derive an optimal query execution plan. The data lakehouse should possess a high-speed data caching layer to speed up data access for frequently accessed data.

Examples of existing lakehouse architectures

A few commercially available cloud-based offerings do satisfy the requirements of a data lakehouse to some extent, if not completely. Some of them are listed in this section.

Amazon Athena is an interactive query service provided by AWS as part of its managed services. AWS is backed by the open source scalable query engine Presto and lets you query data residing in S3 buckets. It supports a metadata layer that's backed by Hive and lets you create table schema definitions. However, query engines such as Athena cannot solve all the problems of data lakes and data warehouses. They still lack basic data management features such as ACID transactions and performance improvement features such as indexes and caching.

The cloud-based commercial data warehouses known as Snowflake come a close second as it offers all the features of a traditional data warehouse, along with more advanced features that support artificial intelligence, machine learning, and data science. It combines data warehouses, subject-specific data marts, and data lakes into a single version of the truth that can power multiple workloads, including traditional analytics and advanced analytics. However, Snowflake does not provide data management features; data is stored within its storage system and it doesn't provide the same features for data stored in data lakes. Snowflake might also not be a good fit for large-scale ML projects as the data would need to be streamed into a data lake.

Google BigQuery, the petabyte-scale, real-time data warehousing solution, offers almost all the features that a data lakehouse does. It supports simultaneous batch and streaming workloads, as well as ML workloads using SQL- and query-like language via its BigQuery ML offering, which even supports AutoML. However, even BigQuery requires data to be stored in its internal format, and it doesn't provide all the query performance-boosting features for external data stored in data lakes. In the following section, we will explore how we can leverage Apache Spark, along with Delta Lake and cloud-based data lakes, as a data lakehouse.

Apache Spark-based data lakehouse architecture

Apache Spark, when combined with Delta Lake and cloud-based data lakes, satisfies almost all the requirements of a data lakehouse. We will explore this, along with an Apache Spark-based reference architecture, in this section. Let's get started:

- Delta Lake, via its transaction logs, fully supports ACID transactions, similar to a traditional data warehouse, to ensure data that's written to Delta Lake is consistent and that any downstream readers never read any dirty data. This also allows multiple reads to occur and writes data to the same dataset from multiple Spark clusters, without compromising the integrity of the dataset.

- Apache Spark has always been data storage-agnostic and can read data from a myriad of data sources, This includes reading data into memory so that it can be processed and then writing to the results to persistent storage. Thus, Apache Spark, when coupled with a distributed, persistent storage system such as a cloud-based data lake, fully supports decoupling storage and compute.

- Apache Spark supports multiple ways of accessing data stored within Delta Lake, including direct access using Spark's Java, Scala, PySpark, and SparkR APIs. Apache Spark also supports JDBC/ODBC connectivity via Spark ThriftServer for BI tool connectivity. Delta Lake also supports plain Java APIs for connectivity outside of Apache Spark.

- Delta Lake supports its own built-in metadata layer via its transaction log. Transaction logs provide Delta Lake with version control, an audit trail of table changes, and Time Travel to be able to traverse between various versions of a table, as well as the ability to restore any snapshot of the table at a given point in time.

- Both Apache Spark and Delta Lake support all types of structured and unstructured data. Moreover, Delta Lake supports schema enforcement, along with support and schema evolution.

- Apache Spark has support for real-time analytics via Structured Streaming, and Delta Lake fully supports simultaneous batch and streaming.

Thus, Apache Spark, along with Delta Lake coupled with cloud-based data lakes, supports in-memory data caching and performance improvement features such as data-skipping indexes and collecting table and file statistics. This combination makes for a great candidate for a data lakehouse.

> **Note**
>
> Spark Structured Streaming only supports micro-batch-based streaming and doesn't support event processing. Also, Apache Spark and Delta Lake together make SQL query performance very fast. However, Spark's inherent JVM scheduling delays still introduce a considerable delta in query processing times, making it unsuitable for ultra-low latency queries. Moreover, Apache Spark can support concurrent users via multiple clusters and by tuning certain Spark cluster parameters, though this complexity needs to be managed by the user. These reasons make Apache Spark, despite being used with Delta Lake, not suitable for very high concurrency, ultra-low latency use cases. Databricks has developed a next-generation query processing engine named Photon that can overcome these issues of open source Spark. However, Databricks has not released Photon for open source Apache Spark at the time of writing.

Now that you have seen how Apache Spark and Delta Lake can work together as a data lakehouse, let's see what that reference architecture looks like:

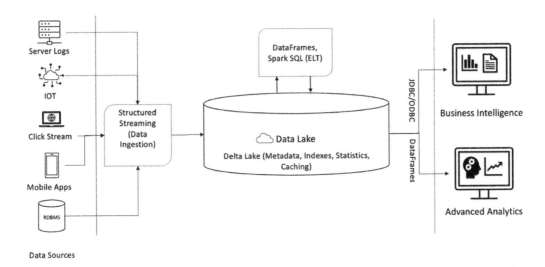

Figure 14.4 – Data lakehouse powered by Apache Spark and Delta Lake

The preceding diagram shows a data lakehouse architecture using Apache Spark and Delta Lake. Here, data ingestion can be done in real time or batch using Structured Streaming, via regular Spark batch jobs, or using some third-party data integration tool. Raw data from various sources, such as transactional databases, IoT data, clickstream data, server logs, and so on, is directly streamed into the data lakehouse and stored in Delta file format. Then, that raw data is transformed using Apache Spark DataFrame APIs or using Spark SQL. Again, this can be accomplished in either batch or streaming fashion using Structured Streaming. Table metadata, indexes, and statistics all are handled by Delta Lake transaction logs, and Hive can be used as the metastore. BI and SQL analytics tools can consume the data in the data lakehouse directly using JDBC/ODBC connections, and advanced analytics tools and libraries can directly interface with the data in the lakehouse using Spark SQL or DataFrame APIs vis the Spark clusters. This way, the combination of Apache Spark and Delta Lake within the cloud, with object stores as data lakes, can be used to implement the data lakehouse paradigm. Now that we have implemented a reference Data Lakehouse architecture, let's understand some of its advantages.

Advantages of data lakehouses

Data lakehouses address most of the challenges of using data warehouses and data lakes. Some advantages of using data lakehouses are that they reduce data redundancies, which are caused by two-tier systems such as a data lake along with a data warehouse in the cloud. This translates to reduced storage costs and simplified maintenance and data governance as any data governance features, such as access control and audit logging, can be implemented in a single place. This eliminates the operational overhead of managing data governance on multiple tools.

You should have all the data in a single storage system so that you have simplified data processing and ETL architectures, which also means easier to maintain and manage pipelines. Data engineers do not need to maintain separate code bases for disparate systems, and this greatly helps in reducing errors in data pipelines. It also makes it easier to track data lineage and fix data issues when they are identified.

Data lakehouses provide data analysts, business executives, and data scientists with direct access to the most recent data in the lakehouse. This reduces their dependence on IT teams for data access and helps them with timely and informed decision-making. Data lakehouses ultimately reduce the total cost of ownership as they eliminate data redundancy, reduce operational overhead, and provide performant data processing and storage systems at a fraction of the cost compared to certain commercially available specialist data warehouses.

Despite all the advantages offered by data lakehouses, the technology is still nascent, so it might lag behind certain purpose-built products that have had decades of research and development behind them. As the technology matures, data lakehouses will become more performant and offer connectivity to more common workflows and tools, while still being simple to use and cost-effective.

Summary

In this chapter, you saw the challenges that are faced by data warehouses and data lakes in designing and implementing large-scale data processing systems that deal with large-scale data. We also looked at the need for businesses to move from advanced analytics to simple descriptive analytics and how the existing systems cannot solve both problems simultaneously. Then, the data lakehouse paradigm was introduced, which solves the challenges of both data warehouses and data lakes and how it bridges the gap of both systems by combining the best elements from both. The reference architecture for data lakehouses was presented and a few data lakehouse candidates were presented from existing commercially available, large-scale data processing systems, along with their drawbacks. Next, an Apache Spark-based data lakehouse architecture was presented that made use of the Delta Lake and cloud-based data lakes. Finally, some advantages of data lakehouses were presented, along with a few of their shortcomings.

Other Books You May Enjoy

If you enjoyed this book, you may be interested in these other books by Packt:

Interactive Dashboards and Data Apps with Plotly and Dash

Elias Dabbas

ISBN: 9781800568914

- Find out how to run a fully interactive and easy-to-use app
- Convert your charts to various formats including images and HTML files
- Use Plotly Express and the grammar of graphics for easily mapping data to various visual attributes
- Create different chart types, such as bar charts, scatter plots, histograms, maps, and more
- Expand your app by creating dynamic pages that generate content based on URLs
- Implement new callbacks to manage charts based on URLs and vice versa

Hands-On Data Analysis with Pandas - Second Edition

Stefanie Molin

ISBN: 9781800563452

- Understand how data analysts and scientists gather and analyze data
- Perform data analysis and data wrangling using Python
- Combine, group, and aggregate data from multiple sources
- Create data visualizations with pandas, matplotlib, and seaborn
- Apply machine learning algorithms to identify patterns and make predictions
- Use Python data science libraries to analyze real-world datasets
- Solve common data representation and analysis problems using pandas
- Build Python scripts, modules, and packages for reusable analysis code

Packt is searching for authors like you

If you're interested in becoming an author for Packt, please visit `authors.packtpub.com` and apply today. We have worked with thousands of developers and tech professionals, just like you, to help them share their insight with the global tech community. You can make a general application, apply for a specific hot topic that we are recruiting an author for, or submit your own idea.

Share your thoughts

Now you've finished *Essential PySpark for Scalable Data Analytics*, we'd love to hear your thoughts! Scan the QR code below to go straight to the Amazon review page for this book and share your feedback or leave a review on the site that you purchased it from.

`https://packt.link/r/1-800-56887-8`

Your review is important to us and the tech community and will help us make sure we're delivering excellent quality content.

Index

A

accuracy metrics 119
ACID transactions 276, 277
Adaptive Query Execution 35
ADLS 27
Altair 234
alternating least squares
  used, for collaborative filtering 181, 182
Amazon Athena 278
Amazon QuickSight 260
American National Standards
    Institute (ANSI) 243
analytical data stores
  building, with cloud data lakes 58
Apache Airflow 43
Apache Arrow 216
Apache Hive 249
Apache Hive compatibility
  reference link 249
Apache Kafka 25
Apache Parquet 37
Apache Spark
  about 8, 9, 27, 32, 39, 148
  as distributed SQL engine 257
  Distributed Computing 8
Apache Spark 1.3 245

Apache Spark 3.0
  features 20
Apache Spark, and Delta Lake
  as data lakehouse 280
Apache Spark-based data lakehouse
    architecture 279, 280
Apache Spark Cluster
  architecture 11
  Cluster Manager 12
  Spark Driver 11
  Spark Executors 12
  working with 12-15
Apache Superset 260
application programming
    interface (API) 257
arbitrary Python code
  scaling out, with pandas UDF 216
arbitrary updates and deletes
  in data lakes, with Delta Lake 68-71
artificial intelligence (AI) 263, 272
association 120
association rules
  about 180
  building, with machine learning 180
assortment optimization 184
Autoscaling 43

AWS S3 27
AWS Sagemaker 203
Azure Blob 27
Azure ML 203

B

batch inferencing
  with offline feature store 144, 145
Batch Layer 49, 50
batch processing
  about 39
  data ingestion pipelines, building in 39
  data ingestion, using 39
  unifying, with Delta Lake 73
  unifying, with Lambda Architecture 48
batch processing, types
  full data load 40
  incremental data load 40-43
BI and DW architecture 272, 273
binary classification
  about 159
  implementing, with decision trees 161
  implementing, with logistic
    regression 159, 160
bisecting K-means
  using, for hierarchical
    clustering 177, 178
bronze data 85
business intelligence (BI) 272
business intelligence tools 223

C

CAP theorem 59
Catalyst 16, 246
Catalyst optimizer 246, 247

categorical variable
  transforming, into vector with
    OneHotEncoder 139
categorical variables
  encoding 138
  transforming 136
central processing unit (CPU) 246
Change Data Capture (CDC) 62, 102-105
checkpointing 44
classification 158
classification models
  training, with gradient boosted
    trees 168, 169
classification models, applications
  email spam detection 171
  financial fraud detection 171
  industrial machinery and equipment,
    failure prediction 171
  object detection 171
cloud-based data lakes
  advantages 31
cloud data lakes
  challenges 58-62
  challenges, overcoming
    with Delta Lake 62
  used, for building analytical
    data stores 58
clustering
  about 120
  using, with machine learning 175
clustering applications
  customer churn analysis 184
  customer segmentation 183
  insurance fraud detection 185
  retail assortment optimization 184
clustering techniques
  hierarchical clustering 177, 178
  K-means 175-177

Cluster Manager 43
collaborative filtering
  with alternating least squares 181, 182
columnar storage
  about 245
  versus row-based storage 244, 245
comma-separated values (CSV) 248
commits 65
Community Edition of Databricks 12
Continuous Delivery for Machine
    Learning (CD4ML) 203, 204
continuous integration and continuous
    delivery (CI/CD) 204
continuous variables
  transforming 139
cost per acquisition (CPA) 183
crontab 43
cross-validation 119, 192, 196, 214
customer churn models 121
customer churn rate 184
customer lifetime value (CLV) 170
customer lifetime value estimation 170
customer lifetime value models 121
customer segmentation 183

D

data
  cleaning 55
  consolidating, with ETL 74-78
  de-duplicating 82, 83
  extracting, from operational systems 55
  ingesting, from data sources 25
  ingesting, from file-based
      data sources 27, 28
  ingesting, from message queues 28, 29
  ingesting, from relational
      data sources 26
  ingesting, into data lakes 31
  ingesting, into data sinks 30
  ingesting, into data warehouses 30, 31
  ingesting, into in-memory data stores 32
  ingesting, into NoSQL data store 32
  integrating 55
  integrating, with data federation 79, 80
  integrating, with data virtualization
      techniques 79
  loading, into data warehouse 56
  selecting, to eliminate redundancies 82
  transforming 55
Databricks Community Edition
  about 224
  SQL Workbench/J, connecting
      to 260-262
  Tableau Online, connecting to 264-266
Databricks Filesystem (DBFS) 28, 194
Databricks JDBC/ODBC interface 258
Databricks public documentation
  reference link 270
Databricks Runtime 217
data cleansing
  about 78, 81, 128
  used, for making raw data
      analytics-ready 81
Data Definition Language (DDL) 242, 243
data federation 79
DataFrames
  about 246
  big data processing 15
data ingestion
  with batch processing 39
data ingestion, in real time
  with structured streaming 43
data ingestion pipelines
  building, in batch processing 39
  building, in real time 39

data integration
  about 74
  used, for consolidating data 74
data lakehouse architecture 277, 278
data lakehouse paradigm 276
data lakehouses
  advantages 282
  requisites 276, 277
data lake reliability
  improving, with Delta Lake 65
data lakes
  about 25, 245
  challenges 274, 275
  data reliability challenges 59-61
  file formats, using for data storage 33
data manipulation 129
Data Manipulation Language
    (DML) 242-244
Data Munging 127
Data Parallel Processing
  about 5, 213
  with MapReduce paradigm 6, 7
  with RDDs 9
Data Parallel Processing, issues
  Map stage 6
  Reduce stage 6
  Shuffle stage 6
data partitioning
  about 38, 86
  ELT processing performance,
    optimizing 86, 87
data preparation 127
data preprocessing 127, 128
data sinks 30
Data Sources 29
data standardization 84, 85
data, transforming with Spark DataFrames
  actions 17

lazy evaluation 17, 18
  transformations 16
data virtualization
  about 79
  advantages 79
  disadvantages 79
data virtualization techniques
  used, for integrating data 79
data visualization 222
data visualization techniques
  with PySpark 224
data visualization tools, types
  about 222
  Business intelligence tools 223
  notebooks 224
  observability tools 223
data warehouses
  about 30, 245
  challenges 272, 273
  data, loading into 56
data warehousing 74
data wrangling
  with Apache Spark 127
  with MLLib 127
date variables
  transforming 140
decision trees
  about 156, 228
  used, for implementing binary
    classification 161
  used, for implementing linear
    regression 157
Deep Learning 120
Delta
  as offline feature store 145
Delta Lake
  about 50, 63, 148, 155, 248, 279, 280

arbitrary updates and deletes,
    in data lakes 68-71
schema enforcement 145
schema evolution 145
schema evolution support 67, 68
streaming workloads 146
support for simultaneous batch 146
Time Travel 71, 72, 146
used, for enabling schema
    validation 66, 67
used, for simplifying Lambda
    Architecture 98-102
used, for unifying batch processing 73
used, for unifying streams processing 73
Delta Lake, integrating
  with machine learning
    operations tools 146, 147
Delta tables
  metadata 145
  structure 145
Delta transaction log 63-71
demand forecasting 121
deserialization 216
DevOps engineers 223
dimensionality reduction
  about 182
  reference link 182
Dimensional Modeling 20, 30
discrete variables
  encoding 138
Distributed Computing
  about 4, 5, 28, 213
  with Apache Spark 8
distributed hyperparameter
    tuning 214, 216
Domain Specific Language (DSL) 16

dynamic file pruning
  reference link 88
dynamic price optimization 170
dynamic pricing 170

E

ELT processing performance
  optimizing, with data partitioning 86, 87
email spam detection 171
embarrassingly parallel computing
  used, for model training 213
embarrassingly parallel processing 123
Enterprise Decision Support
    System (Enterprise DSS)
  about 24, 91
  architecture 25
Estimator 126, 135
event time 106
experiments
  tracking, with MLflow 191-197
exploratory data analysis
  about 208
  with pandas 209
  with PySpark 210
external table 100
Extract, Load, and Transform (ELT)
  about 54, 56, 57
  advantages 58
Extract, Transform, Load (ETL)
  about 54, 55
  advantages 56
  disadvantages 56
  used, for consolidating data 74-78

F

feature extraction 133-136
features
  about 133, 154, 158
  assembling, into feature vector 140, 141
feature scaling 141
feature selection 142, 143
feature store
  about 144, 155
  as central feature repository 143, 144
feature transformation 136
feature vector 126
file-based data sources
  about 27
  data, ingesting from 27, 28
file data source 247, 248
file formats
  used, for data storage in data lakes 33
financial fraud detection 122, 171
full data load 40

G

Gaussian mixture model (GSM) 179, 180
gold data 85
Google BigQuery 279
Google Cloud AI 203
Google Data Studio 260
gradient boosted trees
  about 167
  used, for training classification
    models 168, 169
  used, for training regression
    models 167, 168
Grafana 223
GraphFrames 246
graphical user interface (GUI) 267

grid search 214
grouped pandas UDFs
  about 216
  reference link 216

H

Hadoop Distributed File System
    (HDFS) 27, 274
hierarchical clustering
  about 177
  with bisecting K-means 177, 178
higher-order functions 10
histograms 227
HIVE 70
Hive data source 249
HiveServer2 257, 263
Hive Thrift JDBC/ODBC Server 257
HTML
  used, in interactive visuals 229, 230
hyperparameters 119, 135
hyperparameter tuning 123, 198, 214

I

IBM Cognos 223
incremental data load 40-43
inferencing 144
information extraction
  with natural language processing 122
in-memory databases
  about 32
  for ultra-low latency analytics 33
in-memory data stores
  data, ingesting into 32
inner join 252
input/output (I/O) 246
interactive visuals

with HTML 229, 230
with JavaScript 229, 230
Internet of Things (IoT) 97

J

Java 246
Java Database Connectivity (JDBC) 248
JavaScript
  used, in interactive visuals 229, 230
JavaScript Object Notation (JSON) 248
Java virtual machine (JVM) 247, 268
JDBC data source 248
JDBC/ODBC 277
Job Scheduler 43
join hint 253
joins 244, 253
Jupyter notebooks 224

K

Kafka 29
Key Performance Indicators (KPIs) 223
K-means clustering 175-177
Koalas
  used, for upgrading pandas
    to PySpark 217, 218

L

Label 119, 154, 158
lakehouse architectures
  examples 278, 279
Lambda Architecture
  about 48, 61, 98
  simplifying, with Delta Lake 98-102
  used, for unifying batch processing 48
  used, for unifying real time 48

Lambda Architecture, components
  Batch layer 49
  Serving layer 50
  Speed layer 49
lambda functions 10
late-arriving data
  about 105, 106
  handling 106
  stateful streams processing,
    with watermarking 106
  stateful streams processing,
    with windowing 106
latent Dirichlet allocation (LDA)
  about 178
  used, for topic modeling 178, 179
linear regression
  about 155
  implementing, with decision trees 157
  implementing, with Spark
    MLlib 155, 156
logistic regression
  about 158
  used, for implementing binary
    classification 159, 160
Looker 223

M

Machine Learning
  about 118
  scaling 123
  used, for building association rules 180
machine learning life cycle 188-190
machine learning operations tools
  Delta Lake, integrating with 146, 147
machine learning process 132, 133
machine learning visualizations
  reference link 229

MapReduce paradigm
  used, for Data Parallel Processing 6, 7
market basket analysis 122, 182
Matplotlib 231
Memcached 33, 93
message queues
  about 25, 28
  data, ingesting from 28, 29
Metabase 260
metastore 70, 248
micro-batch 44
Microsoft Power BI 223
MicroStrategy 223
ML algorithms 119
ML algorithms, business use cases
  applications 121
  customer churn models 121
  customer lifetime value models 121
  demand forecasting 121
  financial fraud detection 122
  market basket analysis 122
  shipment lead-time prediction 122
ML algorithms, scaling
  techniques 123, 124
ML algorithms, types
  reinforcement learning 120
  supervised learning 119
  unsupervised learning 120
MLflow
  about 146, 190, 211
  components 191
  used, for tracking experiments 191-197
mlflow. command 197
MLflow Model 197, 198
MLflow Model Registry
  about 199
  used, for tracking model
    versions 199-201

MLflow projects
  about 204
  reference link 205
MLflow Tracking 192, 197
MLflow Tracking Server
  about 211
  reference link 192
model inference 119
model inferencing
  scaling out 211, 212
Model Registry Workflows
  reference link 201
model scoring 119, 144
model training
  with embarrassingly parallel
    computing 213
model tuning 198
multi-class classification models
  training, with random forests 166
multi-hop architecture
  about 109-113
  prerequisites 111
multinomial classification 160
MySQL 26

N

Naïve Bayes
  about 162
  implementing, with Spark MLlib 163
natural language processing
  used, for information extraction 122
near real-time analytics systems 94
non-parametric learning algorithm 153
NoSQL 93
NoSQL databases
  for operational analytics 32

NoSQL data store
  data, ingesting into 32
NumPy
  reference link 237

O

object detection 171
observability tools 223
offline feature store
  used, for batch inferencing 144, 145
offline model inferencing
  with batch processing 201
OneHotEncoder
  used, for transforming categorical
    variable into vector 139
online feature store, for real-time
    inferencing 147, 148
online inferencing in real time
  components 148
online model inferencing
  with real-time 202
Operational System 26
operational systems
  data, extracting from 55
Optimized Row Columnar (ORC) 245
optimizer hints 253

P

pandas
  about 236, 237
  PySpark, converting into 238, 239
  upgrading, to PySpark with
    Koalas 217, 218
  used, for exploratory data analysis 209
  versus PySpark 236

pandas UDF
  used, for scaling out arbitrary
    Python code 216
parametric learning algorithm 153
Parquet 245
Parquet file 37
partition pruning 38, 86
petabytes (PB) 263
Pipelines 126, 127
Plotly 233
predicate 86
predicate pushdown 86
principal component analysis (PCA) 182
Prometheus 223
Pyodbc 268
PyPI 217
PySpark
  about 12, 58, 212
  converting, into pandas 238, 239
  used, for exploratory data analysis 210
  used, in data visualization
    techniques 224
  used, in Python data visualizations 231
  versus pandas 236
PySpark native data visualizations
  about 224-228
  interactive visuals, with JavaScript
    and HTML 229, 230
Python 246
Python applications
  connecting, to Spark SQL
    with Pyodbc 268, 269
Python data visualizations
  declarative visualizations,
    with Altair 234, 236
  interactive visualizations,
    with Plotly 233, 234

scientific visualizations, with
    Seaborn 232, 233
two-dimensional plots, creating
    with Matplotlib 231, 232
with PySpark 231

Q

Qlikview 223
Q-Q plots 227
quantile plots 227
query hints 253

R

random forests
  used, for training multi-class
      classification 166
  used, for training regression models 165
raw data
  transforming, into meaningful data 54
raw data analytics-ready
  making, with data cleansing 81
RDDs
  Data Parallel Processing 9
real time
  data ingestion pipelines, building in 39
  unifying, with Lambda Architecture 48
real-time analytics industry use cases
  about 96
  financial fraud detection 97
  IT security threat detection 98
  real-time predictive analytics,
      in manufacturing 97
  vehicles, connected in
      automotive sector 97
real-time data analytics system 90, 91

real-time data analytics
    systems architecture
  about 90
  streaming data sinks 93
  streaming data sources 91, 92
real-time data consumers 96
real-time transactional systems 93, 94
real-world supervised learning
    applications
  about 169
  classification applications 171
  regression applications 169
recommendation systems 185
recommender system 181
Redash 260
Redis 33, 93
regression
  about 154
  linear regression 155
regression models
  training, with gradient boosted trees 168
  training, with random forests 165
regression models, applications
  customer lifetime value estimation 170
  dynamic price optimization 170
  shipment lead time estimation 170
reinforcement learning 120
relational database management
    system (RDBMS) 242, 257
relational data sources
  about 26
  data, ingesting from 26
residuals 228
resilient distributed datasets (RDDs) 245
ROC curves 228
row-based storage
  about 245
  versus columnar storage 244, 245

S

SAP Business Objects 223
Scala 246
scalable ML algorithms 124
scalar pandas UDFs
  about 216
  reference link 216
scatter plots 227
schema evolution
  about 67
  with Delta Lake 67, 68
schema validation
  enabling, with Delta Lake 66, 67
Seaborn 232
semi-structured data formats 36
serialization 216
Serializer/Deserializer (SerDes) 249
Service-Level Agreements (SLAs) 58
Serving layer 50
shipment lead time estimation 122, 170
show() function 76
Sigmoid function 158
silver data 85
singular value decomposition (SVD) 182
Spark
  about 198
  SQL, using on 18, 19
Spark 2.3 216
Spark DataFrames
  data, transforming with 15, 16
Spark DML 251, 252
Spark Global Temp View 50
Spark ML 246
Spark MLLib
  about 119, 124
  used, for implementing linear
    regression 155, 156

used, for implementing Naïve Bayes 163
Spark MLLib, components
  Estimator 126
  Pipelines 126
  Transformer 125
Spark ML library 213
Spark Sessions 50
Spark SQL
  about 210, 245, 246
  big data processing 15
Spark SQL data sources
  about 247
  file data source 247, 248
  Hive data source 249
  JDBC data source 248
Spark SQL DDL 250
Spark SQL engine 246
Spark SQL language reference 249
Spark SQL performance
  optimizing 252, 253
Spark SQL performance-tuning
  reference link 253
Spark Structured Streaming 280
Speed layer 49, 50
SQL analysis tools 259
SQL hints 253
SQL query optimizer 246
SQL syntax
  reference link 252
SQL Workbench/J
  about 259, 260
  connecting, to Databricks
    Community Edition 260-262
  reference link 260
Star/Snowflake schemas 277
stateful streams processing
  with watermarking 106-109
  with windowing 106-109

StopWordsRemover
  used, for removing words 137
streaming data sink
  about 93
  near real-time analytics systems 94
  real-time transactional systems 93
streaming data sources 91, 92
stream processing engines
  about 95, 96
  real-time data consumers 96
streams processing
  unifying, with Delta Lake 73
StringIndexer
  used, for encoding string variables 138
structured data storage formats 37, 38
Structured Query Language
      (SQL) 26, 242, 246
structured streaming
  about 43, 44, 47, 95, 213, 246
  data, loading incrementally 45-47
structured streaming programming guide
  reference link 47
sub-queries 244
supervised machine learning
  about 119, 152
  non-parametric learning algorithm 153
  parametric learning algorithm 153
supervised machine learning, applications
  classification 158
  regression 154
Support Vector Machines (SVM)
  about 163
  implementing 164

T

Tableau 223
Tableau Online
  about 263, 268
  connecting, to Databricks
      Community Edition 263-266
text
  tokenization, into individual terms 136
Time Travel
  about 71
  with Delta Lake 71, 72
time variables
  transforming 140
topic 29
topic modeling
  about 178
  with latent Dirichlet allocation 178, 179
total cost of ownership 58
training dataset 134
Train-Validation Split
  reference link 198
Transactional System 26
transaction log 63
Transformer 125, 135
tree ensembles 164
Tungsten 37
tuning 119

U

Uniform Resource Locator (URL) 249
union() function 76
unstructured data storage formats
  about 34, 35
  disadvantages 34

unsupervised learning, real-
    world applications
  association rules 185
  clustering applications 183
  collaborative filtering 185
unsupervised machine learning 120, 174
user-defined function
    (UDF) 202, 212, 247

V

VACUUM command
  reference link 73
Vega engine 234
video on demand 182

W

watermark 41
watermarking
  used, for stateful streams
    processing 106-109
windowing
  used, for stateful streams
    processing 106-109
words
  removing, with StopWordsRemover 137
Worker Nodes 7
write-ahead logging (WAL) 63
write-ahead logs 44

Z

Zeppelin notebooks 224

Made in the USA
Middletown, DE
19 January 2022

59147318R00179